Through biblical scholarship and carefu[...] job in highlighting for us the place and [...] work of God throughout Scripture. I highly recomm[...] wish to expand their understanding of the interwoven nature of God's dealings with the nations throughout biblical history and the place of Africans and Africa in it.

—**Dr Joshua Bogunjoko**
International Director, SIM (Serving In Mission)

Africans and Africa in the Bible by scholar and missionary Tim Welch has comprehensively surveyed all of the numerous, but often overlooked, references to Africans and to Africa in the Old and the New Testament. This volume will be of special value and interest to both Christians and non-Christians on the African continent.

—**Dr Edwin Yamauchi**
Author of Africa and the Bible, *editor of* Africa and Africans in Antiquity

By simply and faithfully placing the biblical data regarding Africans and Africa before the reading public, Tim Welch has rendered a great service to the body of Christ. The many years he has spent in Africa, reading the Bible from within that context and together with Africans who love the Scriptures, have yielded this wonderful and timely document which should add fresh impetus to what God is already doing in his global mission through the African people. Reading this has been energizing and empowering.

—**Mutua Mahiaini**
International President, The Navigators

Truly amazing . . . an essential read for anyone interested in knowing the place of Africans and Africa in the Bible. An inspiring, eye-opening, and stimulating book for this time when Christianity is the fastest growing religion in Africa.

—**Dr Daniel Bourdanné**
General Secretary, International Fellowship of Evangelical Students (IFES)

In this wonderful book, Tim Welch helps us to understand how Africa played a significant role in the story of God's people. It provides the foundation on which Africa continued to shape Christian thought during the first millennium.

—**The Rt Rev Dr Mouneer Hanna Anis**
Bishop of the Anglican Diocese of Egypt with North Africa and the Horn of Africa

Tim Welch's *Africans and Africa in the Bible* is for both the novice and the scholar. He meticulously explores the evidence for what can truly be considered African in the Bible and what cannot. His appendices provide indices of Africa in both Testaments, identifying where in the biblical text Africa or Africans are referenced as well as a second list identifying Africa and Africans alphabetically. The result is a large body of evidence that shows Africa's contribution to the biblical narrative – but without being overly Afrocentric as can sometimes happen in such studies. His work will add to the mounting conviction that Africa is indeed an integral part of the biblical narrative of God's salvation of his people. Africans and the West both need to hear the message that Christianity is not just the "white man's religion", but is the truth that spans cultures, races, color, geography, and prejudices. I heartily recommend this work as part of anyone's library who wants to be literate about Africa's contribution to the Christian world.

— Rev Dr Joel Elowsky
Researcher, Center for Early African Christianity, Yale University
Professor of Historical Theology, Concordia Seminary

Christianity had been portrayed as a foreign religion to Africa and Africans until we started discovering numerous references in both the Old and New Testaments to names of people from places we know now as the continent of Africa. These people were associated with God's mission over the ages. As Africans, these discoveries fuelled our enthusiasm to take further initiatives in carrying out God's mission through his church on earth. *Africans and Africa in the Bible* by Tim Welch has added more impetus to such enthusiasm.

—Rev Dr Reuben Ezemadu
Continental Coordinator, Movement for African National Initiatives (MANI)

Tim Welch has done an extensive and thorough work in reminding readers that Africans are not just recent recipients of the gospel message; rather, they are an integral part of that message. His meticulous research on Africans in the Bible should motivate the African church and increase awareness of Africa's rich biblical history, as it shows that Christianity has deep roots in African soil! What a blessing for the African church!

—Joanna Ilboudo
Executive Director, ACTS-Burkina Faso

Africans and Africa in the Bible by Tim Welch is a "Wow!" book for those of us who live and work in the African context. As he himself says, "it is time for the Church in Africa to recognize its very rich biblical heritage." He does a magnificent job putting together what ancient and modern scholarship has to say about each person and place. The book is a massive contribution to our understanding of the role Africa and Africans played in Scripture. Just his end material, listing every place in Scripture where Africans or places in Africa are mentioned, is worth the price of the book. It belongs in the library of every pastor, missionary, scholar, seminary, and Bible school student.

—Dr Howard Brant
Senior Church and Mission Consultant, Addis Ababa, Ethiopia

Tim Welch has done an amazing study in *Africans and Africa in the Bible*. The research is profound, biblical, and scholarly, meeting the need of anyone who is looking to see how the Bible and Christianity relate to Africa. For those who minister in Africa and among the African diaspora, the book tells about the role played by Africans in the unfolding story of God's plan. It applies to all spheres of ministry: church, missions, and theological education. I warm-heartedly recommend this book to all and especially to those who wrestle with the idea of Christianity being a "Western Religion".

—Dr Siegfried Ngubane
Director, SIM Southern Africa

This book is destined to prove a tremendous companion and friend to all African students of the Bible: pastors, theological educators, students, and lay people. As the church in Africa moves onto centre stage in world Christianity in a new and very different kind of "Afrocentrism", this book will give confidence to African scholars and church leaders to take pride in their continent and their ancestors who formed part of the story of the making of the people of God. Through meticulous but accessible and fair scholarship, Welch has pealed back hundreds of years of Euro/American-centric layers which have hidden from view the presence and influence of black people in the Scriptures. To misquote the late Francis Schaeffer, "We were there and we were not silent"! It is my sincere hope that this book will further encourage African students of the Bible to relax their reliance on colonial Christianity and instead learn to sink their gospel roots directly into the soil of the Bible and its world.

—Rev Joe Kapolyo
Lead Minister, Edmonton Baptist Church, London;
former Principal of the Theological College of Central Africa (Ndola, Zambia)

Many people in our African continent think the Bible and the Christian religion came to us from white men. In *Africans and Africa in the Bible,* Tim Welch has done an excellent job of research and sound analysis to show that we were incorrect to think that way. I recommend this book to every pastor, Bible teacher, and Bible student, both white and black, working in Africa, which will help Africans see and believe in their central role in the eternal good counsel of Jehovah's own will.

—Simon Mvondo Edzoa
President of Cameroon Biblical Seminary

This is an amazing book highlighting the role of Africans dealing with God's revelation and its transformation, from the very onset of Christianity. This is inspirational!

—Rev Johnson Asare
National Director, Markaz Al Bishara (Ghana)

AFRICANS AND AFRICA IN THE BIBLE

An Ethnic and Geographic Approach

Tim Welch

OASIS INTERNATIONAL LIMITED
Satisfying Africa's Thirst for God's Word

AFRICANS AND AFRICA IN THE BIBLE:
An Ethnic and Geographic Approach

ISBN 13: 978-1-59452-751-7
ISBN: 1-59452-751-2

This revised and amplified edition first appeared in French as *L'Afrique et les Africains dans la Bible*, published by the Centre de Publications Evangéliques (CPE) in Abidjan, Côte d'Ivoire in 2001. For questions, contact Tim Welch at tim.welch@sim.org.

Oasis International is a ministry devoted to fostering a robust and sustainable pan-African publishing industry. For more information, go to oasisint.net.

Translation from French: Philip, Janet, and Tim Welch

Ethiopian girl photo 10696108 © Edwardje - Dreamstime.com
River Nile in Egypt photo 113313322 © Marabelo - Dreamstime.com
Monk at Abuna Yemata Guh photo 1073995910 © iStock.com/benedek

19 20 21 22 23 24 25 BPI 10 9 8 7 6 5 4 3 2 1

DEDICATION

This book is dedicated to my African friends who have shown by their love for the Lord, as well as by their family life, that they are an integral part of the gospel message:

Moïse and Fanta Doumbouya
Younoussa and Alphonsine Djao
Joshua and Joanna Bogunjoko
Jules and Jacqueline Ouoba
Abdoulaye and Elisabeth Sangho
Soungalo and Adèle Soro
Mutua and Stephanie Mahiaini
Kwame and Jackie Busumbru
Robert and Grace Setor
Gilbert and Stella Okoronkwo
Jérémie and Marie-Claire Agré
Daniel and Halymah Bourdanné
Dieudonné and Madeleine Ngumbi
Solomon and Alexandrine Andriatsimialomananarivo
Cosette Kashalé and her late husband Dibinga
Pierre and Édith Rabé

TABLE OF CONTENTS

FOREWORD

Why a book on Africa and the Bible? Surely the Bible in the Old Testament is about the land of Israel, the Philistines, Phoenicians, and the great empires of Mesopotamia and beyond—Assyria, Babylonia, and Persia? Does not the New Testament focus on Palestine, Asia Minor, Greece, and Rome? Is Africa even in the Bible's scope of interest?

In *Africans and Africa in the Bible*, Tim Welch answers that last question with a resounding "Yes!" The entire canon, but especially the Old Testament, has an amazingly large number of references to the African continent and to Africans. In fact, I would hazard a guess that the reader will be astonished at the amount of people and places that are mentioned and that play an important role in the biblical story.

This book is important for at least two reasons. To begin with, the author is committed to demonstrating that the Bible and the Christian faith are not the "white man's" scripture and religion. As this work makes abundantly clear, Africa, particularly north and north-east Africa (present day Egypt, Libya, and Sudan), is central to many of the Bible's narratives. *Africans and Africa in the Bible*, in other words, is *missiologically significant*.

In addition, this work is *educationally helpful*. It offers a treasure chest of information about Africans who intersect Old Testament accounts and appear at key moments in the New Testament. For the Old Testament, Welch deals with, among others: Moses's Cushite wife, Phinehas, the multiple Pharaohs, Ebed-Melech who came to Jeremiah's aid, and Zephaniah's father Cushi. For the New Testament, he cites, for example, the Egyptians and Libyans present at Pentecost, the Ethiopian eunuch baptized by Philip in Acts 8, and Simeon called Niger who was a leader in the church at Antioch (Acts 13:1).

This informational feast is not just about people but also about places. Welch explains, for instance, why Egypt and Libya must be included in discussions about things African in the Bible, even as some would deny or minimize their African identity. He clarifies how Cush is better understood as being located in the area of modern Sudan, not Ethiopia. The African cities of Alexandria and Memphis and places like Goshen and Put are identified and their impact revealed. What is more, this volume closes with five appendices! The first lists in canonical order all the references to Africans and Africa in the Bible, the second is a concordance of verses mentioning Africans, whereas the third lists African place names. The fourth appendix registers some names that are disputed, and the fifth compares how African people and places in the Bible are translated in four English versions.

In recent years Africa has begun to take a higher profile in worldwide evangelical academic circles, although some of the topics of study differ from that of this book. One could mention theologian Thomas C. Oden's investigation of Africa's impact on Christianity (*How*

Africa Shaped the Christian Mind and *The African Memory of Mark: Reassessing Early Church Tradition*) and Jehu Hanciles's contribution to diaspora missiology (*Beyond Christendom: Globalization, African Migration, and the Transformation of the West*). Historian Philip Jenkins has done much to raise awareness of how the church is growing in the Global South, including Africa (*The Next Christendom: The Coming of Global Christianity* and *The New Faces of Christianity: Believing the Bible in the Global South*).

In terms of publications on Africa and the Bible, two come to mind when talking about non-African authors: J. Daniel Hays's *From Every People and Nation: A Biblical Theology of Race* and Edwin Yamauchi's *Africa and the Bible*. From the pen of an African, perhaps *Africa and the Africans in the Old Testament* by the Nigerian David Tuesday Adamo is best known. Tim Welch is well-placed to add the fruit of his own research to this field. The material presented here in *Africans and Africa in the Bible* appeared initially in a slimmer volume in French; that material is now much expanded. Though not an African, he has served for many years in Côte d'Ivoire, working hard to facilitate projects at local, national, and continent levels that yield a truly contextualized African flavour to the study of the Bible.

This volume is careful, thorough, and irenic in tone. It deserves to be considered as a valuable resource alongside of the works by Hays, Yamauchi, and Adamo. As one of Tim's former professors at Denver Seminary, it gives me great joy to heartily commend *Africans and Africa in the Bible* to the reader. There is much to learn in its pages!

M. Daniel Carroll R. (Rodas), PhD
Blanchard Professor of Old Testament
Wheaton College and Graduate School
U.S.A.

PREFACE

I am the first one to admit that it would have been preferable to have an African write a book on Africans and Africa in the Bible. I have written such a text not because I think that I know more about this subject than my African brothers and sisters. Rather, it is because I find the subject matter both interesting and quite overlooked. I began research on this topic while studying at Denver Seminary (USA) for a course on the Old Testament in 1998. After finishing a short paper on Africans in the Old Testament, and following my return to Africa, I showed the paper to the director of the *Centre de Publications Evangéliques*. He encouraged me to do more research on the matter and then present it as a manuscript for publishing. Fortunately, he is a patient man; it took me over three years to fulfil his request. The printing in Hong Kong also took time. *L'Afrique et les Africains dans la Bible* finally appeared on bookshelves in Africa in early 2003.

On the other hand, it is not necessarily a bad thing that a white man should write about Africans in the Bible. I am not writing this book in order to "defend my own skin", as a friend of mine told me. I have nothing to gain *personally* from taking the positions I take in this book, and I hope that will guarantee a certain objectivity throughout this work. That is for the reader to decide.

It is possible that some readers will find my approach far too technical despite their overall interest in the topic of Africans in the Bible. I encourage those readers to first read the fifth chapter, the conclusion, which will hopefully motivate them to return to the earlier chapters and give them specific examples which will help them answer the most basic of questions: "So what?" These earlier chapters should aid in understanding how Africans in the Bible related to God, to Israel and to the church.

At times in this book I will refer to an article which is found on a compact disc (CD) instead of on a printed page. I realize that this might complicate life for the person who wants to verify the accuracy of what I have written, and I therefore ask him or her in advance to please forgive me for this inconvenience.

Because this book first appeared in French, a number of the passages I quote are from books written in French. Where necessary, I have translated these articles into English myself. Hence any errors in translation are my responsibility and not that of the French-speaking author.

I have chosen to use a British (as opposed to American) orthography for this text, since many English-speaking African readers live in countries which have adopted that same orthography. However, when citing the Bible or works written by Americans, I have not modified the spelling of words so as to fit with British rules, much to the chagrin of my computer spell-checker.

There are five appendices at the back of the book. The first one is the most extensive, as it lists all the references (both direct and indirect) to African people or places in the Bible. They are listed in order of appearance in the Scriptures. I have done my best to ensure the accuracy of those references, but I admit that an error may have crept in here and there, especially since I used several French Bibles as the initial sources for this list. Any such errors in this or the other appendices should be brought to the attention of the author.

The second and third appendices cover all the Bible references to African people or African place names that I could find. The sheer number of references is quite impressive, and their simple presence supports the major thesis of this book, which is: **Christianity is not just a white man's religion. It also qualifies as an African religion.** Finding and classifying all of the Bible references was an arduous task, and it is quite possible that I have left some references out or made a mistake in listing others. Remember, however, that one version of the Bible does not always number verses in the same way as another version. Again, I have opted for the numbering used by the NIV.

The fourth appendix lists the names of people that certain scholars – especially Afrocentric theologians – consider to be Africans, but that other scholars question. Their inclusion in this list does not necessarily mean that I do not consider them as African, but rather that many others do not.

There are several ways to spell proper names and place names, depending on the Bible one uses. The King James Bible uses a different spelling at times from the New International Version, or the New English Bible from Today's English Version. In this book I have chosen to use the orthography found in the NIV because that seems to be the English Bible the most commonly used in Africa. The fifth appendix gives the orthography of all four of the above-named versions of the Bible in English.

The reader will quickly see that there are numerous endnotes in this book. The reason for all these notes is, first of all, to give an ampler defence of my reasoning, and secondly, to allow the reader to know what titles to obtain in order to do his or her own research and find out more on a given subject.

My hope is that this book will become a practical tool for every Christian – pastor or layperson – who wants to know more about the role Africans have played in the Bible story. May each reader come to understand that God himself inspired the biblical authors to mention Africans and Africa throughout the pages of Scripture.

Tim Welch
Abidjan, Côte d'Ivoire
February, 2014

ACKNOWLEDGEMENTS

While an author is the person who collects and organizes the necessary ideas to formulate them into a book, I suspect that no book has ever been written without the help and influence of people from the outside. At least this one was not.

Therefore, I want to thank all the staff at INADES (the African Institute for Economic and Social Development) in Abidjan, Côte d'Ivoire, for it was at their library that I found almost all of the French titles that I quote in this book. Thanks to them, the research for this book was considerably expanded and, I hope, improved upon. I can only hope that a growing number of African authors, both French-speaking and English-speaking, will come to the fore and do a much better job than I have as they write on relevant theological issues. I also want to express my sincere gratitude to Richard Avit in Abidjan who went out of his way to help me with all the citations from the Bible dictionaries in French that I have used in this book.

I want to especially thank Dr J. Daniel Hays, professor at Ouachita Baptist University (USA), for the help he gave me by sending photocopies of his articles on Cushites in the Scriptures, as well as for the numerous email messages he sent to me, explaining the meaning of certain proper names found in the Old Testament and giving me his reasoning for the position he has taken on certain biblical persons. His advice and ideas allowed me to know the thinking of a true expert in this field. In addition, he gave me permission to quote extensively from his book, *From Every People and Nation: A biblical theology of race*, a book I highly recommend to any person interested in the area of race relations.

Two other renowned scholars, Dr Alfred Kuen and Dr Edwin Yamauchi, also granted permission to quote extensively from their works, *Nouveau Dictionnaire Biblique, édition révisée* and *Africa and the Bible*, respectively. Dr Yamauchi responded with amazing speed and grace to emails from a totally unknown person. My sincere gratitude is extended to both of these men who are among the leading experts in their field.

I also want to thank my former Old Testament professor at Denver Seminary, Dr Daniel Carroll R. He is the one who suggested this topic to me in the first place in 1998, and he is also the one who put me in touch with Dr Hays. His encouragement over the years has been a real motivation to me. Thank you for your friendship.

I am very grateful to Greg Burgess, who not only put me in contact with Oasis International, but also advocated with them on my behalf. I also want to thank Matthew Elliott and his staff at Oasis for taking on this book. I am especially grateful to Hannah Rasmussen, who spent countless hours reading, rearranging, questioning and improving significantly the text of this book. Without her thorough yet kind and gracious expertise, this book would be far inferior in quality. Thank you!

I am indebted to my son, Philip, for the motivation he provided by telling me how many of his friends wanted to see this book appear in English, and also for his help in translating a significant part of the text from French into English. Competent, loving children are a real blessing from the Lord. My daughter Katie, my daughter-in-law Kazy and my son-in-law Kurt have also blessed my life in innumerable ways which have, directly or indirectly, led to my being able to complete this book.

Finally, my deepest and most sincere thanks go to my wife, Janet. She too spent a great number of hours translating this book into English and for that I am most grateful. But far more than that, she accompanied me for almost a third of a century in the West African country of Cote d'Ivoire. That life was not always very tranquil or calm, and she experienced medical emergencies with our children, the loss of beloved friends, separation from family, political upheaval on more than one occasion, and other trying circumstances that would make most people throw up their hands and scream, "Enough!" But she did not do so; rather she remains a constant student of culture, a lover of people, a thoughtful and creative helper, and in my opinion the far better missionary between the two of us. I continue to grow in my respect and love for her, and I thank the Lord daily for giving me such a marvellous life companion.

1

INTRODUCTION

A common criticism of Christianity heard in Africa is that it is a "white man's religion." People assume that Europeans or Americans brought Christianity to the African continent. However, a quick survey of church history clearly shows that a significant number of Africans were already Christian many centuries *before* the arrival of the first Western missionaries and more than five centuries before the birth of Islam. The kingdom of Axum (in present-day Ethiopia) became Africa's first Christian kingdom when its king, Ezana, converted around the year 350.[1] Certain African Christians defended the faith with reasoned intelligence, combating the polytheism of the Roman Empire. During Christianity's first five centuries, men such as Tertullian, Clement, Origen, Cyprian, and Augustine – all sons of Africa – wrote very influential and scholarly works that helped the Christian church throughout the world lay a solid foundation upon which it could build.[2] It is interesting to note that the first churches to use Latin in regular worship services were not in Italy, but in North Africa, in the region of Carthage (Tunisia).[3] In addition, some scholars hold that many of Christianity's great intellectual struggles occurred first in Africa and were only debated subsequently in Europe. For such people, "Africa played a decisive role in the formation of Christian culture. Decisive intellectual achievements of Christianity were explored and understood first in Africa before they were recognized in Europe, and a millennium before they found their way to North America."[4]

In his article on the state of the gospel in Africa today, Dr Tite Tiénou said, "The recognition of Africa as one of the heartlands of the Christian faith implies that Christianity is an African religion."[5] Indeed, the extensive number of African Christians confirms the tremendous influence the gospel has had in modern-day Africa.

The goal of this book, however, is not to explain the role Africans have played in church history or to chronicle the development of the African church in the 21st century. Rather, **its purpose is to show the extent to which Africans and the African continent are part of the biblical story**. Numerous references to Africans and Africa are found in the Bible, both in the New Testament and in the Old, demonstrating that Africans are not only recipients of the gospel message, but they are also an integral part of it. Christianity has deep roots in African soil and qualifies as an "African religion" as a result. Christianity is as African as any African traditional religion.

My sincere wish is that the reader will come to appreciate how much the Bible speaks about Africans, and that this appreciation will help us all to understand that Africans, as descendants of Ham, are not cursed as some theologians assert in misinterpreting Genesis 9:25.[6] Instead Africans, like every other race of people in this world, are accountable to God for their actions, whether good or bad. At times the people of Africa are the object of God's blessing and other times the object of his wrath. Sometimes God uses Africans to bless his people (whether that be Israel or the church), and at other times he uses Africans to punish his people. Examples from each of these categories will be looked at in the following pages.

But before going any further, we need to examine a very basic question. The Bible often mentions Egyptians, Libyans, Ethiopians/Cushites, and other peoples from Africa. Ethiopians and others from south of the Sahara are readily considered to be black (see Jeremiah 13:23 where the prophet comments proverbially on the "blackness" of "Ethiopians"). But can we legitimately consider North Africans, because of their lighter skin and more Arabic culture, as truly African?

There are some theologians, known as "Afrocentric" theologians, who hold that Africans from south of the Sahara played a significant role in the development not only of Ethiopia but also of Egypt and North Africa. For example, black American theologian Cain Hope Felder said, "With the 1962 archaeological discoveries at Qustul, Upper Nubia [present-day Sudan], we now have strong evidence that ancient Egyptian civilization was prefigured and shaped by developments to the south, in Nubia."[7] They conclude, therefore, that ancient Egypt had its roots in black Africa and that Egyptians can be legitimately called African.

This conclusion is not limited to Afrocentric theologians. Roughly 2500 years ago, around 460 BC, the Greek historian Herodotus stated, "Egypt derived from the culture of greater Ethiopia."[8] The most well-known African scholar who deals with this subject, Cheikh Anta Diop from Senegal, also insists that Egyptians are Africans. He writes:

> In examining the varied representatives [from Egypt], it follows that Egypt was necessarily populated by a [black] race which had subdued the proto-Indoeuropean and Semitic groups who, by their random travels, had infiltrated the [Nile] valley.
>
> In reality, all the representatives who are undeniably part of the proto-dynastic and even dynastic kings (1st, 2nd, 3rd dynasties) are of the [characteristically black] type. That is the case for Lord Tera-Neter (temple of Aunu in the city of Hemen near Luxor); for King Narmer (the "Menes" of Egyptian texts) who unified the country for the first time; for King Khasekhen of the 2nd dynasty; for King Zozer of the 3rd dynasty, etc.[9]

Other scholars, however, including some black scholars, are not in entire agreement with this conclusion. African-American classics scholar Frank Snowden Jr. rejects the identification of Egyptians as blacks, according to Yamauchi.[10] Another is Nigerian scholar David Tuesday Adamo who states, "one must avoid another type of counter prejudice by African or black scholars who maintain that all the people of the Near East, Africa, and Greece were originally black".[11] Some scholars think that these Afrocentric theologians are guilty of over-simplifying things by calling Egyptians "black". For example, Edwin Yamauchi states, "as to the question of whether the Egyptians were black, the answer is not so simple as Afrocentrists assert . . . Cheik Anta Diop, whom Afrocentrists adopt as their intellectual star, is not a trustworthy guide in either linguistics or history . . . He simply makes too many unsupportable statements."[12] Finally, Thomas Oden, an enthusiastic proponent of the African role in the development of early Christianity, nonetheless warns against "Afrocentric exaggeration" and deterioration into an "exuberant Afrocentrism".[13]

I agree that many Afrocentric theologians do exaggerate at times by claiming a black presence and an African contribution just about everywhere in the Bible. For instance, Alfred Dunston claims that the Midianites in Exodus 2, were a tribe of black people, or at least that there were numerous blacks living among them.[14] For Charles Copher, Moses, Aaron, and Miriam are black people.[15] For Walter McCray, the Canaanites are "an explicitly black people"; Nimrod was "one of our great black ancestors"; and the Chaldeans, along with Nebuchadnezzar and Belshazzar, "should be classified as biblical blacks".[16] Others consider the Shulamite woman to be black, since she says, "Dark am I" in Song of Songs 1:5.[17] In the introduction to *The Original African Heritage Study Bible*, Cain Hope Felder states that Jesus was a black man.[18]

Because it is so easy to find example after example of the "exuberant Afrocentrism" Oden warns against, the unfortunate result is that many people simply dismiss all claims for an African presence in the Scriptures as an over-exaggeration by theologians with an axe to grind, thus robbing the Word of God of its intellectual integrity and objectivity. Such a reaction tends to "throw the baby out with the bath water", as they say, for those passages which demonstrate a legitimate African presence are immediately associated with the exaggerated claims of a virtual African omnipresence in the Bible, and consequently all claims are considered unfounded and illegitimate.

Certain general sources, such as *The Times Atlas of World History* and the *Compton's Interactive Encyclopedia*, refer to Egyptians not as "black" but as "Afro-asiatic", which means a cross of African peoples and Semitic peoples from Asia.[19] Some experts agree. Raymond Mauny, after giving several possibilities for the origin of the Egyptian people, states, "Egypt, at the crossroads of three continents, the land where races and civilizations cross-breed, such is the logical vocation of this country. One component wanting to monopolize the whole is to run counter to the truth."[20] In other words, in a country where black, brown, and white people have intermarried for years, no one race can claim the Egyptians as belonging solely to them.

The *New Bible Dictionary* speaks of the "first real Egyptians" as those called the Taso-Badarians, a people who established the first pre-dynastic culture. It goes on to say that these people seem to be of African origin, along with two other cultures called Naqada I and Naqada II. It was only around the year 3000 BC that Asiatic peoples from Mesopotamia arrived and merged with this pre-dynastic people.[21]

What is interesting is that the French revised version of the *New Bible Dictionary*, the *Nouveau dictionnaire biblique révisé*, gives a different explanation of the origin of the Egyptians. An English translation of this text states:

> In prehistoric times, Ham's descendants of the white race moved into Egypt in successive waves and supplanted the natives. Later, other invaders from Babylon, Semites for the most part, occupied Egypt and influenced its language. During this same period, Nubians also intermixed with the Egyptians.[22]

So with regard to the origin of the Egyptian people, the French-language version of the *New Bible Dictionary* emphasizes their Asiatic ancestry while the English-language version emphasizes their African ancestry. In both cases, however, they speak of the merging and intermixing of peoples. We can therefore conclude that in a technical sense Egyptians are an "Afro-asiatic" people no matter who occupied the land first, because of their history of mixing people groups. Even Cheikh Anta Diop, who insists upon the characteristically black features of the early Egyptian kings, admits that such cross-breeding took place, all the while maintaining that this cross-breeding never eliminated black features from the Egyptian people:

> Indeed Egyptian cross-breeding fanned out over the course of history, no one denies it, but it is noteworthy that it never succeeded in overwhelming the racial constants of the earlier population, specifically those of Upper Egypt. The skin colour of Egyptians lightened with time, like that of blacks from the [Caribbean] Antilles, but Egyptians never stopped being [blacks].[23]

H. R. Hall speaks of ethnicity in Egypt and among the royal families of Egypt and Cush in his article on Egypt up to the time of Alexander the Great. Like Diop, he concludes, "there is clear evidence of [characteristically black] features, frequently from intermarriages, at all levels of Egyptian society."[24] Therefore, the most logical conclusion seems to be that the Egyptians were a mixed race, and neither 100 per cent Asian nor 100 per cent African people.

Scholar and renowned Egyptologist E. A. Wallis Budge agrees with this conclusion. "Many facts go to show the persistence of the [black] influence on the beliefs, and manners, and customs of the Dynastic Egyptians".[25] Budge, who studied and translated numerous hieroglyphic texts, held that the Egyptians considered themselves to be descendants of Punt (present day Somalia).

Margaret Bunson, author of *The Encyclopedia of Ancient Egypt*, speaks of the pre-dynastic peoples of ancient Egypt, specifically of the peoples called Badarians (4500–4000 BC), and those belonging to Naqada I (4000–3500 BC) and Naqada II (3500–3000 BC), mentioned above. She affirms that "the manufactured pottery of the Badarians demonstrates sophistication and artistry" and that it was during the "cultural sequence" of Naqada II that we see evidence of the "changes brought about in contacts with other peoples and other lands".[26] She also maintains that when the two Egypts – Lower Egypt in the north and Upper Egypt in the south – united around 3000 BC, it was a matter of the southern kingdom dominating the northern peoples.

> There is evidence that Lower Egypt was not actually a kingdom when the armies from the south came to dominate the region and to bring about a unified nation (c. 3000 BCE) . . . The concept of Lower Egypt starting as a kingdom with its own geographical and social uniqueness quite probably was a fabrication with religious and political overtones . . . It is not certain that there was any sort of provincial designation in the northern lands in the Predynastic Period either. The *nomes*, or provinces, date to the first dynasties, and it is possible that Lower Egypt was not one unified region at all . . . The *nomes*, or provinces, were established originally by the rulers of the first dynasties or perhaps were in existence in earlier eras. It is probable that Upper Egypt was advanced in that regard.[27]

In short, Egypt felt the influence of Asiatic peoples both during and after the period 3500–3000 BC, but these people who migrated there found a culture that was already quite developed, and the driving force behind the unification of the two Egypts around 3000 BC came from the south – from the kingdom of Upper Egypt – and not from Lower Egypt in the north.

The French Bible dictionary, *Dictionnaire biblique pour tous*, agrees with Bunson and the *New Bible Dictionary* concerning the origin of the Egyptians. An English translation of it says:

> The first Egyptians who settled in the Nile valley are called Taso-Badarians and they seem to be of African origin. These communities grew, along with their local sanctuaries and their beliefs in life after death. The first Pharaoh of all of Egypt was apparently Narmer from Upper Egypt, who conquered the rival kingdom from the delta and founded the first dynasty.[28]

In Egypt, the south conquered the north, and not vice-versa.

Some people like to emphasize that a large number of Asiatic people came to Egypt and intermarried with the locals, concluding that such a cross-breeding excludes them from being called "African"; they insist on calling them "Afro-asiatic", as already noted above. But if one holds that Egyptians are really more Asian than African, then it seems logical to me that we cannot call English or French people "Europeans", but rather we must call them "Eurasians." After all, at the time that Asians came to settle in Egypt (around 3000 BC), there were very few "Europeans." According to the *Times Atlas of World History*, the first four major civilizations began in Egypt, Mesopotamia, India, and China.[29] It is from those four regions of the world that different invasions and migrations took place, also in the third millennium before Christ, and that people from the Middle East began to migrate to Europe, to the regions north and west of the Black Sea. The fact that we call certain languages "Indo-European" languages (such as English, French, Sanskrit, and Persian) shows that a link has existed between Europe and Asia for several millennia. Asiatic peoples migrating to Europe found "European peasant farmers" living there – to quote the term used on a map in the *Times Atlas of World History* – people who lived in small villages as opposed to developed cities. "In northern and western Europe . . . the population was too small and scattered to necessitate elaborate organization."[30]

So we see that Europe, like Egypt, experienced large migrations of Asiatic peoples around 3000 BC. However, I know of no scholar who insists that Europeans today must be called "Eurasian" or "Euro-asiatic" because of this historical linkage. If that is not necessary for Europeans, I fail to see why it is necessary for Egyptians. Perhaps one can better understand why certain Afrocentric theologians like Randall Bailey complain that in theological books, "One notes a similar tendency to exclude and minimize exploration of the subject of African influence . . . There are those efforts to move Egypt out of Africa by arguing for a sharp distinction between sub-Saharan Africa and Egypt."[31]

There are also non-Afrocentric theologians who not only agree with the idea of a Eurocentric bias in theology, but who go even further in their criticism of certain "scholars" and their prejudices in centuries gone by. For example, J. Daniel Hays, one of the world's leading experts on Cushites, attests that:

Many European and American scholars of the 19th and early 20th centuries were blatantly racist. This is particularly true concerning early European Egyptologists, who attempted to appropriate Egyptian culture as 'Western' and to distance the Egyptian cultural advances as far as possible from any African connections.[32]

Robert Draper, who is not a theologian but a political analyst, also speaks of this tendency among 19th-century historians when he speaks of the "bigoted worldview of the times."[33] Robert A. Bennett, Jr, mentions how "modern attitudes have produced a theology, almost, of the African's inferiority from the biblical curse of Canaan (Gen. 9:25, sic, not Ham)" and then goes on to speak of the "more insidious racism" when historians try "to excise Egypt and its culture from Africa".[34] The lingering influence of these dated ideas is still difficult to combat today, even among committed Christians.

Bennett's comment on trying to separate Egypt from Africa leads to another important argument. In addition to the ethnic argument as to why Egyptians and other North Africans should legitimately be called "African", there is also an argument based on geography that needs to be examined, and in my opinion this argument is as solid as it is straightforward. It is obvious if you look at a map – ancient or modern – that Egypt is a part of Africa. How can it be considered otherwise? It is not like the Indian subcontinent, which was physically added to Asia by the movement of tectonic plates. North Africa has always been a part of Africa.

French Egyptologist Jean Leclant does not agree with the idea that Egyptians should be called blacks, but nonetheless accepts that they should be called Africans.

If in fact Egyptians, those of the pyramids and those of our era, are clearly not [blacks], it remains that ancient Egyptian civilization is an African civilization *par excellence*. Egypt is, before anything else, African ground. And the civilization of the Pharaohs can serve as an introduction to understanding the black world.[35]

Thomas Oden, a theologian who has spent years studying Africa's influence in the development of Christian theology, also speaks to this element of geography. He questions those who speak of "two Africas", one in the north and one in the south. One of his conclusions goes to the heart of the matter: "North Africa is no less African than sub-Saharan Africa." A little later in his book he states, "Futile efforts to detach North Africa from 'the real Africa' have failed. The continental geography itself overcomes all parochial arguments. It is just one continent now and always has been."[36]

For these many reasons, I conclude that the Ethiopian people (or more correctly, the Cushite people) mentioned in the Bible are an African people group who came from present-day southern Egypt and northern Sudan. While I realize opinions are divided on this point, I maintain that Egyptians can legitimately be called African even if their race is a cross-breed between Semitic and Hamitic peoples. In my opinion, the word "African" is not necessarily synonymous with "black", a viewpoint that distinguishes my position from that of a number of Afrocentric theologians. That does not change the fact that Egyptians have significant black African roots and have had a physical presence on the African continent for over five millennia. My approach is as much a geographical one as an ethnic one, and I believe both are valid. These two factors together allow us to legitimately consider Egyptians and other people groups from North Africa as Africans.

In light of the above explanation of the word "African", let us now look at the Scriptures to see the extent of the African presence in the Bible.

---

1   Mark Shaw, *The Kingdom of God in Africa* (Grand Rapids: Baker Books, 1996), 62-65.

2   Origen was "the founder of biblical exegesis", and "alongside Tertullian, the defender of the North African church, Cyprian became its organizer and Augustine its great theologian". Ype Schaaf, *L'histoire et le rôle de la Bible en Afrique* (Dokkum: Editions des Groupes Missionnaires, 2000), 17, 20.

3   Bruce Shelley, *Church History in Plain Language* (Dallas: Word Publishing, 1982), 46.

4   Thomas C. Oden, *How Africa Shaped the Christian Mind* (Downers Grove: InterVarsity Press, 2007), 9.

5   Tite Tiénou, "The State of the Gospel in Africa," *Evangelical Missions Quarterly* 37, no. 2 (April 2001): 154.

6   For a good explanation of how this verse has often been misinterpreted, I highly recommend the following books: Tokunboh Adeyemo, *Is Africa Cursed?* (Nairobi: CLMC, 1997), especially chapter 2 (11-19); Edwin Yamauchi, *Africa and the Bible* (Grand Rapids: Baker Academic, 2004), especially the first chapter, "The Curse of Ham"; J. Daniel Hays, *From Every People and Nation: A biblical theology of race* (Downers Grove: InterVarsity Press, 2003), especially chapter 3, "Creation, blessing, and race". Hays says that current Old Testament scholarship holds that it is "exegetically ridiculous" to apply the curse of Ham to Africans (53).

7   Cain Hope Felder, *Troubling Biblical Waters* (Maryknoll: Orbis Books, 1989), 9.

8   Felder, *Troubling Biblical Waters*, 9.

9   Cheikh Anta Diop, *Antériorité des civilisations nègres: mythe ou vérité historique ?* (Dakar: Présence Africaine/edition Club Africain du Livre, 1972), 27-28.

10 Frank M. Snowden Jr., *Blacks in Antiquity* (Cambridge, MA: Harvard University Press, 1970), 8, quoted in Yamauchi, *Africa and the Bible*, 212, 220.

11 David T. Adamo, *Africa and the Africans in the Old Testament* (Eugene: Wipf and Stock Publishers, 1998), 44.

12 Yamauchi, *Africa and the Bible*, 212-213. For a serious critique of Afrocentric interpretation, see 205-213. Chapter 8 of *Africa and the Bible* was originally published as Edwin Yamauchi, "Afrocentric Biblical Interpretation," *Journal of the Evangelical Theological Society* 39, no. 3 (1996): 397-409.

13 Oden, *How Africa Shaped the Christian Mind*, 76-77, 91-92.

14 Alfred Dunston, *The Black Man in the Old Testament and Its World* (Philadelphia: Dorrance and Company, 1974), 97.

15 Charles B. Copher, "The Black Presence in the Old Testament," in *Stony the Road We Trod: African-American Biblical Interpretation,* ed. Cain Hope Felder (Minneapolis: Fortress Press, 1991), 156.

16 Walter McCray, *The Black Presence in the Bible* (Chicago: Black Light Fellowship, 1990), 56, 69, 71.

17 Robert A. Bennett, Jr., "Africa and the Biblical Period," *Harvard Theological Review* 64 (1971), 489.

18 Cain Hope Felder, "Introduction" in *The Original African Heritage Study Bible*, ed. Cain Hope Felder (Iowa Falls: World Bible Publishers, 1998), xiv-xv.

19 Geoffrey Barraclough, ed, *The Times Atlas of World History* (Maplewood: Hammond, 1979), 45; "Ancient Egypt," *Compton's Interactive Encyclopedia* 3rd ed. (Carlsbad, CA: Compton's NewMedia, Inc. 1994).

20 Raymond Mauny, *Bulletin de l'IFAN, B* (July-October 1960), no. 3-4, quoted in Diop, *Antériorité*, 243.

21 "However, just prior to (and during) Egypt's abrupt emergence into history with the founding of a literate pharaonic monarchy, there is slight evidence for infiltration of new people from outside Egypt . . . perhaps of Asiatic origin." Kenneth A. Kitchen, "Egypt," in the *New Bible Dictionary* (Grand Rapids: Eerdmans, 1962), 338-339.

22 "Egypte," in the *Nouveau dictionnaire biblique révisé,* ed. René Pache (Saint-Légier, Switzerland: Editions Emmaüs, 1992), 384.

23 Diop, *Antériorité*, 244.

24 H. R. Hall, "Egypt to the Coming of Alexander," *Cambridge Ancient History* 6 (1933), 137-166, quoted in Hays, *From Every People and Nation*, 37. I highly recommend the second chapter of Hays's book, "The ethnic make-up of the Old Testament world."

25 Ernest Alfred Wallis Budge, *The Egyptian Sudan*, vol. I (New York: AMS Press, 1976), 512-513, quoted in David T. Adamo, 15.

26 Margaret Bunson, *The Encyclopedia of Ancient Egypt*, rev. ed. (New York: Facts on File, Inc., 2002), 118-119.

27 Bunson, *The Encyclopedia of Ancient Egypt,* 115, 117. Another source says "the Nubian cultures of this period [Naqada II], which are found as far south as Khartum [sic], are not sharply distinct from those of Egypt". John Baines and Jaromír Málek, *Atlas of Ancient Egypt* (New York: Facts on File, 1980), 30.

28 "Egypte," in the *Dictionnaire biblique pour tous* (Valence, France: Éditions LLB, 1994), 159.

29 Barraclough, ed, *Times Atlas of World History*, 52-53, 60-61.

30 Barraclough, ed, *Times Atlas of World History*, 52.

31 Randall Bailey, "Beyond Identification: The Use of Africans in Old Testament Poetry and Narratives," in *Stony the Road We Trod: African-American Biblical Interpretation*, ed. Cain Hope Felder (Minneapolis: Fortress Press, 1991), 167.

32 Hays, *From Every People and Nation*, 26.

33 Robert Draper, "Black Pharaohs," *National Geographic* 213, no. 2 (February 2008), 40.

34 Bennett, "Africa and the Biblical Period," 485.

35 Jean Leclant, "Un tableau du Proche-Orient à la fin du XVIIIe siècle," *Bulletin de la Faculté des Lettres de Strasbourg* 39, no. 5 (February 1961), 252, quoted in Diop, *Antériorité*, 69.

36 Oden, *How Africa Shaped the Christian Mind*, 79, 83.

2

AFRICANS
IN THE OLD TESTAMENT

The first reference to African people in the Old Testament is found in Genesis 10, a chapter sometimes called "the Table of Nations". The three sons of Noah were Shem, Ham, and Japheth, and Genesis 10 deals with their descendants. Genesis 10:6 states that Ham's sons were Cush, Mizraim, Put, and Canaan. These first three sons of Ham are traditionally identified as the ancestors of all African peoples, while Canaan's descendants settled in the Middle East.

The tribe of Cush settled in "Ethiopia", a term referring primarily to the upper Nile region, including southern Egypt and the northern part of Sudan, roughly between the first and the fifth cataracts on the Nile, but perhaps also including a part of the Arabian Peninsula.[1]

It is important to remember that "Ethiopia" in the Bible does not refer to the same region as the present-day nation of Ethiopia. Lower Cush (the northernmost area) was initially called Wawat and was situated between the first and fourth cataracts along the Nile. Upper Cush (the southernmost area) was referred to simply as Cush and was located above the fourth cataract. "Upper" and "lower" are geographical terms that refer to relative elevation above sea level, and not to points on a compass. Hays states that "during the 18th dynasty in Egypt [roughly the time of Moses], these terms [Wawat and Cush] represented two distinct provinces, but the terms soon became interchangeable. The southern area became more powerful and dominant, and thus the name Cush became the common word used in Egyptian texts for the entire region."[2]

The tribe of Mizraim settled in Egypt. In the ancient Near East, Egypt included the flat delta region of the Nile (known as Lower Egypt) and the long, narrow area of land along the Nile valley as far south as the first cataract (known as Upper Egypt). The *New Bible Dictionary* describes Egypt in the following way:

> Among the Egyptians' own names for their homeland, the commonest were: *Kmt* ("Kemyt"), "the black land" (referring to the rich, black soil), *t'wy* ("tawy"), "the two lands" (of the Upper Egyptian valley and the Lower Egyptian delta), and *T'-mr'i* ("To-meri"), "Egypt", the exact literal meaning of which is uncertain . . . Historically ancient Egypt consists of the long,

narrow Nile Valley from the first cataract at Aswan . . . to the Memphis/
Cairo district, plus the broad, flat triangle (hence its name) of the Delta
from Cairo to the sea. The contrast of valley and delta enforce a dual nature
upon Egypt.[3]

The tribe of Put settled in either Libya or Somalia (this will be discussed in more detail later).

Canaan, as already mentioned, settled in Palestine and Phoenicia, not in Africa. Since
Genesis 10:6 treats Ham's "African sons" in the order of Cush, Mizraim, and Put, that is the
order in which they will be discussed here.

A. Descendants of Cush (Sudan or "Ethiopia")

The descendants of Cush are referred to as "Cushites" in the Hebrew Bible as well as in
Egyptian and Akkadian literature. There are 48 Old Testament references in Hebrew to
either the noun "Cush" or its adjective form "Cushite"[4] and nine additional times the noun is
referenced as a proper name for a person instead of a region. However, if we add the indirect
references to this people or place, as well as the references to specific Cushites, there are a
total of 135 Old Testament references to Cush or Cushites in the Old Testament in the NIV
Bible.

It is interesting to note how certain versions of the Bible translate the Hebrew word כּוּשִׁי
(*kushi*, Cushite):

Bible translation	Generally translated as	Noteworthy exceptions
New English Bible (NEB)	Cushite	Proper name "Cushi" (2 Samuel 18; Jeremiah 36:14; Zephaniah 1:1) "Nubian" (Jeremiah 13:23)
King James Version (KJV)	Ethiopian	Proper name "Cushi" (2 Samuel 18; Jeremiah 36:14; Zephaniah 1:1)
New American Standard Bible (NASB) and Revised Standard Version (RSV)	Ethiopian	"Cushite" describing Moses's wife (Numbers 12:1) "the Cushite" (2 Samuel 18) "Cushi" (Jeremiah 36:14, Zephaniah 1:1)
New International Version (NIV)	Cushite	"Ethiopian" (Jeremiah 13:23) "Nubian" (Daniel 11:43)
Today's English Version (TEV)	Sudanese or Sudan	"Cushite" (Numbers 12:1) "black man" (Jeremiah 13:23)

These different translators undoubtedly had good reasons for translating the same Hebrew
word six different ways: Ethiopian, (the) Cushite, Cushi, Nubian, black man, Sudanese. But

it does make for a certain amount of confusion when trying to ascertain who is involved in these different passages.

Early in Genesis a question arises concerning Cush. Is the man called Cush in Genesis 10:7 the same Cush found in Genesis 10:8? Logically, one would think that should be the case. But a problem is introduced when we see that Nimrod, Cush's son in verse 8, is not a part of the list of Cush's sons in verse 7. Also, the sons of Cush in verse 7 live in Arabia and north-east Africa, whereas Nimrod lives in Mesopotamia, according to verse 10. Another complicating factor is the existence of the "land of Cush" in Genesis 2:13, a verse which speaks of the Garden of Eden and presumably puts Cush in the same region of Mesopotamia as the Tigris and Euphrates rivers.[5] A much later Old Testament verse, Micah 5:6, also links Nimrod with Assyria (on the upper Mesopotamian plain). These various factors link Nimrod and his father, Cush, with Mesopotamia and therefore not with Africa.

Opinions are divided as to whether one or two people are named Cush in these verses. Some believe that two different people are named Cush and that one is an African and the other an Asian.[6] Others think that there is only one person named Cush, and that he is most likely an African who then migrated, or whose sons migrated, to Mesopotamia.[7] Whatever the solution to the puzzle of Genesis 10:7-8 may be, after Genesis 10 (which relates to a time period around 2500 BC), we lose sight of these "other Cushites" in the Bible, since in the Old Testament the term "Cushite" consistently refers to a black person from the upper Nile region in Africa and not to someone from Arabia or Mesopotamia.

Certain scholars maintain that Moses's Cushite wife is an exception to that rule, but it seems most probable that she is an African woman instead of an Arabian woman (see the discussion later in this chapter).

The tribe of Cush settled in "Ethiopia", a term which describes the "region south of Egypt (Nubia or northern Sudan) called Ethiopia by classical authors and thus by some Bible translators, *but not referring to present day Ethiopia*."[8] If we compare the region of Cush to a modern map, it would be more geographically accurate to translate "Cushite" as "Sudanese", rather than "Ethiopian" as is used in many Bibles. A note in the French *Parole Vivante* New Testament says, "Ethiopia in the Bible does not designate the modern-day country but rather ancient Nubia, in the middle of Sudan, about 800 km south of Egypt."[9] The conscientious reader must always remember that the "Ethiopians" of the Bible would today be called Sudanese, and this would be true for both the Old and New Testaments.

According to J. Daniel Hays, the Cushites settled the region along the Nile River known as the Kerma Basin located in present-day Sudan. Kerma, just south of the third cataract, became the capital city, and prospered from 2500–1500 BC. He goes on to say:

> This culture excelled in art as well as in the manufacture of bronze items, especially weapons. These people were famous especially for their ceramics, producing some of the most advanced pottery of that period. Perhaps the most important commodity in Cush was gold. Gadd writes that this region was "the general gold mine of the ancient world."[10]

Hays also notes that there is "evidence that Cush was integrally involved in the chariot trade of the ancient Near East, particularly in the development of specially bred chariot horses."[11]

We need to remember that these Cushites – famous for their weapons, pottery, ceramics, gold and horses – were black people. According to one lexicon, the Hebrew word "Cush" equals "black".[12] The fact that Cushites were very dark had even become proverbial by Jeremiah's day (around 600 BC), as we see in Jeremiah 13:23, which states, "Can the Ethiopian change his skin or the leopard its spots?" Today's English Version even translates this verse as, "Can a black man change the color of his skin . . . ?" This illustrates that during Jeremiah's time, "Cushite" was synonymous with "black".

Hays explains that "two lines of evidence demonstrate that the Cushites were black people with classic [black] features. First, Egyptian, Greek, and Roman art presents the Cushites as black. Second, numerous ancient literary texts also refer directly and indirectly to the black skin colour and other [characteristically black] features of the Cushites."[13] As proof, he cites the work of scholars who have specialized in Egyptian art and literature, such as Strouhal, Aldred, Eggebrecht, Ranke, James, Snowden, and Bugner.

In spite of the above evidence, there has been widespread debate over the descendants of Cush. Even though it is generally accepted that Cush settled in northern Sudan, his descendants mentioned in Genesis 10:7 – five sons and two grandsons – are often associated with tribes that settled in Arabia. The note in the *NIV Study Bible* says that these seven Cushite nations were *all* located in Arabia.[14] However, if all seven of Cush's sons and grandsons settled in Arabia, then there would have been *no* Cushites in Africa once Cush himself died (assuming he himself lived there). But since there is so much evidence for black Cushites in Africa, somewhere along the line they must have migrated from Arabia to Africa, an event not recorded in the Table of Nations (Genesis 10). While possible, this explanation strikes me as quite tenuous.

A more plausible explanation of how so many Cushites ended up in Africa is that, while four of Cush's sons and their descendants lived in Arabia, the descendants of Seba, Cush's first son, remained in Africa, living in the northeast corner of the continent. Scholars who hold to such an explanation[15] base their reasoning in part on verses like Isaiah 43:3 and 45:14, which speak of Seba, Nubia/Cush, and Egypt together. From this it seems probable that Cush and his eldest son inhabited the regions of the upper Nile while his other sons and grandsons migrated to the Arabian Peninsula.

This conclusion is supported by historical evidence that indicates "Ethiopia" and southern Arabia shared the same culture. One scriptural passage that could purportedly support this idea is 2 Chronicles 21:16, which speaks of "the Arabs who lived near the Cushites". Strabo, the Greek historian who lived just before the time of Christ, spoke of the "the Ethiopians that are . . . 'sundered in twain' naturally by the Arabian Gulf . . . some of them live in Asia, others in Libya [Africa] though they differ in no respect from each other."[16] It must be remembered that the Greeks called all black people "Ethiopian", a term meaning "the burnt faces".

The Senegalese author Cheikh Anta Diop also speaks of the unity of these two regions, saying, "up to the birth of Muhammad, southern Arabia is inseparable from Ethiopia; their historical destiny was a common one, and Ethiopia's sovereignty over Arabia was only at times barely interrupted".[17] David T. Adamo, who, like Diop, holds to an "Afrocentric reconstruction of the history of ancient Israel" says, "it is possible that from Kerma the Cushite kingdom, with its administrative centre in Kerma or Meroe, extended to part of Arabia."[18]

The Rev Father Jean-Baptiste Coulbeaux says in his book on the history of Ethiopia, "'Cush' and 'Ethiopian' are equivalent terms, designating one and the same race. As such, they refer equally to the Cushites of Arabia and to those of the African continent . . . The children of Cush were indeed scattered, some in Arabia and some in Africa".[19] Even though Diop and Coulbeaux do not agree as to who was sovereign over whom – Coulbeaux maintains that the Cushites from Arabia became so dominant when they migrated to present-day Ethiopia that it could be considered a conquest[20] – both views illustrate how much the two regions were intertwined. The fact that several Ethiopian languages are Semitic languages[21] is evidence in favour of Coulbeaux's position. Nonetheless, this linguistic link serves as another indication of the connection between these two regions.

To conclude, the descendants of Cush were black people who lived both in Africa and Arabia. There seems to be too much evidence to only put them on one side or the other of the Red Sea. However, *over time* these two branches were seen as two separate peoples, most likely due to the fact that those Cushites in Arabia intermarried with other, primarily Semitic,[22] peoples for many generations while those in Africa did not. This eventually led to a difference in skin colour, facial features, linguistic patterns, and cultural values between these two Cushitic peoples.

Having established who the Cushites were, we now turn to what the Bible says about them. Like the Libyans, Cushites were renowned as good soldiers. Several of the verses that mention Libyans also mention Cushites who were employed as mercenaries. It seems that for a time the military might of the Cushites surpassed that of the Libyans, since the nations of Cush and Egypt are described as the "boundless strength" of the city of Nineveh (Nahum 3:9). Furthermore, Cushite archers were renowned for their accuracy throughout the ancient Near East. Welsby also tells us there are accounts of elite Cushite cavalry units, particularly known for the training of their chariot horses. Assyrians and others often imported Cushite chariot horses by way of Egypt.[23]

It is understandable why many kings of Israel were tempted to turn to the military might of Egypt and Cush/Sudan. This is one reason why the Old Testament prophets warned the people of Israel to place their faith in God instead of in powerful, yet unreliable, regional powers.

Isaiah 18:1-7 confirms that the country of Cush was viewed as a regional power that dominated other nearby kingdoms. In Isaiah's day the kings of Cush reigned over all of Egypt. The second part of Isaiah 18:2 mentions Cush: "Go, swift messengers, to a people tall and smooth-skinned, to a people feared far and wide, an aggressive nation of strange speech, whose land is divided by rivers." These same adjectives are used again in verse 7 to reinforce the truth of the prophet's words. Cushites are here described as tall and smooth-skinned. The Greek historian Herodotus says that Cushites/Nubians/Ethiopians are "the largest and most beautiful of men".[24] As previously mentioned, the black colouring of their skin had become proverbial and the word "Cushite" was synonymous with "black".

During the 18th, 19th, and 20th Egyptian dynasties, around the time between Moses and David, Hays tells us, "many Cushites lived in Egypt at this time, some slaves taken in war, but others as free members of society. They are depicted as house servants, workers, soldiers, and police. Cushite soldiers could attain high rank, even ascending to the Pharaoh's personal bodyguard."[25]

Later, during the 25th dynasty, several black Pharaohs came to power in Egypt, roughly concurrent with the reigns of kings Ahaz and Hezekiah in Judah. They reigned for over 75 years over all of Egypt. Robert Draper, in his article titled "Black Pharaohs" in *National Geographic*, explains to what extent these Pharaohs from Nubia (southern part of modern Egypt, northern part of modern Sudan) dominated the political life of the region:

> The black Pharaohs reunified an Egypt in shambles, and filled its countryside with glorious monuments, thus creating an empire that stretched from present day Khartoum to the Mediterranean in the north. They stood up to the bloodthirsty Assyrians, and maybe even delivered the city of Jerusalem. Their chapter in history has only recently been told. Archaeologists have only been exploring their stories for four decades, noting that these black Pharaohs did not spring from a void. Rather they rose from a robust African civilization that flourished on the banks of the Nile for almost 2500 years, dating back to at least the first Egyptian dynasty.[26]

Hays agrees with Draper concerning both the impact and the timeframe of the Cushite/ Nubian civilization. He summarizes the history of the Cushites, saying:

> The Cushite civilization extended over a period of more than 2500 years. Its populace was urbane, civilized, literate, artistic, and religious. During this era Cush was a major actor on the geopolitical stage of the ancient Near East – and she is owed her proper place in history alongside the Egyptians, Assyrians, Babylonians, Hittites, Hebrews, and other important peoples of the ancient world. This was a black civilization, African on African soil, known and respected throughout antiquity. The ancient Near East, the "cradle of civilization", was without a doubt multiracial.[27]

If more proof were needed, an additional witness to the importance of this region is found in the work of the ancient geographer, Eratosthenes, who was born in Cyrene (in modern-day Libya) and studied in Alexandria in Egypt. He was the first person to have the idea of subdividing the surface of the earth by using imaginary parallel lines – lines that we call latitude and longitude today – in order to better know the distance and the direction between two known points. However, on Eratosthenes's map, these lines of latitude and longitude were not placed at regular intervals like on modern maps. Rather, they crossed well-known places in the ancient world. His longitudinal lines went through "ancient, familiar, and prominent places – Alexandria, Rhodes, Meroe (the capital of ancient Ethiopian kings), the Pillars of Hercules, Sicily, the Euphrates River . . . The result was an irregular network, serving human convenience by superimposing a neat grid on the earth's spherical surface."[28] It is interesting to note that Eratosthenes marked his map with these lines around 240 BC, more than 400 years after the 25th dynasty and the height of Cushite influence. Even after all that time, Meroe (the name later given to southern Cush) was still considered to be a well-known and important region.

Now let us look at specific Cushite people in the Old Testament.

Moses's Cushite wife

The first use of the word "Cushite" in the Old Testament describes Moses's wife. "Miriam and Aaron began to speak against Moses. They blamed him for his Cushite wife (for he had married a Cushite woman)" (Numbers 12:1). Some believe this "Cushite wife" refers to Zipporah, Moses's wife who is also mentioned in Exodus 2:21 and 4:24-26, in which case "Cushite" would be synonymous with "Midianite". If this is the case, then Moses's Cushite wife was Arab, not African. A note in *La Bible en français courant* translates to say, "Cushite here probably means 'belonging to the tribe of Cushan' (compare Habakkuk 3:7)."[29] Another French Bible explains, "if the name Cushite often refers to the Nubian peoples of the Upper Nile, it applies no less to the nomadic tribes indistinguishable from the Midianites".[30] This argument is based on only one verse that mentions Cushan and Midian together (Habakkuk 3:7). If both these tribes were Asiatic from the Middle East, and if "Cushite" can apply to someone from Cushan as well as from Cush, then Moses's wife could have been Arab instead of African. However if this is the case, it is the only instance in the entire Bible where "Cushite" refers to someone from Cushan. Every other time, it refers to the people of Cush, that is, people of the region south of Egypt and north of Sudan, called "Ethiopia" at that time.

Other scholars, however, do not believe the term "Cushite" refers to someone from the tribe of Cushan. A note linked to Numbers 12:1 in the *NIV Study Bible* reads, "Cush was the first son of Ham, the father of the southernmost peoples known to the Hebrews (Gen 10:6-7) living in the southern Nile valley. Moses's wife Zipporah may be referred to here . . . It is more likely, however, that the reference is to a new wife taken by Moses, perhaps after the death of his first wife."[31]

J. Daniel Hays, an author who has written extensively about Cushites, believes that Moses married a black woman from Cush, the civilization south of Egypt. He explains:

> During the 18th, 19th, and 20th Egyptian dynasties (1552–1069 BC), Cush was under direct Egyptian control, and was practically part of Egypt. Thousands of Cushites lived in Egypt, and they penetrated all layers of society. Since Moses was born and raised during this period in Egypt (many scholars place the Exodus in the 13th century BC), he surely knew many Cushites."[32]

We cannot forget that a sizable melting pot existed in Egypt, and that a large part of it left with the Israelites. Exodus 12:38 says, "A mixed crowd also went with them" (RSV) or "Many people who were not Israelites went with them" (NLT). Regarding the Hebrew word for "mixed crowd", Hays says "the clear stress of the Hebrew term used (*'ēreb*) is that these people were non-Israelites." He cites Brueggemann in saying that "the phrase suggests that this is no kinship group, no ethnic community, but [rather] a great conglomeration of lower-class folk . . . This term is important for the view that earliest Israel was not an ethnic community."[33] I agree that this term refers to a "great conglomeration" of folks, although the Hebrew term does not imply that they were "lower-class" as Brueggemann suggests. At times in the Old Testament, derivatives of this word are even used to mean "captain, chief".[34] The New Living Translation of this verse says that "Many people who were not Israelites went with them." Many verses in the Pentateuch refer to the immigrant populations living among the Israelites. It is very likely that Moses's "Cushite wife" was part of this "mixed crowd" of people following the ways of God.

Hays points out other logical problems with the view that Moses's "Cushite wife" refers to Zipporah. Why is Moses's father-in-law referred to as a "Midianite" in Numbers 10 if his daughter is a "Cushite" in chapter 12? Furthermore, why would Aaron and Miriam wait 40 years before speaking out against his wife? Their complaint would make more sense if they were complaining about a marriage that had just happened rather than one that had happened forty years earlier. Numbers 12:1 also implies a recent marriage. Frankly, these arguments seem more solid to me than those based on a single obscure verse in Habakkuk that was written more than 600 years later.

The Bible does not clarify why Miriam and Aaron spoke against this woman. The fact that she was black seems like a pretext for rebelling against Moses's authority (see Numbers 12:2). Young agrees that it was a convenient pretext, and their true reason for complaining was their jealousy of Moses's position.[35] Also, Snowden maintains that marriages between blacks and other ethnic groups, especially Egyptians, were not exceptional.[36] Why then complain about something that was common practice?

However, some scholars maintain that Aaron and Miriam's complaint was racist, and that the siblings' only basis for objection was that Moses had married a black woman.[37] Others rule out this possibility.[38] Others say that the problem was the woman's distant and prideful attitude, not racism.[39] Hays suggests that Miriam did not want another woman intruding in their "small circle of power", since she, Moses, and Aaron were all siblings. But this was no simple case of jealousy. Rather, she wanted Moses to follow the example of the Pharaohs who often married their sisters to consolidate power. Perhaps Miriam saw the Cushite woman as a rival who had taken her place.[40] All of these reasons are impossible to prove since the Bible does not actually spell out Miriam or Aaron's motivations; such theories are merely conjecture.

To summarize, this passage indicates that it is very probable that Moses – considered by many to be the greatest prophet of the Old Testament – had a black wife. I personally opt for this interpretation. It follows the broader usage of the term "Cushite" and it seems certain that the "mixed crowd" that accompanied the Israelites in the Exodus included Cushites. The use of the word "Cushan" in Habakkuk 600 years later is too chronologically distant from the book of Numbers to guarantee the accuracy of the possible linguistic convention. That said, it must be acknowledged that some descendants of Cush did settle in Arabia; this woman could have been one of them. Less probably, perhaps "Cushite" really could refer to someone from Cushan. In either case, this would be the *only* reference in the Old Testament where Cushite does *not* mean someone from Africa. It is impossible to know conclusively whether Moses's "Cushite wife" was from Africa or Arabia, but the evidence favours the interpretation that she was African.

Phinehas

The second Cushite person in the Old Testament is practically hidden. You must study the meaning of his name to discover his Cushite origins. This man is Phinehas, son of Eleazar and grandson of Aaron (Exodus 6:25). His mother was the daughter of Putiel.

The name Phinehas is borrowed from the Egyptian language. The Egyptian word for "Cushite/Nubian" is *nehsiu*, and the article "the" is the prefix *ph-*. Phinehas therefore means "the Cushite".[41] It is the first time we see this name in the Old Testament. But how is it that

Aaron's grandson has a name that means "the Cushite"? The logical answer is that his mother was Cushite, or in other words, that Putiel's daughter was black. As I mentioned previously, "Cushite" in biblical times could refer to someone from Cush, or proverbially to someone with dark skin. We will see later in this chapter that Putiel may have been a Somali or a Libyan, that is, a man with a dark complexion. Some scholars hold that Putiel was Egyptian, but this would still likely mean that he was dark in complexion. If Putiel's wife (Phinehas's grandmother) was a Cushite, his daughter would be some combination of Cushite and Libyan/Somali/Egyptian, thus also very dark-skinned. It seems logical then that Phinehas was very dark skinned, which he got from his mother's side, and that this characteristic is what earned him his name. Hays agrees when he speaks of a mixed marriage between a Hebrew (Eleazar, Phinehas's father) and a Cushite (Phinehas's mother) to explain why their son is called "the black man".[42] In any case, it is safe to conclude that this man was dark-skinned and part African.

Phinehas's righteous character is apparent in Numbers 25. The Israelites had begun intermarrying with Moabite and Midianite women. Many Israelite men had begun to adopt the religious practices of their new wives, most of whom worshipped the Baal of Peor. Worshipping the Baal of Peor involved debauchery, which combines the sins of idolatry and sexual immorality. As a result, God's wrath was kindled against the Israelites and he sent a plague on all of Israel. Many people died. To end the plague, which was killing many innocent people along with the guilty, Moses commanded the tribal leaders to put all the guilty parties to death.

But before this order could be carried out, an Israelite named Zimri brought a Midianite woman into his tent – not far from Moses, the elders, and the entire congregation – to sleep with her. Perhaps because Zimri was a prince of the tribe of Simeon, he thought he could act with impunity. Whatever his reasoning, it was an act of blatant disobedience, a public disavowal of the covenant between God and his people. He was openly mocking God.

When Phinehas saw what was happening, his zeal for God and for justice drove him to intervene. He seized a spear and entered the tent. He pinned the couple together with the spear, killing them both. An act of blatant defiance required an act of extreme jealousy for God. Phinehas's zealous deed and his obedience to Moses's orders saved thousands of lives. As soon as he killed the guilty couple, the plague stopped. His righteous anger against sin went together with his love for his people. God did not wait for the deaths of all the other guilty people before stopping the plague. His anger immediately turned away from the Israelites.

The result of Phinehas's zeal was that God formed a "covenant of peace" with him, a perpetual "covenant of a lasting priesthood" with his descendants (Numbers 25:12-13). The Old Testament uses the word "covenant" to describe God's relationship with Israel, but that covenant was replaced by the new covenant. God made an everlasting covenant with only a few individuals: Noah, Abraham, Isaac, David, and Phinehas. We must not overlook the fact that of these five, one was an African. It can be conjectured that perhaps Phinehas was chosen to make the yearly sacrifice of atonement for Israel's sins as high priest (see Leviticus 16), because he had made atonement for the Israelites by stopping the plague (Numbers 25:13). Phinehas fulfilled the function of high priest for almost 20 years, if not longer, after the death of his father Eleazar (Joshua 24:33). God kept his covenant with Phinehas. "His descendants held the high priesthood until the Romans destroyed the Temple in AD 70, except for a short period when the house of Eli served as high priests."[43]

Phinehas is known for other exploits in the Old Testament as well. He was part of an army of 12,000 soldiers in a battle against the Midianites (Numbers 31:6). He later acted as the spokesman for God. On behalf of the people, Phinehas asked God what to do about the depravity of the Benjamites (Judges 20:27-28). At God's command, Phinehas told the children of Israel to attack the Benjamites because of their depravity, resulting in their near destruction.

We should not, however, make the mistake of characterizing Phinehas as a belligerent person. In Joshua 22, we see him take the role of national mediator. The whole assembly of Israel wanted to go to war against the tribes east of the Jordan, because those tribes had constructed an altar. Instead of getting carried away with emotion, Israel decided to listen to the explanation of the tribes east of the Jordan. They sent a delegation of chief men, led by Phinehas. When the tribes explained their pure motives, the delegation realized that by listening before going to war, they had avoided a serious mistake. As a sign of his humility and in his work as a peacemaker, Phinehas admitted that Israel was wrong to want to attack the eastern tribes, who had acted faithfully toward God (Joshua 22:30-33). In Phinehas's life, Wenham mentions his "courage and decisiveness are apparent".[44]

The Bible itself makes three interesting comments on Phinehas. Psalm 106:30-31 says, "But Phinehas stood up and intervened, and the plague was checked. This was credited to him as righteousness for endless generations to come." Only one other person is mentioned having something credited to them as righteousness: Abraham. In the same way that Abraham's faith was "credited to him as righteousness" (Genesis 15:6 and Romans 4:3, 5), Phinehas's zeal was also credited to him as righteousness.

Secondly, 1 Chronicles 9:20 says, "In earlier times Phinehas son of Eleazar was in charge of the gatekeepers, and the Lord was with him." The two books of Chronicles were written more than 600 years after the death of Phinehas. The author of these books does not mention Phinehas's exploits, as the psalmist did. He does not even mention the troubles with the Midianites. But two characteristics are remembered: he was the leader of certain men who had an important responsibility, and God was with him. We remember him for his leadership, and we remember him for his intimate relationship with God. What a fitting tribute for this African man who guided the people of Israel through a turbulent time in their history!

The last prophet of the Old Testament, Malachi, refers to Phinehas as "Levi":

> And you will know that I have sent you this admonition so that my covenant with Levi may continue," says the Lord Almighty. "My covenant was with him, **a covenant of life and peace**, and I gave them to him; this called for **reverence** and he revered me and stood in awe of my name. **True instruction** was in his mouth and **nothing false** was found on his lips. He walked with me in peace and **uprightness**, and turned many from sin.
>
> For the lips of a priest ought to preserve **knowledge**, and from his mouth men should seek instruction – because he is the messenger of the Lord Almighty. (Malachi 2:4-7, emphasis added)

Only the descendants of Levi could perform the functions of priests and make the required sacrifices. Aaron was a descendant of Levi. But it is important to note that nowhere in the Old Testament is there an explicit description of such an alliance with Levi as the one mentioned in Malachi 2:5-6. However, the exact words "covenant of peace" are used by God regarding Phinehas in Numbers 25:12, when God says, "Therefore . . . I am making my covenant of peace with him." As a grandson of Aaron, and therefore a direct descendant of Levi, it seems that this verse is speaking of Phinehas. Some commentaries and Bibles draw the same conclusion.[45] This passage also says that "Levi" "turned many from sin". We see no example of this recorded in the life of Levi. But God says, "Phinehas son of Eleazar, the son of Aaron, the priest, has turned my anger away from the Israelites; for he was as zealous as I am for my honor among them, so that in my zeal I did not put an end to them" (Numbers 25:11). The similar wording and circumstances make it clear that the "Levi" in Malachi is not Levi after all, but rather his descendant, Phinehas. By using the name "Levi" which represents all priests, Malachi implies that all priests should be characterized by these verses which describe Phinehas. Along with Zadok (see Ezekiel 43:19 and 44:15), Phinehas is one of only two high priests used as a model for the entire Old Testament priesthood.

So we see that Phinehas is the priest that God himself presents as a model for all priests to follow if they want to live in truth, peace, uprightness, knowledge, and a reverence for God.

The Queen of Sheba

Another woman of the Old Testament demonstrates yet again the problem of knowing where the descendants of Cush emigrated. Scholars debate whether the Queen of Sheba, mentioned in 1 Kings 10 and 2 Chronicles 9, was African or Arab.

It is unclear whether Sheba is in Africa or Arabia partially because the Bible mentions two places with similar names, Sheba (1 Kings 10; 2 Chronicles 9; Psalm 72:10) and Seba (Psalm 72:10; Isaiah 43:3). Even though they are two distinct places, English translations often use "Sabean" for people from either Sheba or Seba, which confuses it further (Job 1:15; Isaiah 45:14; possibly Ezekiel 23:42).[46] The French *Bible d'étude Semeur 2000* states that Seba refers to a "people living undoubtedly in Africa, probably in northern modern-day Sudan",[47] and some scholars agree. But where was Sheba located?

Certain Church fathers, like Josephus, Origen, and Jerome identify Sheba with Africa. Diop also considers the evidence to point towards Africa rather than Arabia: "It thus appears, from the slim historical sources we possess, that it is more to Ethiopia and not 'Sabean' Arabia that we must attach the Queen of Sheba."[48] Diop offers no proof to sustain his hypothesis, however. Coulbeaux solves the problem, at least for himself, by explaining that she was queen of two regions: "Solomon's royal visitor, the *Makkeda* of the Abyssinians [and] the *Belkis* of the Arabs, was in effect ruler of the Sabeans on both coasts of the Red Sea. She therefore satisfies the demands of the double legend of two countries united under a single sceptre."[49]

Despite the opinions of these authors, as well as the words of the "Kebra Nagast", the national saga of Ethiopia,[50] most recent Bible dictionaries identify Sheba with Arabia. The *Bible d'étude Semeur 2000* says people from Sheba were "a nomadic people living in southern Arabia . . . They were merchants".[51] Bright places it in eastern Yemen.[52] Hays, who is normally very favourable towards defending Africa's place in the Bible, concludes by saying, "Although there is a valid argument that she [the Queen of Sheba] was from black Africa, the evidence seems stronger that she lived in southwestern Arabia, and the majority of Old Testament scholars maintain this view."[53] So although it is impossible to pinpoint the geographic locale of the Queen of Sheba, her African origin seems unlikely.

Joab's Cushite servant

During King David's reign, an African served Joab, David's general. He is called simply "the Cushite" (2 Samuel 18:21-32). When Joab killed Absalom, David's rebellious son, he had to send a messenger to inform David. He knew that the news would not please the king. Instead of sending his usual messenger, Ahimaaz, he sent the Cushite in his place. This could possibly indicate Joab's scorn for Cushites; he knew that if the king reacted badly to the news of his son's death, the messenger's life could well be in jeopardy. In that case, he would prefer to send a foreigner than an Israelite. Hays, however, suggests another possibility: "Perhaps, like Ebed-Melech 300 years later, this Cushite was one of the few not overawed by the king [David] – one who was not afraid of the king and who could thus speak forthrightly, even to the point of delivering the news of the death of the king's son."[54]

The Cushite promptly and faithfully did what he was asked to do, regardless of the potential danger. Ahimaaz was also sent to warn David, and actually arrived first by taking another route. But he could not or would not clearly communicate the message, and David had to await the Cushite's arrival to discover the fate of his son. We can see that the Cushite responded to David's questions with tact, trying to reassure David in such a delicate moment. David finally accepts the fact of his son's death from the words of the Cushite. Even though it was a bitter message to hear, David does not harm the messenger. It seems David had more regard for the Cushite than his general did.

Zerah

In 2 Chronicles 14:9-15, we hear of another Cushite, Zerah, who is an enemy of the people of Israel. This man was the commander of an African army that attacked Asa, king of Judah, around 900 BC. Zerah was probably a military commander dispatched by the Libyan Pharaoh Osorkon I, since Libyans and Cushites often deployed together on the field of battle (i.e., 2 Chronicles 16:8). Zerah was the commander of a vast army which was supplemented by 300 chariots. But King Asa called upon the Lord and Zerah's army was defeated at Mareshah (2 Chronicles 14:11). Despite their defeat, this account shows us, according to Hays, that the Cushites played an important geopolitical role in the Near East, and in Israel in particular.[55]

So

The Old Testament mentions another Pharaoh about whom we know very little. So, king of Egypt, received a request for aid from Hoshea, the last king of the northern kingdom of Israel (2 Kings 17:1-5), although Hoshea was a vassal of the Assyrian king Shalmaneser V. It is unclear whether So came to his aid, since the king of Assyria put Hoshea in prison. Scholars propose several explanations for whom So might have been:

1. The last Libyan Pharaoh, Osorkon IV (727-716 BC);
2. Tefnakht, of the 24th dynasty, who lived in the Delta city of Sais;
3. A lesser, unidentified "kinglet" of the eastern delta region;

4. So, vocalized Sewe' or Siwe', the Cushite general who eventually became Pharaoh Shaba(ka)/Shaba(ko);

5. Sibe/Siwe, the commander in chief (tartan) of the Egyptian army which, allied with Hanin king of Gaza, was defeated in battle at Raphia in 720 BC by Sargon II, king of Assyria;

6. So is not a proper name, but rather a transcription from Egyptian and refers to the "so" (or vizier) of the king of Egypt, who was Osorkon IV.[56]

That same source concludes that the most plausible possibilities are the first and third.

Although the biblical text calls him "So, king of Egypt", it is possible that he was not an Egyptian at all. In his book *Africa and the Bible*, Yamauchi treats him in the chapter on Cushites and states that some scholars identify him with the Cushite ruler Piankhy.[57] As just seen, the *New Bible Dictionary* says that he was perhaps the last Libyan Pharaoh, Osorkon IV, and it allows that others see him as the Cushite Pharaoh, Shabaka.[58]

The New English Bible takes a minority viewpoint, translating part of 2 Kings 17:4 as "to the king of Egypt at So" instead of "to So, king of Egypt". In this case, So is a place in Egypt, not a person.

We do not know whether So was Egyptian, Libyan, or Cushite, but he was an African ruler in the Bible.

Shabaka, Shebitku, and Tirhakah

As we have already seen, the Pharaohs in Egypt were not always Egyptians. Cushite Pharaohs began to rule in the 25th dynasty, with the first two Pharaohs, Kashta and Piankhy, ruling over Cush (northern Sudan along with southern Egypt), including the city of Thebes. The *Bible d'étude Semeur 2000* proposes, "It could be a question of internal struggles which saw Egyptian infighting around 716 BC at the end of the 24th dynasty, allowing the Ethiopian [Cushite] kings of the 25th dynasty to impose their rule over the whole country."[59] Whether it was due to the internal weakness of the 24th dynasty or the military superiority of the 25th dynasty, the subsequent Cushite Pharaohs of the 25th dynasty expanded their rule to include all of Egypt. The Old Testament mentions some of these Cushite Pharaohs who ruled over all of Egypt, probably referring to Shabaka, Shebitku, and Tirhakah.

Shabaka or his successor Shebitku could be the Pharaoh in Isaiah 18–20 and 30–31. During Isaiah's time, Assyria had conquered the Northern Kingdom (Israel) in 722 BC, leaving the Southern Kingdom (Judah) vulnerable. Just a few years later, these Cushite kings came to power in Egypt, with Shabaka being the first Cushite Pharaoh to rule over all of Egypt. "Almost all the distinctive characteristics of Kushite rule in Egypt, in administrative control, royal regalia, iconography, and artistic style, were formulated under Shabako."[60] Hezekiah became king of Judah at roughly the same time. According to the *NIV Study Bible*, "King Hezekiah of Judah was under great pressure to make an alliance with Egypt. Isaiah urgently warned against such a policy."[61] This pressure to form an alliance may have occurred early in his reign, since Hezekiah's father, King Ahaz, had already offered gifts to the king of Assyria (2 Chronicles 28:21). If so, Hezekiah would have been dealing with Pharaoh Shabaka. A note in the *NIV Study Bible* for Isaiah 30:1 tends to confirm this: "After Shabaka became Pharaoh . . . the smaller nations in Aram (Syria) and Canaan sought his help against Assyria. Judah apparently joined them."[62]

So we see that Judah ended up concluding an alliance with a Cushite Pharaoh of Egypt because of the threat from Sennacherib, king of Assyria. Initially Hezekiah was willing to pay a heavy tribute of gold and silver to Sennacherib (2 Kings 18:13-16). Assyrian annals, however, speak of other objects of value furnished by Hezekiah: couches and chairs inlaid with ivory, elephant hides, and ebony wood. Hays notes that "the fact that Hezekiah has treasures that are connected to Africa (ivory, elephant hides, ebony-wood) correlates well with our earlier observation that relations between the Cushites and the Judahites were close at this time".[63]

Despite all this tribute paid by Hezekiah, around 701 BC the Assyrian army laid siege to Jerusalem. The Assyrian messenger warned the king of Judah to not put his trust in Egypt and its Pharaoh, just as Isaiah warned, but for totally different reasons (2 Kings 18:21; Isaiah 36:6). The Pharaoh in question is Shebitku, fourth Pharaoh of the 25th dynasty. As a result of the alliance with Judah, Shebitku sent his younger brother, Tirhakah, as the head of the Egyptian army, to fight the Assyrians.[64] The *NIV Study Bible* note on Isaiah 37:9 explains: "In 701 BC, he [Tirhakah] was actually a prince (the brother of the new Pharaoh Shebitku, who sent him with an army to help Hezekiah withstand the Assyrian invasion); he did not become king until 690. But this part of Isaiah was not written before 681 . . . so it was natural to speak of Tirhakah as king."[65] The fact that he came from Cush explains why in these two verses he is called "the king of Cush" instead of the king of Egypt. At the end of the day, the prophet Isaiah was proven right: Tirhakah's army was not trustworthy, for it was badly defeated by Sennacherib at the battle of Eltekeh. God himself then proceeded to destroy the Assyrian army (Isaiah 37:36-37).

In spite of the defeat of Prince Tirhakah's army, we see in the Bible that the king of Judah made an appeal to an African kingdom, and that the African monarch Shebitku allied himself with the people of God and even sent aid when these allies were threatened, despite potentially dangerous consequences.

The Bible speaks little of Tirhakah, but other sources speak of his reign. Citing several sources, Yamauchi speaks of Tirhakah as the most important Pharaoh of the 25th dynasty, a man known for his athleticism, his piety, and the many construction projects completed during his reign.[66]

Cushi, great-grandfather of Jehudi

Jeremiah 36:14 mentions Jehudi, son of Nethaniah, son of Shelemiah, son of Cushi. Normally, the name Cushi means "the Cushite" in Hebrew, that is, a black person from the region of modern-day northern Sudan. So the name Cushi means "the black man". However, there are several possibilities as to the interpretation of this name. According to Hays:

> In this context there are at least four plausible reasons for naming someone *Cushi*: the individual was *actually* a Cushite from Cush; the individual had a Cushite mother, father, or grandparent, and therefore *looked* like a Cushite; the individual had Judahite parents, but was *born* in Cush; or the individual was named *in honour* of the Cushites, since they were a powerful military ally in the struggle against the Assyrians. Since numerous Cushite soldiers, diplomats, and traders were in Judah, and likewise, Judahite diplomats

and traders must have been in Egypt and Cush, any of the four scenarios described above would have been possible.[67]

It must be said that naming someone "the black man" who is not black would naturally create a lot of confusion. Giving someone that kind of a *nickname* later in life could certainly be a possibility, but here this verse is speaking of a proper name that is part of a genealogy. Hebrew genealogies do not normally deal with nicknames. I tend to think the first two possibilities are the most likely: either Cushi really was a black Cushite, or his father or mother was a black Cushite.

There is one example in the psalms of a Hebrew man from the tribe of Benjamin named Cush (the title to Psalm 7). In spite of his name, he is not a black man, since the text says he is a Benjamite. However, his name is "Cush", the name of a country, and not "Cushi", which means Cushite/black man. Using the country name, Cush, as a proper name seems to correspond better to the idea of being named in honour of a country than does using the name Cushi. To use a modern-day illustration, if someone wanted to name a son after the "Arab spring" of 2011, it would seem more logical to name a son "Egypt" than to name him "Egyptian". The former would lead to less confusion than the latter. In the same way, Hays's first two possibilities still seem more plausible and probable for someone named Cushi, so the latter two possibilities seem more plausible for someone named Cush.

Ebed-Melech

One Cushite in the Bible truly distinguished himself in the service of the Lord, although he is unknown to most Christians. This man was Ebed-Melech (Jeremiah 38–39). Interestingly, in chapter 37 an African (Pharaoh Hophra) was unable to come to the aid of the people of God despite his vast army and military might. But in the next chapter, an African saved the life of God's prophet through diplomacy and personal courage.

Ebed-Melech (which means "servant of the king" in Hebrew) was an "official in the royal palace" in Judah, under King Zedekiah (38:7). Many newer translations of the Bible refer to Ebed-Melech as "an important palace official", and *La Bible en Français Courant* calls him "a trusted man in the royal palace". Many of the older versions of the Bible call him "a eunuch of the king's house". According to the *Nouveau dictionnaire biblique révisé*, a eunuch is someone who has been castrated, but "according to [the Jewish historian] Josephus, castration was not practiced by the Jews on either men or animals, and the spirit of the Law was opposed to such treatment in Israel . . . Eunuchs often occupied high places and commanded vast authority."[68] This may explain why these different translations of the Bible translate this word differently. Hays concludes that:

> The most plausible explanation . . . is to understand Ebed-Melech as a military officer. Perhaps he led a contingent of Cushite soldiers. He may even have been in charge of the royal bodyguards. He is probably the ranking representative of the Egyptian army in Jerusalem, the equivalent of a modern military attaché. This would explain why he could obtain an audience with Zedekiah and why Zedekiah acquiesced so quickly [to Ebed-Melech's proposal].[69]

As an "important palace official" and "a trusted man in the palace", Ebed-Melech quickly became aware that Jeremiah had been taken by the king's ministers and thrown into a mud-filled cistern. He went to King Zedekiah, who was holding court at the Benjamin gate. A city gate was often used by kings and officials as a kind of open courtroom.[70] There Ebed-Melech publicly denounced the king's ministers, knowing that they wanted to put Jeremiah to death as a traitor. By pleading Jeremiah's case, he obtained permission from the king to have Jeremiah removed from the cistern. In doing so he was careful not to further injure the prophet. He provided "old rags and worn-out clothes and let them down with ropes to Jeremiah in the cistern. Ebed-Melech the Cushite said to Jeremiah, 'Put these old rags and worn-out clothes under your arms to pad the ropes.' Jeremiah did so" (Jeremiah 38:11-12). This thoughtful and practical act shows the high regard Ebed-Melech had for the prophet, even though it cost him; from that point on he lived in fear of these ministers of the king (Jeremiah 39:17).

God blessed Ebed-Melech. In Jeremiah 39:15-18, God promised to deliver him from the misery that was about to befall Jerusalem (which was under siege from the Babylonian army at the time – about 587 BC) His life would be spared; he would not die by the sword. What a relief to know he had protection from his enemies, both the Babylonians and the scheming ministers loyal to King Zedekiah.

God told Ebed-Melech why he chose to bless him: "because you trust in me" (Jeremiah 39:18). God rewarded his faith, a faith proven by his courage before the king and his ministers and proven by his compassion toward Jeremiah. David Adamo sums it up well when he says:

> When some scholars examined "Ebed-Melech's courage, dispatch, compassion, and his ability to bring out the best in" one of the kings of Israel, they considered this story in Jeremiah 37:7-13 as "one of the fairest stories in the Old Testament." Moved to save the life of another and acting without calculation or counting the cost, an unknown black man emerges "from obscurity to immortality."[71]

Cushi, Zephaniah's father

Another man named Cushi appears in Zephaniah 1:1. He was the father of the prophet Zephaniah. The same comments concerning ethnicity that applied to Cushi the great-grandfather of Jehudi (see above), also apply to this man named Cushi. The main difference is that here he is the father, and not the great-grandfather, of the person being discussed. If Zephaniah's father was himself a Cushite, that means that his son was half black African and half Judahite. Or, if Zephaniah's father was the son of a mixed marriage between a Judahite and a Cushite, that would mean that Zephaniah was 25 per cent black African. Either way, he was partly Cushite/black.

If, on the other hand, Zephaniah's father was given the name Cushi because he was born in Cush of Jewish parents, or because his parents wanted to honour the country of Cush, then there would be no link between Zephaniah and any supposed Cushite ethnicity. But, as stated earlier, giving a name that means "black man" to a non-black man would definitely create confusion. A person could easily earn such a nickname for being born in Cush or for honouring the Cushites, but this verse does not treat nicknames. Rather it treats proper names that are part of an official genealogy of the prophet.

If Cushi was himself a Cushite, then one of his parents would also have been a Cushite, unless he had been adopted by a family from Judah, which seems unlikely. Since Cushi's father is named Gedaliah, which is a Hebrew name, it seems unlikely that Gedaliah was a Cushite. A more likely explanation would be that Gedaliah took a Cushite wife, and that is why their son was named Cushi. This explanation corresponds better, in my opinion, with the list of the four other Hebrew names given in this genealogy.

The prophet Zephaniah mentions Cush in his book on two other occasions. The first time deals with the Cushites who were struck down by God as a punishment for their ways, and it is a probable reference to the Cushite Pharaohs who ruled over Egypt during the 25th dynasty (Zephaniah 2:12). The second reference concerns a promise that God makes to Cush (Zephaniah 3:9-12). This very positive promise will be considered in more detail in chapter four.

B. Descendants of Mizraim (Egypt)

Several descendants of Mizraim are mentioned in Genesis 10:13-14. The first ones mentioned are the Lydians (called "Ludites" or "the Ludim" in many versions). These people will be discussed in section D of this chapter.

Other descendants of Mizraim mentioned in these two verses – all of whom are considered as African peoples – are the Anamites, Lehabites, Naphtuhites, Pathrusites, and Casluhites:

- The Anamites settled to the west of Egypt, near the city of Cyrene[72] (which is 160 kilometres north-east of the present-day city of Benghazi, Libya).

- The Lehabites were tribes who may have inhabited the Libyan desert. Many scholars equate them with the "Lubim", who are generally identified with Libyans.[73] The "Lubim" are mentioned in 2 Chronicles 12:3 and 16:8. While the King James Version and the New American Standard Version use the Hebrew transliteration "Lubim" in these verses, most other versions opt for the word "Libyans". Some Bible dictionaries refer to them as probably being the same people as the Lehabites.[74]

- The Naphtuhites were a people who lived in either Lower Egypt (that is, the delta region)[75] or in central Egypt.[76]

- The Pathrusites (meaning "those from Pathros") were inhabitants of Upper Egypt, roughly the southern region of the Nile valley between Cairo and Aswan. Pathros means "the southern land" and is the Hebrew name for Upper Egypt, where the city of Thebes was located.[77] Some feel that Pathros was the traditional birthplace of the nation of Egypt.[78]

- The Casluhites were a people who either descended from the Egyptians or were conquered and then assimilated by them. Perhaps they inhabited the Mediterranean region of Casiotis, stretching from the eastern mouth of the Nile delta to Philistia.[79] They were apparently the direct ancestors of the Philistines, a people who were linked to "various Hamitic peoples" and who "were not a single group with a single origin or living only in one period of time in southwestern Canaan. They appear rather to have been an amalgamation of several different peoples, and the Philistines descended from the Casluhites [appear] to be different from those who came from Caphtor [Crete]."[80]

The Caphtorites are also mentioned in this passage. Although they are not considered to be an African people, they were nonetheless a people who descended from Mizraim (Egypt) and then migrated later to the island of Crete in the Aegean Sea. Caphtor is the ancient name for Crete. Certain Bibles, such as the Today's English Version and the *Bible d'étude Semeur 2000* in French, actually use the terms Crete/Cretans instead of Caphtorites. This people gave rise to the Minoan civilization in the 2nd millennium BC.

Perhaps it is surprising to realize that an African presence is far more prevalent in the Old Testament than in the New. This is due to the fact that the people of Israel spent more than 400 years in Egypt (Genesis 37 – Exodus 14). The proper name "Egypt" (*Mizraim* in Hebrew) actually means "two Egypts" since it includes both parts of that country, Upper Egypt (the Nile valley) and Lower Egypt (the delta region). Egypt is either mentioned directly or referred to indirectly 658 times, and Egyptian(s) are mentioned or referenced 291 times, for a total of 949 times in the Old Testament alone. One author states that "Egypt, in her relationship to Israel, receives more coverage in the pages of the Old Testament than any other nation."[81]

Four times in the Psalms, Egypt is referred to poetically by the term "Ham" (Psalm 78:51; 105:23, 27; 106:22). Four other times, the word *rahab* is used in poetic passages to represent Egypt (Psalm 87:4; 89:10; Isaiah 30:7; 51:9). This word means "braggart" and it also refers to a mythological sea monster.

Space does not permit me to comment on each and every reference in the Bible to Egypt or an Egyptian. But in the following section I will try to highlight the Egyptians who are the most noteworthy.

Pharaoh during the time of Abraham

Genesis 12 introduces the first African about whom we know more than just his name and region of residence. This is the same chapter where we see Abraham, the father of the Jewish people, for the first time. This African is the Egyptian Pharaoh who dealt kindly with Abraham because of Sarah, Abraham's wife. This Pharaoh was very generous with the Jewish patriarch, giving him "sheep and cattle, male and female donkeys, menservants and maidservants, and camels" (Genesis 12:16).

This Pharaoh was also an upright man; some might even say more upright than Abraham. Abraham was not totally honest with Pharaoh, hiding from him the fact that Sarah was his wife. When Pharaoh took Sarah into his palace as his own wife, God inflicted Pharaoh's household with serious diseases. After learning the truth, Pharaoh summoned Abraham and ordered him to leave, allowing him to take not only his wife but also "everything he had" (Genesis 12:20). This Pharaoh was upright, honest, and generous, a man who did not seek revenge even when he had been wronged. A note in the *NIV Study Bible* says that "Egyptian ethics emphasized the importance of absolute truthfulness, and Abram was put in the uncomfortable position of being exposed as a liar."[82]

We do not know which particular Pharaoh this was. According to Bright, it could have been one of the Pharaohs of the 12th dynasty such as Senusret I or Amenemhet II, since the 12th dynasty was inaugurated near the beginning of the 20th century BC, roughly the time Abraham was born. He concludes that the evidence "argues strongly that the events of

Genesis 12–50, are to be placed between the 20th and 16th centuries. They fit splendidly in that period".[83]

In speaking of these 12th dynasty Pharaohs, Bright says:

> The Pharaohs of the 12th Dynasty undertook many ambitious projects designed to further the national prosperity. An elaborate system of canals turned the Fayum lake into a catchment basin for the Nile floods and reclaimed many acres of land for cultivation. A chain of forts across the Isthmus of Suez guarded the land from the incursions of Semitic bands. The copper mines of Sinai were once again opened and exploited. Trade moved up the Nile into Nubia, through the Wadi Hammamat and down the Red Sea to Punt (Somaliland), across the seas to Phoenicia and Crete, and even as far as Babylonia . . . Egypt, in short, enjoyed a prosperity seldom matched in all of her long history. With it, the peaceful arts flourished. Medicine and mathematics reached the climax of their development. Literature of all sorts was produced, including didactic works, tales and autobiographical narratives, poems and prophetic texts. It was a golden age of Egyptian culture.[84]

If Bright is correct in his dating of the time period for Abraham's sojourn in Egypt, then it is easy to understand why this Pharaoh could afford to be generous with Abraham.

Hagar

After Abraham's and Sarah's stay in Egypt, they returned to Canaan. Sarah was not able to have children, so she decided to give her Egyptian servant Hagar to Abraham to "build a family through her" (Genesis 16:2). Hagar gave birth to Ishmael, Abraham's first son. But before Ishmael's birth, Hagar began to despise Sarah, and Sarah began to mistreat Hagar. So Hagar fled from Sarah and Abraham and went into the desert. The Lord sent an angel to Hagar, to counsel her to return to Sarah and to tell her about her son Ishmael. He also gave a promise to this African woman: "I will so increase your descendants that they will be too numerous to count" (Genesis 16:10). God repeated this promise to Hagar the second time that she fled from Sarah and feared for the life of her son (Genesis 21:18). Four people in the Old Testament received a promise from God that their descendants would become a great nation: Abraham (Genesis 12:2; 13:16; 15:5; etc.), Isaac (Genesis 26:4, 24), Jacob (Genesis 28:14; 35:11; 46:3), and Hagar (Genesis 16:10). We often forget that one of these four people was a woman from Africa.

Wives of Ishmael and Joseph

Abraham was not the only person to take an Egyptian for a wife. Both Ishmael and Joseph took an Egyptian wife. We do not know the name of Ishmael's wife (Genesis 21:21), but Joseph's wife was named Asenath (Genesis 41:45, 50). She was the daughter of Potiphera, a priest who lived in the city of On (Heliopolis) and served the sun god Ra.

Potiphar and his wife

Before being named Pharaoh's second-in-command, Joseph was a slave in the household of a certain man named Potiphar. We do not know very much about Potiphar, other than the fact that he was the captain of the guard under Pharaoh (Genesis 39:1). He recognized that God was with Joseph, and as a result Joseph found favour in his eyes. Unfortunately, Potiphar's wife found Joseph to be very favourable in her eyes too. She was more than willing to be unfaithful to her husband by trying to sleep with Joseph. She tried day after day to get him to go to bed with her. But Joseph always refused, knowing that sleeping with her would be an affront to Potiphar and a sin against God. Frustrated by being turned down, Potiphar's wife invented an accusation against Joseph, claiming that he had tried to molest her. Potiphar became very angry and sent Joseph to prison. Potiphar and his wife, therefore, do not have a very good reputation. The husband did not investigate a criminal matter very thoroughly, and the wife was a lying, unfaithful woman.

Pharaoh during the time of Joseph

Within the same story (Genesis 39–50), we meet the next African in the Bible: the Pharaoh who ruled during the time of Joseph. Scholars' views are divided concerning the identity of this Pharaoh. Many scholars believe that the ancestors of Israel entered Egypt during the Hyksos rule.[85] The term "Hyksos" means "foreign chief"[86] or "shepherd king".[87] The Pharaohs used this term for the Asiatic princes from the Middle East, who were most likely of Semitic origin. They invaded Egypt in the 18th century BC and ruled there for more than a century. In other words, the majority of scholars believe that the Pharaoh during the time of Joseph was not an African but rather an Asiatic ruler of Egypt.

Some scholars disagree. The *Nouveau dictionnaire biblique révisé* says, "it is supposed that Joseph was the prime minister under the reign of a Hyksos Pharaoh, but this could also have occurred earlier, under the 12th dynasty."[88] Many scholars put the Hyksos Pharaohs during the 15th and 16th dynasties. *Harper's Bible Dictionary* says, "nothing in the patriarchal narrative need necessarily be dated to the Hyksos period in Egypt."[89] So it cannot be determined for sure if the Pharaoh who made Joseph his "prime minister" was African or Asiatic. It all depends on where Joseph is placed in Egypt's chronology. Like the chronology in the *NIV Study Bible*, I hold to the view that Joseph served under an African Pharaoh and not under a Hyksos Pharaoh. It seems likely that the Hyksos Pharaohs reigned in between the times of Joseph and Moses.

This Pharaoh, like his predecessor 200 years earlier during the time of Abraham, was a very generous man. When Joseph's brothers asked if they could reside in Egypt, Pharaoh told Joseph, "the land of Egypt is before you; settle your father and your brothers in the best part of the land" (Genesis 47:6-11). He was also a good administrator, for he made sure that those "with special ability" were put in charge of his own livestock (Genesis 47:6). Pharaoh was looking for people of competence who could oversee his affairs.

This Pharaoh (and perhaps his predecessors as well) allowed the people to own their own land. It was only when the famine became extremely severe that the people decided to sell their land to their king (Genesis 47:19-20). Today, we often assume that the king/Pharaoh always owned all the land and the people simply worked on it as serfs or slaves. But that was not the case here. This Middle Kingdom ruler allowed private property, demonstrating a fair and rather enlightened form of land administration. Also, this Pharaoh was lenient with the priests, allotting them a regular amount of food during the famine (Genesis 47:22).

Finally, we see that this Pharaoh was kind toward foreigners. Not only did he offer the best land to Joseph's brothers, he also gave Joseph's father an extravagant state funeral:

> So Joseph went up to bury his father. All Pharaoh's officials accompanied him – the dignitaries of his court and all the dignitaries of Egypt – besides all the members of Joseph's household . . . Chariots and horsemen also went up with him. It was a very large company . . . When the Canaanites who lived there saw the mourning . . . they said, "The Egyptians are holding a solemn ceremony of mourning" (Genesis 50:7-11).

A man of generosity, a responsible and fair administrator, a friend of foreigners – this was the Pharaoh who made Joseph his trusted advisor and second-in-command.

The prison warden and the captain of the guard

Any leader of a country needs able administrators, and the same was true of the Pharaohs of Egypt. Two men who served under the Pharaoh during Joseph's time were his prison warden and the captain of the guard (Genesis 39–40). Even though Potiphar was also a captain of the guard under Pharaoh (Genesis 39), it seems very unlikely that he is the *same* captain of the guard mentioned in chapter 40. He probably would not throw Joseph in prison at the end of chapter 39 and then at the beginning of chapter 40 treat him kindly and give him additional responsibility.

Once Potiphar had Joseph put in prison, each of these two officials recognized him to be a trustworthy person. As a result, the prison warden entrusted the oversight of all the prisoners to Joseph. He delegated to Joseph the daily administration of the prison, and he did not have to worry about supervising Joseph's activities or decisions. Likewise, the captain of the guard put Pharaoh's two prisoners – the cupbearer and the baker – under Joseph's supervision while they were under a kind of house arrest. So both the prison warden and the captain of the guard discerned praiseworthy qualities in a prisoner, and both of them treated Joseph honourably, respecting him for his competence and character.

Pharaoh's cupbearer and baker

Pharaoh's cupbearer and baker were high officials serving in the royal court. One day they did something to greatly offend Pharaoh. He became extremely angry with his officials. He had them arrested and held in the house of the captain of the guard. After a certain amount of time – presumably after investigating the matter – Pharaoh released the royal cupbearer and let him resume his official duties. The royal baker, on the other hand, was put to death, which implies that he was the guilty party concerning the serious offense against Pharaoh. The cupbearer was innocent and the baker was guilty. However, the cupbearer still had his faults, since he forgot to speak to Pharaoh on Joseph's behalf as Joseph had requested (Genesis 40:23). Because he forgot, Joseph spent two more years in prison. Eventually he remembered Joseph and told Pharaoh how Joseph had interpreted his dream, setting the stage for Joseph's introduction to Pharaoh and subsequent rise to power.

Egyptian physicians

At Joseph's request, his father, Jacob, was embalmed in Egypt by Egyptian physicians (Genesis 50:2, 3) and Joseph's body was also embalmed upon his own death (Genesis 50:26). Embalming is the process of preserving a dead body, often via surgical means, in order to prevent decay. Whereas many cultures from the ancient Near East only applied spices and perfumes before wrapping bodies in cloth, the Egyptians were quite developed in their techniques of preserving the human body. The *Encyclopedia Britannica* says,

> The beginnings of the art and techniques of embalming are associated principally with ancient Egypt where . . . a dry soil and climate encouraged its development . . . The highly skilled and trained embalmers took exquisite care to preserve [the body] . . . It is held that embalming skill reached a peak during the New Kingdom period between 1738 and 1102 BC.[90]

Embalming a corpse probably had not yet reached its peak during Joseph's lifetime, assuming that he lived in Egypt prior to the New Kingdom. The Hebrew verb for "embalm" is only found in Genesis 50, suggesting that this practice was very Egyptian and "was clearly done only because of the linkage of these prominent patriarchs with Egyptian life and culture".[91] Even though the Jews did not normally practice embalming, Joseph's years in Egypt evidently persuaded him to ask that his father's body be preserved in that way, which would then allow for his family to make the trip back to the land of Canaan for burial.

The Pharaohs after Joseph

Over a long period of time, the Pharaohs in Egypt changed their attitude toward the Hebrews living in their country. "A new king, who did not know about Joseph, came to power in Egypt" (Exodus 1:8). This "new king" came to power about 200 years after Joseph's death. The people of Israel's enslavement did not occur overnight, but came about gradually as the Egyptians began to increasingly fear their growing number.

The *NIV Study Bible* and the *Nouveau dictionnaire biblique révisé* identify this new king as probably being "Ahmose, the founder of the 18th dynasty, who expelled the Hyksos (foreign – predominantly Semitic – rulers of Egypt)."[92] Other sources list other Pharaohs as this "new king". Bright favours Sethos I.[93] The *Bible d'étude Semeur 2000* mentions both Ahmose and Sethos I as possibilities, and adds Thuthmosis III as yet another option.[94] So we see that some scholars favour Ahmose and Thuthmosis III who ruled in the early or mid-18th dynasty, while others favour Sethos I who ruled in the early 19th dynasty. The problem is that there could be as many as 250 years in between these two time periods. The earlier Pharaohs (Ahmose and Thuthmosis III) ruled in the mid-16th or mid-15th century BC, respectively, while the later one (Sethos I) ruled in the early 13th century BC. Obviously, determining the appropriate Pharaoh depends on when one thinks the Exodus took place.

Whoever this Pharaoh was, he imposed forced labour upon the Hebrews and oppressed them ruthlessly. With their labour, he constructed two great Egyptian cities, Pithom and Rameses, used for the storage of grain and other supplies (Exodus 1:11). The *Nouveau dictionnaire biblique révisé* says this about these two cities:

> [Pithom is], with Raamses,[95] one of the two store cities that Israelite slaves built in Egypt for the Pharaoh (Exodus 1:11). Edward Naville . . .

discovered ancient Pithom, on the southern bank of the fresh water canal going from Cairo to Suez via the Wadi Tumilat . . . Vast underground structures are located to the northeast of the temple of Tum. The walls of these structures are nearly 2.75 metres thick; they are made of crude bricks linked together by a thin layer of mortar. Interestingly, certain bricks do not contain any straw (cf. Exodus 5:10-12). These walls enclose a large number of rectangular premises with no doors; they are accessed from the top. Naville believes that these are the granaries where Pharaoh stored the supplies necessary for his troops, or for caravans being readied to cross the desert on their way to Syria.[96]

The Pharaoh who imposed this heavy labour upon the Israelites (or perhaps it was his successor) was so fearful of the Hebrews' potential power that he ordered that every new-born Hebrew boy must be thrown into the Nile (Exodus 1:22). It was into this kind of environment that Moses was born in Africa.

Hatshepsut, Pharaoh's daughter

Here we meet an African woman who changed the course of history: Pharaoh's daughter. The *Nouveau dictionnaire biblique révisé* and the *NIV Study Bible* both identify her as the daughter who later became Queen Hatshepsut,[97] a woman who was a very dominant figure in Egyptian politics, holding the throne for 22 years in place of her nephew and son-in-law, Thuthmosis III. She completed many civil construction projects across Egypt and improved Egypt's trade relations with her foreign neighbours.[98] But well before those things happened, this princess decided to have mercy on a baby boy, in spite of her father's orders to throw all newborn Hebrew boys in the Nile. Like the midwives Shiphrah and Puah before her, she did not respect Pharaoh's orders. Aware that the baby was "one of the Hebrew babies" (Exodus 2:6), she kept the child and took him as her son. By saving the life of the baby Moses, this African woman opened the door for the Jewish people to become the nation of Israel.

Shiphrah and Puah

It isn't clear whether Shiphrah and Puah are Egyptians or not. Most texts refer to the "midwives of the Hebrews" in Exodus 1:15. Does this mean that they are Hebrews themselves, or are they Egyptians working for the Hebrews? By contrast the *Bible du Semeur 2000* translates this passage as "two midwives for the Hebrews", and provides a note saying they were "probably midwife overseers. For some they have Egyptian names, for others they have Semitic names."[99] Their being Egyptian seems more logical, given the fact they had an audience with Pharaoh himself, and given the nature of his order to these women. But a note in the NIV Study Bible says these two women's names were "Semitic and not Egyptian names".[100] So who is right? If we conclude that Shiphrah and Puah are Egyptians, there may have been *three* African women who changed the course of history in the first two chapters of Exodus.

The Pharaohs of Egypt

The following table shows the dates of the reign for different Pharaohs. These dates are approximate and are not accepted by everyone. Certain names are also subject to debate.[101] *If there is any overlap in dates between dynasties or even within a dynasty, this either indicates the existence of a co-regency in one place, or two Pharaohs who were simultaneously accepted by different parts of the country.*

THE PRE-DYNASTIC PERIOD 6000–3100 BC	
THE EARLY DYNASTIC PERIOD	
3100–2650 BC	
1st Dynasty	
Menes/Narmer	3100–3037
Hor-Aha	3037–?
Djer	?
Djet	?
Queen Mereneith	?
Den	?
Anedjib	?
Semerkhet	?
Qa'a	?
Sneferka	?–2770
2nd Dynasty	
Hotepsekhemwy	2770–?
Raneb	?
Nynetjer	?
Weneg	?
Sendji	?
Neferkare	?
Neferkasokar	?
Hudjefa ("missing name")	?
Nubnefer	?
Sekhemib	?
Khasekhemwy	?–2650
THE OLD KINGDOM 2650–2150 BC	
3rd Dynasty	
Sanakhte	2650–2630

Djoser	2630–2611
Sekhemkhet	2611–2603
Khaba	2603–2599
Huni (Neferkare?)	2599–2575
4th Dynasty	
Sneferu	2575–2551
Khufu	2551–2528
Djedefre	2528–2520
Khafre	2520–2494
Bauefre	2494–2490
Menkaure	2490–2472
Shepseskaf	2472–2467
Djedefptah	2467–2465
5th Dynasty	
Userkaf	2465–2458
Sahure	2458–2446
Neferirkare	2446–?
Shepseskare	?–2419
Neferefre	2419–2416
Niuserre	2416–2396
Menkauhor	2396–2388
Djedkare	2388–2356
Unas	2356–2323
6th Dynasty	
Teti	2323–2311
Userkare	2311–2310
Pepi I	2310–2261
Merenre I	2261–2247
Pepi II	2247–2153
Merenre II	2153–2152
Queen Nitocris	2152–2150

THE FIRST INTERMEDIATE PERIOD 2150–2033 BC	
7th and 8th Dynasties	
Neterkare	2150–?
Menkare	?
Neferkare	?
Neferkare Neby	?
Djedkamaare	?
Nefer-kakhendure	?
Merenhor	?
Sneferka	?
Wadjetkare	?
Qakare Iby	?
9th and 10th Dynasties	
Meryibre Khety	?
Merykare	?
Kaneferre	?
Nebkaure Akhtoy	?
11th Dynasty (Thebes)	
Montuhotep I	2106–2100
Intef I	2100–2090
Intef II	2090–2041
Intef III	2041–2033
THE MIDDLE KINGDOM 2033–1786 BC	
11th Dynasty (all of Egypt)	
Montuhotep II	2033–1982
Montuhotep III	1982–1970
Montuhotep IV	1970–1963
12th Dynasty	
Amenemhat I	1963–1934
Senusret I	1934–1898
Amenemhat II	1898–1866
Senusret II	1866–1862
Senusret III	1862–1843
Amenemhat III	1843–1798
Amenemhat IV	1798

Queen Sobeknefru	1798–1786
THE SECOND INTERMEDIATE PERIOD 1786–1550 BC	
13th Dynasty[102]	
The number of Pharaohs is uncertain, numbering perhaps as many as 70, among whom there are:	
Sobekhotep I	?
Sekhemkare	?
Amenemhat V	?
Sehetibre	?
Iufni	?
Sankhibre	?
Samenkhare	?
Sehetibre	?
Sewadjkare	?
Nedjemibre	?
Wegaf	?
Ameny Intef IV	?
Hor	?
Sobekhotep II Amenemhat VI	?
Khendjer	?
Sobekhotep III	?
Neferhotep I	?
Sobekhotep IV	?
Neferhotep II	?
Sobekhotep V	?
Iayib	?
Ay	?
Sobekhotep VI	?
Sankhreneswadjtu	?
Sobekhotep VII	?
Dudimose	?
14th Dynasty	
Lesser Pharaohs, contemporaries of the 13th dynasty	

15th Dynasty	
A number of Hyksos Pharaohs, including:	
Sheshi	?
Yakubher	?
Khyan	?
Apepi I	?
Apepi II	?

16th Dynasty	
Lesser Hyksos Pharaohs, contemporaries of the 15th dynasty	

17th Dynasty	
Numerous Pharaohs from Thebes, including:	
Sobekemsaf II	?
Intef VII	?
Tao I	?
Tao II	?
Kamose	?

THE NEW KINGDOM 1550–1069 BC	

18th Dynasty	
Ahmose	1550–1525
Amenhotep I	1525–1504
Thuthmosis I	1504–1492
Thuthmosis II	1492–1479
Hatshepsut	1479–1457
Thuthmosis III	1479–1425
Amenhotep II	1425–1401
Thuthmosis IV	1401–1391
Amenhotep III	1391–1353
Amenhotep IV Akhenaten	1353–1337
Smenkhare	1337–1336
Tutankhamun	1336–1327
Ay	1327–1323
Horemheb	1323–1295

19th Dynasty	
Ramesses I	1295–1294

Seti I	1294–1279
Ramesses II	1279–1213
Merenptah	1213–1203
Amenmesses	1203–1200
Seti II	1200–1194
Siptah	1194–1188
Queen Twosret	1188–1186

20th Dynasty	
Setnakhte	1186–1184
Ramesses III	1184–1153
Ramesses IV	1153–1148
Ramesses V	1148–1144
Ramesses VI	1144–1136
Ramesses VII	1136–1128
Ramesses VIII	1128–1125
Ramesses IX	1125–1107
Ramesses X	1107–1098
Ramesses XI	1098–1069

THIRD INTERMEDIATE PERIOD 1069–664 BC	

21st Dynasty	
Smendes	1069–1044
Amenemnisu	1044–1040
Psusennes I	1040–992
Amenemope	993–984
Osorkon the Elder	984–978
Siamun	978–959
Psusennes II	959–945

22nd Dynasty	
Sheshonq I/Shishak	945–924
Osorkon I	924–909
Takelot I	909–?
Sheshonq II	?–883
Osorkon II	883–855
Takelot II	860–835
Sheshonq III	835–783
Pami	783–773

Sheshonq V	773–735
Osorkon IV/So?	735–712
23rd Dynasty	
Several kings reigned from Thebes, Tanis, and elsewhere, concurrently with the 22nd dynasty. These included:	
Pedibastet	828–803
Sheshonq IV	?
Osorkon III	777–749
Takelot III	?
Rudamon	?
Iuput Usermaatre	?
Peftjauabastet	740–725
24th Dynasty	
Two Pharaohs reigned in Saïs, concurrently with the 22nd dynasty:	
Tefnakht	724–717
Bakenrenef/Bocchoris	717–712
25th Dynasty (Nubia and Thebes)	
Kashta	760–747
Piankhy/Piye	747–716
25th Dynasty (Nubia and all of Egypt)	
Shabata/Shabako/Shabaka	716–702
Shabatka/Shebitko/Shebitku	702–690
Taharqa/Tirhakah	690–664
Tantamun	664–657
26th Dynasty	
Nekau/Neco I	672–664
Psamtik I	664–610
Nekau/Neco II	610–595
Psamtik II	595–589
Apries/Wahibre/Hophra	589–570
Ahmose II/Amasis	570–526
Psamtik III	526–525

THE LATE PERIOD 525–343 BC	
27th Dynasty (first Persian domination)	
Cambyse II	525–522
Darius I	521–486
Xerxes	486–466
Artaxerxes I	465–424
Darius II	424–404
28th Dynasty	
Amyrtaeus	404–399
29th Dynasty	
Nefaarud/Nepherites I	399–393
Psammutis	393
Hakor/Achoris	393–380
Nepherites II	380
30th Dynasty	
Nectanebo I	380–362
Teos	365–360
Nectanebo II	360–343
(The names that follow are not those of Pharaohs, but rather of conquerors who dominated Egypt in their respective times.)	
2nd PERSIAN DOMINATION 343–332 BC	
Artaxerxes III	343–338
Arses	338–336
Darius III	336–332
GRECO-ROMAN PERIOD 332 BC–AD 395	
Macedonian Dynasty	
Alexander III (the Great)	332–323
Philip Arridaeus	323–316
Alexander IV	316–304
Ptolemaic Era	
Ptolemy I Soter	304–284
Ptolemy II Philadelphus	285–246

Ptolemy III Euergetes	246–221
Ptolemy IV Philopator	221–205
Ptolemy V Epiphanes	205–180
Ptolemy VI Philometor	180–145
Ptolemy VII Neos Philopator	145
Ptolemy VIII Euergetes	170–163, 145–116
Ptolemy IX Soter	116–107, 88–81
Ptolemy X Alexander	107–88
Queen Cleopatra Berenice	81–80
Ptolemy XI Alexander	80
Ptolemy XII Auletes	80–58, 55–51
Queen Berenice IV	58–55
Queen Cleopatra VII	51–30
Ptolemy XIII Theos Philapator	51–47

Ptolemy XIV	47–44
Ptolemy XV Caesarion	44–30
Roman Emperors	
Augustus	30 BC–AD 14
Tiberius	14–37
Caligula	37–41
Claudius	41–54
Nero	54–68
Galba	68–69
Otho	69
Vitellius	69
Vespasian	69–79
Titus	79–81
Domitian	81–96
Nerva	96–98
. . . and so on until AD 395. Since the era of the NT ends around AD 100, the other emperors are not mentioned here.	

The Pharaoh who drove Moses out of Egypt

Moses spent 40 years in Egypt (Acts 7:23) and during this time a different Pharaoh seems to have ascended to the throne. Some identify this man as Thuthmosis III.[103] This Pharaoh sought the death penalty for Moses after his crime of killing an Egyptian, but Moses fled before he could be apprehended. Cheikh Anta Diop says of this Pharaoh:

> Egypt became a conquering and imperialistic nation only by reaction, in self-defence after the Hyksos occupation of the 18th dynasty; this was especially true of Thuthmosis III, who is often called the Napoleon of antiquity. He conquered Palestine and Syria, pushing the border to the upper Euphrates at Kadesh. This required 17 expeditions. During the eighth, he left Egypt by sea and landed in Phoenicia, where he had boats built in Byblos and carried overland through the desert to the Euphrates; with these he crossed the river and defeated the Mittani.
>
> The renown he gained from this victory assured the subjection of warrior peoples such as the Assyrians, Babylonians, and Hittites, all of whom paid Egypt tribute. As a result, Egyptian domination under Thuthmosis III extended to the base of the Elamite mountain range. The Egyptians practiced a policy of assimilation, taking the young heirs apparent of conquered kingdoms, giving them an Egyptian education, and sending them home to spread Egyptian civilization.[104]

Moses benefited from such an education, though in the end it was he who, with God's help, taught Pharaoh a lesson or two. We see nevertheless what kind of a powerful person Moses had to deal with prior to fleeing Egypt.

The Pharaoh at the time of the Exodus

After Moses fled from Egypt, the reigning Pharaoh passed away (Exodus 2:23). The *Bible d'étude Semeur 2000* says that if this passage is speaking of Thutmosis III's death, "that agrees with the data from Egyptology which teaches us that his reign was very long."[105] Depending on how much longer Thutmosis III lived after Moses's flight, and taking into account Moses's forty years in Midian, the Pharaoh during the time of the Exodus would be either Thutmosis IV or Amenhotep III. The *NIV Study Bible* argues that an earlier ruler, Amenhotep II, was the Pharaoh of the Exodus,[106] but this seems to not allow for enough time to elapse between Moses's birth and return to Egypt eighty years later, based on the preceding timeline of ruling Pharaohs.

Either way, this Pharaoh during the time of the Exodus is the best-known Egyptian in the Bible. The book of Exodus tells us of all the times when Pharaoh opposed Moses and Aaron because his heart was hardened. In contrast to the Pharaohs during the time of Abraham or Joseph, this man was not kind to foreigners. He was also incredibly stubborn. When Moses spoke to him on behalf of God, telling him to let the Israelites go, the answer was an outright "no", despite the signs and wonders performed in his court. It was only when God inflicted the 10 plagues on Egypt, culminating in the death of his firstborn son, that this Pharaoh finally consented and obeyed the command of the Lord.

However, he soon changed his mind and chased after the fleeing Israelites (Exodus 14:5). This decision cost him his army, for as soon as he entered the Red Sea/Sea of Reeds,[107] "the water flowed back and covered the chariots and horsemen – the entire army of Pharaoh that had followed the Israelites into the sea. Not one of them survived" (Exodus 14:28).

Since the crossing of the Red Sea is considered by the Bible itself to be the crowning miracle of the Old Testament – it is mentioned at least 25 times – it is normal that the Pharaoh opposed to the people of Israel should be considered one of the great enemies in the Bible. Judas and Pontius Pilate are perhaps the only two biblical characters more despised than the Pharaoh at the time of the Exodus. He opposed the will of God, reversed his decision to free the Israelites several times, was obstinate and hard-hearted, and tried to annihilate the people of Israel after their departure. All these things explain why this Egyptian man is one of the greatest enemies of God in the Bible.

Egyptian magicians, sorcerers, and wise men

Just prior to the Exodus, Pharaoh summoned his wise men, magicians, and sorcerers, asking them to perform the same miracles as Moses and Aaron. But more than 400 years earlier, during the time of Joseph, we see that the Pharaoh had also called on his wise men and magicians to interpret his dream, which they were unable to do. Their failure led to Joseph becoming the prime minister in Egypt in accordance with the plans the Lord had for him. These accounts show that Egyptian Pharaohs would routinely seek answers to their problems by turning to the wisdom of their advisors or to the supernatural via the occult practices of their magicians and sorcerers.

The Pharaoh at the time of the Exodus relied heavily on such practices. He often called his magicians and sorcerers to duplicate via their mystic methodology the same signs and wonders that Aaron and Moses were able to do by the power of God. Up to a certain point, they were able to do so. They succeeded in changing wooden staffs into serpents (Exodus 7:11-12), turning the water of the Nile River into blood (Exodus 7:22), and making frogs come up onto the land of Egypt (Exodus 8:7). One must admit that the secret powers of these diviners were quite impressive.

These diviners could have been Egyptian or Cushite. Hays writes:

> Cushite magicians had a special reputation in Egypt; they were famous for their power and there were many of them functioning in Egypt (Bresciani 1997: 232-233). There is a strong possibility that some of the "magicians" who confronted Moses in Exodus 7 and 8 were Cushites. The phrase translated "Egyptian magicians" (Exod. 7:11, NIV) literally means "magicians of the Egyptians"; it gives no indication of nationality . . . [A] point of interest is that these "magicians" were also priests. "Magic" and priestly activity cannot be separated. The Hebrew word used for "magician" in Exodus derives from an Egyptian word that refers clearly to a class of priests that studied theology and manipulated spiritual powers . . . While the connection is purely speculative, it is interesting to note the high probability of a Cushite presence among these priests and then the emergence of a central Israelite priest, Phinehas, whose name means "the Negro" or "the Cushite".[108]

We see that African diviners and shamans (also called marabouts) who still practice today have a long, historic tradition. It is not surprising that they are able to produce incredible manifestations of their occult powers through their devotion to evil spirits. But their powers are nonetheless limited compared to the power of the Most High God. God's miracles go far beyond what any African diviner can do, and that was true in the book of Exodus as well. In Exodus 8:18-19, the magicians recognized that "this is the finger of God". Later on, the magicians themselves were afflicted by the boils that God had brought upon them, and we hear nothing further of these sorcerers (Exodus 9:11). This shows that God is more powerful than evil spirits and mystical enchanters. This is even more explicit in the ministry of Jesus in the New Testament, where the crowds exclaim, "He even gives orders to evil spirits and they obey him" (Mark 1:27).

Roughly 700 years after the time of Moses, we see in Isaiah 19:3 that the Egyptians were still consulting their false idols, spirits of the dead, mediums, and spiritists (other versions of the Bible call them charmers, sorcerers, wizards, soothsayers, fortune-tellers, ghosts, witches, necromancers, and clairvoyants). They were trying to predict the future by speaking to the dead. Such practices have continued in modern-day Africa, in spite of the extensive presence of the church. But just as in Exodus 8, God still shows himself to be stronger and more powerful than African diviners. False idols still shudder and tremble before the Lord (Isaiah 19:1). They were impotent to counter the plan God had for Egypt in Isaiah's time, and as a result God delivered Egypt into the hand of Esarhaddon, the king of Assyria, who was a "cruel master" (Isaiah 19:4). All the sorcerers, magicians, and fortune-tellers of that day, just like the sorcerers, marabouts, shamans, and diviners of today, are powerless before the Lord Almighty. The letter of 1 John reminds Christians that "you, dear children, are from God and have overcome [evil spirits and false prophets], because the one who is in you is greater than the one who is in the world" (1 John 4:4).

The Pharaoh at the time of Solomon

Other Egyptian Pharaohs are briefly mentioned in the Old Testament. King Solomon, son of David, "made an alliance with Pharaoh king of Egypt and married his daughter. He brought her to the city of David" (1 Kings 3:1). Immediately following this event God appears to Solomon and tells him, "Ask me for whatever you want me to give you" (1 Kings 3:5). This suggests that the alliance between the two nations was not displeasing to God. Hoffmeier says, "during the united monarchy of Israel, warm relations existed between Egypt and Israel."[109]

Regarding the identity of this Pharaoh, the *Nouveau dictionnaire biblique révisé* suggests:

> [T]his may be Siamen. The name Siamen was proposed because a fragment of a stele [decorative stone slab] found at Tanis in Egypt represents Siamen (of the 21st dynasty), killing an enemy, probably a Philistine. This would correspond to the raid carried out by this Pharaoh against the Philistines during the siege of Gezer, inhabited by Canaanites (1 Kings 9:16). Afterwards, the Pharaoh returned Gezer to Solomon as a dowry for his daughter.[110]

A note in the *NIV Study Bible* explains that this alliance proved Egypt's recognition of the growing power and importance of the Israelite nation. The note continues by saying that the alliance between these two powers allowed both to achieve important political and economic objectives.[111] For example, the town of Gezer was located at the crossroads of two important commercial routes: to the west was a road that started in Egypt and ran north, an important strategic and commercial route for the Pharaoh. To the north of Gezer lay the road connecting Jerusalem to Joppa, a port city on the Mediterranean Sea. Along this road travelled most of the building materials for Solomon's construction projects.[112] This alliance therefore proved beneficial to both parties. About 20 years later Solomon built Pharaoh's daughter her own palace (1 Kings 7:8).

Pharaoh and Queen Tahpenes

Another Pharaoh is referenced in 1 Kings 11:14-22. This Pharaoh is not named (although his wife Tahpenes is!) and it is possible that this is the same Pharaoh from chapter 3, that is, Siamun or Psusennes II. He reigned during the time of David. He acted very similarly to the Pharaoh in Joseph's time. This unknown Pharaoh gave Hadad, a young Edomite man, a house, food, and land. Hadad had fled the terror in Edom when Joab, David's general, sought to kill all the males in the country. Once he arrived in Egypt, Hadad, like Joseph before him, obtained favour in the eyes of the Pharaoh. He even ended up marrying the sister of Pharaoh's wife. Hadad's son was raised by Queen Tahpenes along with Pharaoh's own son. Again, an African king and his wife were very generous and concerned for the well-being of foreigners in their land.

Neco II

Pharaoh Neco II, of the 26th dynasty, left in 609 or 608 BC to help the last king of Assyria, Ashur-Uballit II, who was fighting the Babylonians near the town of Haran (2 Kings 23–24; 2 Chronicles 35). Josiah, king of Judah, and his army forayed out to meet the Egyptian army, "but Neco faced him and killed him at Megiddo" (2 Kings 23:29). Neco II did not want to face Josiah in battle, but Josiah had insisted:

> But Neco sent messengers to him, saying "What quarrel is there between you and me, O king of Judah? It is not you I am attacking at this time, but the house with which I am at war. God has told me to hurry, so stop opposing God, who is with me, or he will destroy you." Josiah, however, would not turn away from him, but disguised himself to engage him in battle. He would not listen to what Neco had said at God's command (2 Chronicles 35:21-22).

We see therefore that an African Pharaoh received a message from God, a message he passed on to the King of Judah. He expected that God's command would be obeyed. But Josiah refused to listen. This African king was the spokesman for God Almighty; Josiah's refusal to listen cost him his life.

Josiah's son, Jehoahaz, was crowned king after his father; however, he only ruled three months before Neco II had him imprisoned and brought to Egypt, where he died. Neco II established Jehoahaz's older brother, Jehoiakim, as king of Judah. Jehoiakim furnished the tribute Neco II had demanded. In 605 BC, Neco II was routed by the heir apparent of Babylon, a prince named Nebuchadnezzar, at Carchemish. So Neco II returned to Egypt, and Jehoiakim became a Babylonian vassal. Three years later Nebuchadnezzar would be back to suppress a revolt in Judah; Jehoiakim was apparently counting on aid from Egypt in his struggle against Babylon. But this aid never came. "The king of Egypt did not march out from his own country again, because the king of Babylon had taken all his territory, from the Wadi of Egypt to the Euphrates River" (2 Kings 24:7). Neco II was able to keep Egypt under control, but he lost the Asian provinces he had previously conquered.

Hophra

One of the last Egyptian Pharaohs was Hophra, who reigned 589–570 BC (Jeremiah 37; 44; Ezekiel 17; 29–32). After his victory in Jerusalem, Nebuchadnezzar established Zedekiah as king of Judah. But, like Jehoiakim before him, Zedekiah revolted against Babylonian rule and turned to Egypt in hopes of military aid, despite the warnings of Ezekiel and Jeremiah to not do so. Hophra and his army attacked the Babylonian army – but without success, as the prophets had predicted (Jeremiah 37:7; Ezekiel 17:17-21; 29:3-16). The defeated Egyptians returned home and the rebellion foundered.

Hophra is especially distinguished in the Bible for his pride. Ezekiel expresses God's words to Pharaoh, comparing the Egyptian empire to a powerful cedar tree:

> Because it towered on high, lifting its top above the thick foliage, and because it was proud of its height, I handed it over to the ruler of the nations, for him to deal with according to its wickedness . . . The sword of the king of Babylon will come against you. I will cause your hordes to fall

by the swords of mighty men – the most ruthless of all nations. They will shatter the pride of Egypt, and all her hordes will be overthrown (32:10-12).

Hophra's pride was so great he even claimed to have created the Nile river (29:3, 9); he believed himself to be a god. God eventually pronounces seven oracles against Egypt and Pharaoh (Ezekiel 29–32). These passages, along with Jeremiah 44:30, speak clearly of Hophra's demise. The *Nouveau dictionnaire biblique révisé* tells of his end: "After a disastrous Libyan campaign and a revolt that resulted in Ahmose becoming co-regent, Hophra was slain in conflict with Ahmose."[113]

Jarha

We have already seen that Egyptians often welcomed Jews and other foreign populations. But Jews also welcomed foreigners and accepted them as members of the chosen people. One example of this is found in 1 Chronicles 2:34-35. Jarha was an Egyptian slave who was permitted to marry one of Sheshan's daughters. Sheshan, who had no sons, chose this Egyptian man to marry into his family and continue the lineage. We know nothing else about Jarha, but the implication is that he must have been a man of some distinction to be chosen by his master to carry the family name rather than a Jewish man. Jarha's son figures among the descendants of Judah, which indicates Jarha had probably converted to Judaism. His story, an Egyptian slave who took a Jewish wife, bears some resemblance to that of Joseph, a Jewish slave who took an Egyptian wife.

Bithiah

Bithiah, a daughter of Pharaoh (we do not know which one), married a Jewish man named Mered (1 Chronicles 4:18). Mered was probably a man of some importance if he could wed Pharaoh's daughter, but this marriage – contrary to that of Solomon – was more than a commercial arrangement. The name Bithiah means "daughter of Jehovah"[114] which indicates she converted and began to worship the covenant God of Israel during her time amongst the Jewish people. As an Egyptian woman, she was welcomed into the assembly of Israel.

C. Descendants of Put/Punt (Somalia or Libya)

In the Old Testament there are nine references to Put or those from Put (also called Libyans/Pul in Isaiah 66:19). The tribe of Put settled in either Libya or Somalia. Based on Persian and Babylonian texts, some consider this son of Ham to be the father of the Libyan tribes west of Egypt. This opinion is held by most experts.[115]

There is, however, a growing minority who do not believe that the tribe of Put settled in Libya. Drawing support from Egyptian texts, they believe instead that the tribe of Put settled in Somalia, and that the terms "Put" and "Punt" referred to in these texts are variations of the same word. The *Nouveau dictionnaire biblique révisé* says,

> The most recent opinion assimilates Put and Punt, to the south and south-east of Cush. Punt is usually identified with the Somalis. According

to Glaser, the name Punt was first used to describe eastern Arabia, then southern Arabia (Scented Coast), and finally the African coast of the Somalis.[116]

Yamauchi explains that there are even more recent theories about the exact location of Punt: "As Punt was, above all, the source of incense for the Egyptians, early scholars identified it with Somalia . . . Recent studies by R. Herzog and K. A. Kitchen indicate that Punt was farther north, in eastern Sudan and northern Ethiopia, extending to the Red Sea, near Port Sudan and Eritrea, where such incense trees also grew."[117]

A note on Genesis 10:6 in the French edition of the Thompson Chain-Reference Bible identifies Put as being "the coast of the Somalis", without even mentioning Libya.[118] Nahum 3:9 and Ezekiel 30:5 both speak of Put and Libya (Lubim/Cub) in the same verse, indicating that these names designate distinct peoples. It is possible, however, that these two distinct people groups inhabited the same region generally referred to as Libya.

Almost everyone agrees that Punt is located on the horn of Africa. The debate is whether Put and Punt refer to the same place/people. Those who answer "yes" see Put as the country of the Somalis or a little further north, while those who reply "no" see Put as a region in eastern Libya or western Egypt. Whatever the solution, both sides can agree that Put/Punt refers to an African people, either Libyan or Somali.

Men of Put were generally viewed as skilled soldiers. Prophets in the Bible call them "soldiers in your army [who] hung their shields and helmets on your walls" (Ezekiel 27:10) and "warriors . . . who carry shields" (Jeremiah 46:9). Since in these examples the soldiers of Put are fighting for Tyre and Egypt respectively, it is fair to say they had a reputation as mercenaries. They allied themselves with many regional powers, like the Cushites (Jeremiah 46:9; Ezekiel 38:5; Nahum 3:9), the Persians (Ezekiel 27:10; 38:5), Egypt (Jeremiah 46:9; Nahum 3:9), Tyre (Ezekiel 27:10), and those from the north by the Black Sea (Ezekiel 38:5). Many times the enemies of Israel employed these African soldiers of fortune.

Putiel

In Exodus 6:25 we read of a man named Putiel. He gave one of his daughters in marriage to Eleazar son of Aaron, making him Eleazar's father-in-law. The name Putiel is interesting, as *-iel* is a Hebrew suffix meaning "of God". For example, Gabriel means "man of God", Daniel means "judge of God", Othniel means "lion of God", etc. So Putiel becomes "Put of God", signifying perhaps a Libyan or a Somali who worships the God of Israel. The fact that Aaron allowed his son to marry Putiel's daughter indicates that this man was someone who was serious in following the God of Israel, and that he had raised his daughter in the same faith.

Hays says that the name Putiel is borrowed from Egyptian with an added suffix.[119] If true, this could mean Putiel was Egyptian and not Somali. But in either case, he was an African who worshipped God.

D. Lubim and Ludim (Libya)

Some of the descendants of Mizraim mentioned in Genesis 10:13-14 are the Lydians (called "Ludites" or "the Ludim" in many versions). Some scholars believe that the Lydians were warriors who came from Africa, since they are associated with Cush/Ethiopia and Put, and these latter two are often mentioned in the context of warfare (i.e. Jeremiah 46:9; Isaiah 66:19; Ezekiel 27:10; 30:5). The *Dictionary of Biblical Languages with Semantic Domains* defines "Ludite" as "Ludite, Lydian, of Lud, i.e. a people residing somewhere in the NE [of] Africa".[120] However, other scholars see the Lydians/Ludites as the indigenous people of the Lydian kingdom in Asia Minor. In fact, most of the references to the Hebrew word לוד (*lud*) are translated in the NIV Bible as "Lydians" instead of "Ludites". Interestingly, that same Bible has notes that say the Lydians of Ezekiel 27:10 were from Asia Minor, while the Lydians of Ezekiel 30:5 are from somewhere in northern Africa,[121] so it evidently sees two distinct groups of Lydian people. The French *Bible d'étude Semeur 2000* explains that these Lydians/ Ludites are "either Lydians [in Asia Minor], or a neighbouring region of Egypt".[122] So it is possible, but not certain, that there are Ludites/Lydians who are an African people from the northeast part of the continent. Almost all the French translations of the Bible and some English ones speak of "Lydia" as being part of Libya, or allow that it could be the case. That is why these verses are included in this chapter.

In the Old Testament there are 25 references to Libyans (Hebrew *lubim* and *ludim*) or to a people supposedly from Libya. Among these, only Pharaoh Shishak is identified by name (1 Kings 11:40; 14:25-26; 2 Chronicles 12:2-9). The other verses which refer to Libyans do so in a very general sense (i.e., 2 Chronicles 12:3; 16:8; Jeremiah 46:9; Isaiah 66:19; Ezekiel 27:10; 30:5; Daniel 11:43; Nahum 3:9) or to Sukkites (2 Chronicles 12:3), a people hard to identify definitively.

It is interesting to note that the single verse Ezekiel 30:5 speaks of all three "Libyan" people: those of Put, Lud (*ludim*), and the Libyans (*lubim/kub*). Of course, it is possible that Put could refer to a non-Libyan people group, as previously discussed.

We should note that ancient Egyptians classified their enemies in three categories: Asians in the north, Cushites in the south, and Libyans in the west. The Libyans appear to have come from Berber peoples, "considered indigenous by some scholars, [who] became well established by the mid-second millennium before the Common Era."[123] Over time these Berbers mixed with black Africans and Egyptians.

Shishak

Shishak is the first Pharaoh to be named in the Bible (1 Kings 11:40). At certain times Egypt had non-Egyptian Pharaohs, as we have already seen in the case of the "Hyksos" Pharaohs who came from the Near East. Shishak was African but not necessarily Egyptian, since he was the first Pharaoh of a Libyan lineage. Yamauchi explains Shishak's origin:

> In Egyptian texts Shishak is called a Great Chief of the Meshwesh, a Libyan tribe. The Meshwesh attacked Egypt during the reigns of Merneptah and Ramses III (c. 1220–1170 BC). After their defeat, the Egyptians used them as mercenaries, settling them in the eastern delta and forcing them to learn Egyptian. Shishak came from a Meshwesh family who had been settled at Heracleopolis for five generations and who occupied high offices there.[124]

A member of a Libyan noble family, Shishak overthrew the feeble 21st dynasty – with which Solomon had made his alliance – and founded the 22nd dynasty, reigning 945–924 BC. Shishak received Jeroboam when Solomon tried to have Jeroboam killed. Five years after Solomon's death, while Rehoboam was king of Judah and Jeroboam was king of Israel, Shishak invaded Judah (1 Kings 14:25; 2 Chronicles 12:1-12). Shishak (and his Cushite and Libyan allies) were the direct instrument of God to punish the infidelity of Rehoboam and the people:

> Because they had been unfaithful to the Lord, Shishak king of Egypt attacked Jerusalem in the fifth year of King Rehoboam. With twelve hundred chariots and sixty thousand horsemen and the innumerable troops of Libyans, Sukkites and Cushites that came with him from Egypt, he captured the fortified cities of Judah and came as far as Jerusalem . . . When Shishak king of Egypt attacked Jerusalem, he carried off the treasures of the temple of the Lord and the treasures of the royal palace. He took everything, including the gold shields Solomon had made. (2 Chronicles 12:2-4, 9)

This powerful king was the first to pillage Jerusalem. He would not be the last, as the people of Judah and their leaders would again and again be unfaithful and be punished by foreign armies, notably the Babylonians. After having defeated Judah, Shishak continued his campaign to the valley of Jezreel and Megiddo in northern Israel. From there he attacked Jeroboam, his former tenant, and quickly defeated him. God seems to have chosen to use Shishak to punish Jeroboam's disobedience (1 Kings 12–14).

The Bible itself does not mention this northern invasion; however, we know it occurred thanks to a large bas-relief found in Thebes that lists 150 towns and villages conquered by Shishak. Bright tells us that "Egyptian armies devastated Palestine from one end to the other . . . The Egyptians pressed on into north Israel, spreading destruction everywhere."[125] Fortunately for Judah and Israel, Shishak could not maintain a long-term military presence, due mostly to his government's internal weakness. He withdrew from Palestine and never came back.

The Sukkites

We mentioned earlier a people group about whom we know almost nothing – the Sukkites. A note in the *NIV Study Bible* for 2 Chronicles 12:3 tells us these were probably Libyan mercenaries elsewhere mentioned in Egyptian texts.[126] The *Nouveau dictionnaire biblique révisé* adds that they were "a people that furnished soldiers to Shishak, king of Egypt, to invade Palestine. They were from an African race."[127] Another possibility is raised by the French *Bible d'étude Semeur 2000* which reads "the old Greek version translated *Sukkites* as troglodytes (cave-dwellers), placing their origins somewhere in the mountainous region on the west coast of the Red Sea."[128] As with the people of Put, there are two possible regions where the Sukkites could have lived: either west of Egypt or on the west coast of the Red Sea.

---

1   See "Kouch," in the *Nouveau dictionnaire biblique révisé*, ed. René Pache (Saint-Légier, Switzerland: Editions Emmaüs, 1992), 726 and related maps which maintain that Cush's descendants settled part of Arabia. As well, see: Reginald S. Poole, "Cush," in *Smith's Bible Dictionary*, ed. H. B. Hackett (New York: Hurd and Houghton, 1875), 519–520; "Cush," *New International Dictionary of the Bible*, eds. J. D. Douglas and Merrill C. Tenney (Grand Rapids, MI: Zondervan, 1987), 244; "Kouch," in the *Dictionnaire biblique pour tous* (Valence, France: Éditions LLB, 1994), 302.

2 J. Daniel Hays, "The Cushites: A Black Nation in Ancient History," *Bibliotheca Sacra* 153, no. 611 (1996), 271.

3 Kenneth A. Kitchen, "Egypt," in the *New Bible Dictionary* (Grand Rapids: Eerdmans, 1962), 337–338.

4 This number comes from James Strong, "כּוּשִׁי, כּוּשִׁי ,כּוּשׁ ,כּוּשׁ," in *Enhanced Strong's Lexicon* (Oak Harbor, WA: Logos Research Systems, 1995), 3568–3571.

5 It should be noted, however, that certain Bibles, such as the King James Version, the Contemporary English Version, and the French *Bible d'étude Semeur 2000* use the term "Ethiopia" instead of "Cush" in Genesis 2:13. The latter gives the following explanation: "Cush, a term which in the rest of the O.T. designates Sudan or Ethiopia. The [Gihon] river would therefore be the Nile. Certain people, however, locate the *land of Cush* in this passage as being in Mesopotamia," Alfred Kuen, Christophe Paya, Hubert Goudineau, Sylvain Romerowski, "Genèse," in the *Bible d'étude Semeur 2000*, ed. Alfred Kuen et al. (Charols, France: Excelsis, 2005), 11.

6 This is the position taken by Ronald Youngblood, "Genesis," in the *NIV Study Bible, 10th Anniversary Edition*, ed. Kenneth Barker et al. (Grand Rapids: Zondervan Publishing House, 1995), 21.

7 This is the position taken by the following: Matthew G. Easton, "Cush," in *Baker's Illustrated Bible Dictionary* (Grand Rapids, MI: Baker Book House, 1978), 177; Poole, "Cush," 519-520; "Cush," in *Nelson's New Illustrated Bible Dictionary*, ed. Ronald Youngblood (Nashville, TN: Thomas Nelson, 1995), 318–319.

8 "Kouch," in the *Dictionnaire biblique pour tous*, 302. Some scholars say the northern part of present-day Ethiopia which falls within the Nile drainage may have been included, but that seems to be a minority view.

9 Alfred Kuen, *Parole Vivante* (Braine-l'Alleud, Belgium: Éditeurs de Littérature Biblique, 1976), 375.

10 Hays, "The Cushites: A Black Nation in Ancient History," 275.

11 Stephanie Dalley, "Foreign Chariotry and Cavalry in the Armies of Tiglath-Pileser III and Sargon II," *Iraq* 47:31–48, quoted in J. Daniel Hays, "The Cushites: A Black Nation in the Bible," *Bibliotheca Sacra* 153, no. 612 (1996), 402.

12 James Strong, "כּוּשׁ," in *Enhanced Strong's Lexicon* (Oak Harbor, WA: Logos Research Systems, 1995), 3568.

13 Hays, "The Cushites: A Black Nation in Ancient History," 272.

14 Youngblood, "Genesis," 21. However, in that same Bible a somewhat contradictory footnote is given by John H. Stek, "Psalms," in the *NIV Study Bible, 10th Anniversary Edition*, ed. Kenneth Barker et al. (Grand Rapids: Zondervan Publishing House, 1995), 852: "[Cush's son, Seba, is] elsewhere in the OT associated with Cush (Genesis 10:7; Isaiah 43:3); it may refer to a region of modern Sudan, south of Egypt." I believe Stek reflects more accurately the ancestry of Seba than does Youngblood.

15 For example, see: Matthew G. Easton, "Seba," in *Baker's Illustrated Bible Dictionary* (Grand Rapids, MI: Baker Book House, 1978), 627; "Seba," in *Nelson's New Illustrated Bible Dictionary*, ed. Ronald Youngblood (Nashville, TN: Thomas Nelson, 1995), 1141; Reginald S. Poole, "Seba," in *Smith's Bible Dictionary*, ed. H. B. Hackett (New York: Hurd and Houghton, 1875), 2899–2901; Orville Nave, "Seba," in *Nave's Topical Bible* (Chicago: Moody Press, 1974), 1150.

16 Quoted in Cain Hope Felder, *Troubling Biblical Waters* (Maryknoll: Orbis Books, 1989), 25.

17 Cheikh Anta Diop, *L'Unité culturelle de l'Afrique Noire* (Dakar: Présence Africaine, 1959), 54.

18 David T. Adamo, *Africa and the Africans in the Old Testament* (Eugene: Wipf and Stock Publishers, 2001), 6, 12.

19 Reverend Father Jean-Baptiste Coulbeaux, *Histoire politique et religieuse de l'Abyssinie : depuis les temps les plus reculés jusqu'à l'avènement de Ménélik II* (Paris: Geuthner, 1929), 80.

20 Coulbeaux, *Histoire politique et religieuse de l'Abyssinie,* 121.

21 John N. Oswalt, "Ethiopia, Cush, Ethiopians," page 435 in vol. 1 of the *Theological Wordbook of the Old Testament*, ed. Laird Harris, Gleason Archer, and Bruce Waltke (Chicago: Moody Press, 1980).

22 For instance, the descendants of Joktan, himself a descendant of Shem (Genesis 10:22-30), resided in southern Arabia. Since descendants of both Ham and Shem lived in Arabia, eventual intermarriage seems likely.

23 Hays, *From Every People and Nation: A biblical theology of race* (Downers Grove: InterVarsity Press, 2003), 89, 97.

24 Alfred Kuen, Hubert Goudineau, Sylvain Romerowski, "Esaïe," in the *Bible d'étude Semeur 2000*, ed. Alfred Kuen et al. (Charols, France: Excelsis, 2005), 986; David T. Adamo, *Africa and the Africans in the Old Testament*, 32.

25 Hays, "The Cushites: A Black Nation in Ancient History," 276.

26 Robert Draper, "Black Pharaohs," *National Geographic* 213, no. 2 (February 2008), 38-59.

27 Hays, "The Cushites: A Black Nation in Ancient History," 280.

28 Daniel J. Boorstin, *The Discoverers* (New York: Random House, 1983), 95-97.

29 *La Bible en français courant* (Pierrefitte France: Alliance Biblique Universelle, 1989), 171 (OT).

30 *La Sainte Bible, version établie par les moines de Maredsous* (Brepols, Belgium: Usines Brepols, 1969), 151. Concerning Moses's wife, the French *Bible TOB* also says that "Cushite could designate a woman belonging to the Midianite tribe of Cushan." *Traduction Œcuménique de la Bible* (Paris: Société Biblique Française/Éditions du Cerf, 1975), 179.

31 Ronald B. Allen and Kenneth L. Barker, "Numbers," in the *NIV Study Bible, 10th Anniversary Edition,* ed. Kenneth Barker et al. (Grand Rapids: Zondervan Publishing House, 1995), 205.

32 J. Daniel Hays, "Moses: The Private Man behind the Public Leader." *Bible Review*, no. 16 (August 2000), 60.

33 Hays, *From Every People and Nation*, 66-67.

34 William White, "רב," pages 826-827 in vol. 2 of the *Theological Wordbook of the Old Testament*, ed. Laird Harris, Gleason Archer, and Bruce Waltke (Chicago: Moody Press, 1980).

35 E. J. Young, "Aaron," page 1 in the *New Bible Dictionary*, ed. J. D. Douglas (Grand Rapids, MI: Eerdmans, 1962).

36 Hays, "The Cushites: A Black Nation in the Bible," 399.

37 Cain Hope Felder, "Race, Racism and the Biblical Narratives," *Stony the Road We Trod: African-American Biblical Interpretation,* ed. Cain Hope Felder (Minneapolis, MN: Fortress Press, 1991), 135. We can note that Hays thinks the most logical reason for Miriam's complaint is racism. Hays, *From Every People and Nation*, 74.

38 Copher does not give an opinion, but he eliminates racism as a cause since he holds that Zipporah, Moses, Aaron, and Miriam are all black people. This kind of reasoning shows that sometimes the Afrocentric theologians have a tendency to exaggerate, in my opinion. Charles B. Copher, "The Black Presence in the Old Testament," *Stony the Road We Trod: African-American Biblical Interpretation,* ed. Cain Hope Felder (Minneapolis, MN: Fortress Press, 1991), 156.

39 Alfred G. Dunston, *The Black Man in the Old Testament and Its World.* (Philadelphia, PA: Dorrance and Company, 1974), 98-99.

40 Hays, *From Every People and Nation*, 76.

41 Kenneth A. Kitchen, "Phinehas," in the *New Bible Dictionary* (Grand Rapids: Eerdmans, 1962), 992; "Phinehas," in *Nelson's New Illustrated Bible Dictionary,* ed. Ronald Youngblood (Nashville, TN: Thomas Nelson, 1995), 989; Hays, "Moses," 62. A good summary of these arguments, both for and against the interpretation of the word *nehsiu* as meaning "the black man" can be found in Adamo, *Africa and the Africans in the Old Testament*, 17-22.

42 Hays, *From Every People and Nation*, 84.

43 "Phinehas," in *Nelson's New Illustrated Bible Dictionary,* 989.

44 Gordon J. Wenham, "Aaron," page 347 in vol. 4 of *New International Dictionary of Old Testament Theology and Exegesis,* ed. Willem VanGemeren (Grand Rapids: Zondervan, 1997).

45 Herbert Wolf and John H. Stek, "Malachi," in the *NIV Study Bible, 10th Anniversary Edition*, ed. Kenneth Barker et al. (Grand Rapids: Zondervan Publishing House, 1995), 1419; John MacArthur, "Malachi," in the *Sainte Bible avec commentaires de John MacArthur* (Geneva: Société Biblique de Genève, 2006), 1355; Craig A. Blaising, "Malachi," in the *Bible Knowledge Commentary*, ed. John F. Walvoord, Roy B. Zuck et al. (Colorado Springs, CO: Victor Books/Scripture Press, 1985), 1579-1580.

46 For example, in Ezekiel 23:42 the *NIV Study Bible* says the Sabeans were "men from Sheba, located at the southwestern corner of the Arabian peninsula (modern Yemen)". Mark Hillmer, "Ezekiel," in the *NIV Study Bible, 10th Anniversary Edition*, ed. Kenneth Barker et al. (Grand Rapids: Zondervan Publishing House, 1995), 1251.

47 Alfred Kuen, Hubert Goudineau, Sylvain Romerowski, "Ezéchiel," in the *Bible d'étude Semeur 2000*, ed. Alfred Kuen et al. (Charols, France: Excelsis, 2005), 1192.

48 Diop, *L'Unité culturelle de l'Afrique Noire*, 54.

49 Coulbeaux, *Histoire politique et religieuse de l'Abyssinie*, 93.

50 The *Royal Order of Ethiopian Hebrews* maintains that the Queen of Sheba gave birth to a boy whose father was King Solomon, and that Emperor Haile Selassie was one of his descendants. For a short explanation of this story, see Ype Schaaf, *L'histoire et le rôle de la Bible en Afrique* (Dokkum, Netherlands: Éditions des Groupes Missionnaires, 2000), 9.

51 Alfred Kuen, Hubert Goudineau, Sylvain Romerowski, "Job," in the *Bible d'étude Semeur 2000*, ed. Alfred Kuen et al. (Charols, France: Excelsis, 2005), 700.

52 John Bright, *A History of Israel*, 2nd ed. (Philadelphia: Westminster Press, 1976), 211.

53 Hays, *From Every People and Nation*, 113.

54 Hays, *From Every People and Nation*, 92.

55 Hays, "The Cushites: A Black Nation in the Bible," 402-403.

56 Kenneth A. Kitchen, "So," in the *New Bible Dictionary, Third edition* (Downers Grove, IL: IVP Academic, 1996), 1115.

57 Edwin Yamauchi, *Africa and the Bible* (Grand Rapids: Baker Academic, 2004), 110.

58 Kitchen, "So," 1115.

59 Alfred Kuen, Hubert Goudineau, Sylvain Romerowski, "Esaïe," 987. The Hebrew text always uses the words "Cush" or "Cushite," not "Ethiopia" or "Ethiopian," in the book of Isaiah.

60 Edna Russmann, "Egypt and the Kushites: Dynasty XXV," in *Africa and Africans in Antiquity*, ed. Edwin Yamauchi (East Lansing, MI: Michigan State University Press, 2001), 118.

61 Herbert Wolf and John H. Stek, "Isaiah," in the *NIV Study Bible, 10th Anniversary Edition*, ed. Kenneth Barker et al. (Grand Rapids: Zondervan Publishing House, 1995), 1038.

62 Wolf and Stek, "Isaiah," 1050.

63 Hays, *From Every People and Nation*, 99.

64 Some scholars say Tirhakah is Shebitku's nephew, not his brother. Edwin Yamauchi, introduction to *Africa and Africans in Antiquity*, ed. Edwin Yamauchi (East Lansing, MI: Michigan State University Press, 2001), 3; Edna Russmann, "Egypt and the Kushites: Dynasty XXV", 118.

65 Wolf and Stek, "Isaiah," 1060.

66 Yamauchi, *Africa and the Bible,* 128-137.

67 Hays, *From Every People and Nation*, 127.

68 "Eunuque," in the *Nouveau dictionnaire biblique révisé*, ed. René Pache (Saint-Légier, Switzerland: Editions Emmaüs, 1992), 443.

69 Hays, *From Every People and Nation*, 136.

70   For other examples of this practice, see Genesis 19:1, Ruth 4:1, and 2 Samuel 15:2.

71   Adamo, *Africa and the Africans in the Old Testament*, 113.

72   Youngblood, "Genesis," 21.

73   T. C. Mitchell, "Lehabim," in the *New Bible Dictionary* (Grand Rapids: Eerdmans, 1962), 728.

74   Matthew G. Easton, "Lubims," in *Baker's Illustrated Bible Dictionary* (Grand Rapids, MI: Baker Book House, 1978), 439; Jerome Smith, ed., "2 Chronicles 12:3," *New Treasury of Scripture Knowledge* (Nashville: Thomas Nelson Publishers, 1992), 485.

75   Youngblood, "Genesis," 21; Kenneth A. Kitchen, "Naphtuhim," in the *New Bible Dictionary, Third edition* (Downers Grove, IL: IVP Academic, 1996), 803.

76   Orville Nave, "Naphtuhim," in *Nave's Topical Bible* (Chicago: Moody Press, 1974), 887.

77   "Pathros," in *Nelson's New Illustrated Bible Dictionary*, ed. Ronald Youngblood (Nashville, TN: Thomas Nelson, 1995), 950.

78   Charles H. Dyer, "Ezekiel," in the *Bible Knowledge Commentary*, ed. John F. Walvoord, Roy B. Zuck et al. (Colorado Springs, CO: Victor Books/Scripture Press, 1985), 1286.

79   "Kaslouhim," in the *Nouveau dictionnaire biblique révisé*, ed. René Pache (Saint-Légier, Switzerland: Editions Emmaüs, 1992), 721.

80   David Howard, "Philistines," page 1049 in vol. 4 of *New International Dictionary of Old Testament Theology and Exegesis,* ed. Willem VanGemeren (Grand Rapids: Zondervan, 1997).

81   James Hoffmeier, "Egypt," page 564 in vol. 4 of *New International Dictionary of Old Testament Theology and Exegesis,* ed. Willem VanGemeren (Grand Rapids: Zondervan, 1997).

82   Youngblood, "Genesis," 25.

83   Bright, *A History of Israel*, 83. Note, however, that others place Abraham's sojourn in Egypt earlier. The Old Testament Chronology in the *NIV Study Bible, 10th Anniversary Edition,* ed. Kenneth Barker et al. (Grand Rapids: Zondervan Publishing House, 1995), places it around 2090 BC, which could have been during the 11th dynasty. As well, the fact that scholars do not agree on the dates of the different dynasties makes it impossible to arrive at an exact identification of this Pharaoh.

84   Bright, *A History of Israel*, 52-53.

85   Bright, *A History of Israel*, 60.

86   Hyksos is defined as "chiefs of foreign lands", "foreign rulers", or "rulers of foreign countries" in the following sources respectively: Kitchen, "Egypt," 342; Bright, *A History of Israel*, 60; "Hyksos," in *Nelson's New Illustrated Bible Dictionary*, ed. Ronald Youngblood (Nashville, TN: Thomas Nelson, 1995), 587.

87   The "Hyksos" are defined as "shepherd princes" by Matthew G. Easton, "Egypt," in *Baker's Illustrated Bible Dictionary* (Grand Rapids, MI: Baker Book House, 178), 221, or "shepherds" by Joseph Thompson, "Egypt," in *Smith's Bible Dictionary*, ed. H. B. Hackett (New York: Hurd and Houghton, 1875), 681-684.

88   "Egypte," in the *Nouveau dictionnaire biblique révisé*, ed. René Pache (Saint-Légier, Switzerland: Editions Emmaüs, 1992), 386.

89   James M. Weinstein, "Hyksos," in *HarperCollins Bible Dictionary*, ed. Paul J. Achtemeier (San Francisco: HarperSanFrancisco, 1996), 444.

90   *Encyclopedia Britannica*, s.v. "Embalming" (Chicago: Encyclopedia Britannica). https://www.britannica.com/topic/embalming (accessed May 8, 2018).

91   Eugene Merrill, "חנט (hnt)," page 197 in vol. 2 of *New International Dictionary of Old Testament Theology and Exegesis,* ed. Willem VanGemeren (Grand Rapids: Zondervan, 1997).

92   Ronald Youngblood and Walter C. Kaiser, Jr., "Exodus," in the *NIV Study Bible, 10th Anniversary Edition*, ed. Kenneth Barker et al. (Grand Rapids: Zondervan Publishing House, 1995), 88, see also "Egypte," in the *Nouveau dictionnaire biblique révisé*, 386.

93 Bright, *History of Israel*, 122.

94 Alfred Kuen, Christophe Paya, Hubert Goudineau, Sylvain Romerowski, "Exode," in the *Bible d'étude Semeur 2000*, ed. Alfred Kuen et al. (Charols, France: Excelsis, 2005), 89.

95 Note also that there is not a common consensus on the spelling of certain names. For instance, Tuthmosis=Thuthmosis=Thutmose; Seti=Sethi=Sethos; Rameses=Ramesses=Raamses; Amenhotep=Amunhotep=Amenophis. I have usually opted for the spelling found in the following two sources: Kitchen, "Egypt," 337–354; Jenny Hill, "Names of the Pharaohs of Ancient Egypt," Ancient Egypt Online, 2016, accessed June 19 2018. http://www.ancientegyptonline.co.uk/names-Pharaoh.html

96 "Pithom," in the *Nouveau dictionnaire biblique révisé*, ed. René Pache (Saint-Légier, Switzerland: Editions Emmaüs, 1992), 1041.

97 "Egypte," in the *Nouveau dictionnaire biblique révisé*, 386; Youngblood and Kaiser, "Exodus," 89.

98 "Egypt: The History of Egypt," in *Nelson's New Illustrated Bible Dictionary*, ed. Ronald Youngblood (Nashville, TN: Thomas Nelson, 1995), 382.

99 Kuen, Paya, Goudineau, Romerowski, "Exode," 89.

100 Youngblood and Kaiser, "Exodus," 88.

101 This list was basically taken from François Boussin, "Les pharaons d'Egypte," Interactive Boussweb, last modified May 25, 1999, accessed May 29, 2018, http://boubouss.perso.infonie.fr/egypte/egypte.htm. Certain modifications to this list were made according to the dates and names given in John Baines and Jaromír Málek, *Atlas of Ancient Egypt* (New York: Facts on File, Inc., 1980), 36-37; Yamauchi, *Africa and the Bible, various pages*. I have usually opted for the spelling found in the following sources: Kitchen, "Egypt," 337–354; Kenneth A. Kitchen, "Pharaoh" in the *New Bible Dictionary* (Grand Rapids: Eerdmans, 1962), 980-981; Hill, "Names of the Pharaohs of Ancient Egypt." Also used: Elise Senakht, "Pharaons de l'Egypte ancienne," Visite Egypte, last modified April 3, 2018, accessed June 20, 2018, http://www.visite-egypte.com/pharaohs.php.

102 Others classify this dynasty as being in the Middle Kingdom instead of the Second Intermediate Period. See for example Baines and Málek, *Atlas of Ancient Egypt,* 36.

103 Youngblood and Kaiser, "Exodus," 89; "Egypte," in the *Nouveau dictionnaire biblique révisé*, 386.

104 Diop, *L'Unité culturelle de l'Afrique Noire*, 154.

105 Kuen, Paya, Goudineau, Romerowski, "Exode," 91.

106 Youngblood and Kaiser, "Exodus," 83.

107 This sea is commonly called the Red Sea, although some Bibles have footnotes saying it could also be called the Sea of Reeds and give several possibilities as to where this crossing may have occurred. Two plausible sites for crossing the Red Sea/Sea of Reeds are the Bitter Lakes or an arm of Lake Menzaleh. See William LaSor, David Hubbard, and Frederic Bush, *Old Testament Survey* (Grand Rapids, MI: Eerdmans, 1982) 128-130.

108 Hays, *From Every People and Nation*, 68.

109 James Hoffmeier, "Egypt," 565.

110 "Pharaon," in the *Nouveau dictionnaire biblique révisé*, ed. René Pache (Saint-Légier, Switzerland: Editions Emmaüs, 1992), 1015. Siamen is also called Siamun. Note that two study Bibles give the names of Smendes and Psusennes II as other possible identities of the Pharaoh in this passage. All three are from the 21st dynasty. Alfred Kuen, Hubert Goudineau, Sylvain Romerowski, "2 Chroniques," in the *Bible d'étude Semeur 2000*, ed. Alfred Kuen et al. (Charols, France: Excelsis, 2005), 468); J. Robert Vannoy, "I Kings," in the *NIV Study Bible, 10th Anniversary Edition*, ed. Kenneth Barker et al. (Grand Rapids: Zondervan Publishing House, 1995), 470.

111 Vannoy, "I Kings," 470.

112 Vannoy, "I Kings," 470.

113 Kenneth A. Kitchen, "Hophra," in the *New Bible Dictionary* (Grand Rapids: Eerdmans, 1962), 536.

114 James Strong, "בִּתְיָה," in *Enhanced Strong's Lexicon* (Oak Harbor, WA: Logos Research Systems, 1995), 1332.

115 For example, "I conclude therefore that Putu-Iaman is likely to have been the Greek colony in Cyrene, north-east Libya in modern terms, and that any connection with Yemen may be ruled out." T. C. Mitchell, "Where Was Putu-Iaman?" *Proceedings of the Seminar for Arabian Studies* 22 (1992): 77, quoted in Yamauchi, *Africa and the Bible*, 184.

116 "Pouth," in the *Nouveau dictionnaire biblique révisé*, ed. René Pache (Saint-Légier, Switzerland: Editions Emmaüs, 1992), 1054.

117 Yamauchi, *Africa and the Bible*, 84-85.

118 Frank Thompson, "Genèse," in *La Bible Thompson avec chaîne de références* (Miami: Editions Vida, 1990), 10.

119 Hays, "Moses," 63.

120 James Swanson, "לוּד," the *Dictionary of Biblical Languages with Semantic Domains: Hebrew (Old Testament)* electronic ed. (Oak Harbor: Logos Research Systems, Inc., 1997), found in the Libronix Digital Library System, version 1.1a, article no. 4276.

121 Mark Hillmer, "Ezekiel," in the *NIV Study Bible, 10th Anniversary Edition*, ed. Kenneth Barker et al. (Grand Rapids: Zondervan Publishing House, 1995), 1256, 1260.

122 Kuen, Paya, Goudineau, Romerowski, "Genèse," 22.

123 Reuben G. Bullard, "The Berbers of the Maghreb and Ancient Carthage," in *Africa and Africans in Antiquity*, ed. Edwin Yamauchi (East Lansing, MI: Michigan State University Press, 2001), 184; Edwin Yamauchi, "Shishak," in *The New International Dictionary of Biblical Archaeology*, E. M. Blaiklock and R. K. Harrison, editors (Grand Rapids: Zondervan, 1983), 412. For more information on Shishak, see "Chichaq," in the *Dictionnaire biblique pour tous* (Valence, France: Éditions LLB, 1994), 101; Yamauchi, *Africa and the Bible*, 188; Richard Patterson and Hermann Austel, "1, 2 Kings," in *The Expositor's Bible Commentary*, Frank Gæbelein, General editor (Grand Rapids, MI: Zondervan, 1988), vol. 4, 124-125.

124 Yamauchi, "Shishak," 412.

125 Bright, *A History of Israel*, 230.

126 Raymond Dillard, "2 Chronicles," in the *NIV Study Bible, 10th Anniversary Edition*, ed. Kenneth Barker et al. (Grand Rapids: Zondervan Publishing House, 1995), 630.

127 "Soukkiens," in the *Nouveau dictionnaire biblique révisé*, ed. René Pache (Saint-Légier, Switzerland: Editions Emmaüs, 1992), 1231.

128 Alfred Kuen, Hubert Goudineau, Sylvain Romerowski, "2 Chroniques," in the *Bible d'étude Semeur 2000*, ed. Alfred Kuen et al. (Charols, France: Excelsis, 2005), 608.

3

AFRICANS IN THE NEW TESTAMENT

After having seen so many references to Africans in the Old Testament, it may be disappointing to discover how few of these passages there are in the New. References to "Egypt" or "Egyptian" are found 949 times in the Old Testament, without counting all the references to Egyptian cities, Pharaohs, or other Egyptian people. In the New Testament, however, there are only 96 references of any kind to an Egyptian place or person. For Cush/ Ethiopia and the Cushites/Ethiopians there are 137 references in the Old Testament, as compared to 25 in the New. There are 40 references to Put/Libya/Somalia and its peoples in the Old Testament and nine in the New. This last number is largely due to the fact that the New Testament mentions the city of Cyrene seven times. I will discuss this city more fully in the next chapter. It is difficult to know where to place the reference to Simeon in Acts 13:1. He was probably African, but we do not know exactly where he came from. If we combine all the New Testament references to Africa or an African – even if their African origin is only probable – we obtain the following result:

Alexandria	4 times
Apollos	29 times
Candace	1 time
Cyrene	7 times
Those from Cyrene	1 time
Deserts	10 times
Egypt	28 times
Egyptian(s)	8 times
Ethiopian(s)	24 times
Hagar	4 times
Libya	1 time
Pharaoh	12 times
Pharaoh's daughter	2 times
Red Sea	4 times
Simeon	1 time
Sinai (Mount or desert)	5 times
Total	141 times

This smaller number of New Testament references, as compared to those in the Old, does not mean that Christianity is any less interested in Africa than Judaism was. When Jesus, at the end of his time on earth, commissioned his disciples to "make disciples of all nations" (Matthew 28:19), Africa was not excluded. In addition, Jesus told his disciples that they would be his "witnesses in Jerusalem, and in all Judea and Samaria and to the ends of the earth" (Acts 1:8). Afterwards, Africa is the first place representing "the ends of the earth" to receive the good news of Jesus Christ (see Acts 8). "Ethiopia" becomes the Church's first foray into cross-cultural missions, even though "Ethiopia" came to Israel instead of vice versa. But before examining this story in detail, we will look in chronological order at the other Africans spoken of in the New Testament.

The day of Pentecost

In Acts 2, we see the disciples filled with the Holy Spirit, who then began to speak of the wonders of God to "God-fearing Jews" who "were staying in Jerusalem". Among them were people from Egypt and the parts of Libya near Cyrene, as well as from many other countries. By a miracle of God, the 120 disciples were able to speak to all these people in their native tongues (*dialektos* in Greek). This means the disciples spoke to the Jews from Egypt in an Egyptian language. They spoke to those from Libya in a Libyan language. Jesus's disciples spoke about him in the mother tongue of each hearer.

The fact that the disciples used various mother tongues, and not Greek or Aramaic, leads me to believe that when this passage speaks of those who lived in Egypt and Libya it is speaking of people of African origin. If these people from Egypt and Libya had been Jews from *Israel* who merely resided in Africa, and not *African* Jews (proselytes), the disciples could have spoken to them in Aramaic or Greek, as Peter did shortly afterwards. The miracle of these "tongues of fire" given by the Holy Spirit would not have been necessary if these people had been Jews from Israel and not natives of Africa who adhered to Judaism.

If on the day of Pentecost those men from "the parts of Libya near Cyrene" had all been Greeks who followed the Jewish religion (since Cyrene was a large Greek colony in northern Africa), the disciples could have easily spoken to them in Greek. After all, Peter, Matthew, John, Jude, and James the brother of Jesus all spoke Greek, as we see by the epistles they wrote in the Greek language shortly afterwards. There would have been no need for a miraculous intervention by the Holy Spirit enabling the disciples to speak to Greek-speakers from Cyrene. But here in Acts 2, this passage emphasizes the fact that all these men coming from different regions of the world heard the disciples speaking in their "own native language", according to verse 8. This fact makes me think that not only were there Israelites living in Egypt and Cyrene who came to Jerusalem to celebrate Pentecost, but there were also native Egyptians and native Cyrenians (that is, Berbers) who were there as well. Verse 10 speaks of "both Jews and converts to Judaism (proselytes)", and I think both groups of people came to Jerusalem from all 15 regions mentioned in this passage.

If this miracle took place, it was to ensure that each listener truly understood the message of salvation in Jesus Christ. Today Bible translators use this same principle, for there is no more effective way to communicate a message than to do it in the listeners' mother tongue.

The result of Pentecost was the birth of the early church in Jerusalem. About 3,000 people were added to that group of 120 believers (Acts 2:41). It is clear that some of these 3,000 people were these same Egyptians and Libyans from Cyrene who had heard the message of Christ in their own language. John Stott, a well-known theologian, said that "nothing could have demonstrated more clearly than this the multi-racial, multi-national, multi-lingual nature of the kingdom of Christ".[1]

These people, including those from Africa, stayed in Jerusalem for a certain time, where "they devoted themselves to the apostles' teaching and to the fellowship, to the breaking of bread and to prayer" (Acts 2:42). Their faith was becoming established.

People from Cyrene and Alexandria

The next time we hear about people from Africa is in Acts 6:9, where we read that men from Cyrene and Alexandria were arguing with Stephen. These were Jews and not the new Christians from Acts 2. These men did not agree with Stephen, "but they could not stand up against his wisdom or the Spirit by whom he spoke" (Acts 6:10). So, they stirred up people against him and even bribed men to lie about him. These men from Africa were involved in the arrest and death of Stephen, possibly as the main instigators.

A deeper look at these two African cities appears in the next section of this book as well. But the main point here is that Cyrene and Alexandria were both founded by the Greeks and remained deeply influenced by the Mediterranean world, first by the Greeks and then by the Romans. The people of these cities spoke the Greek language. One author explains, "The Greek language and culture were not limited to the numerous Greek merchants who settled in Alexandria and the other cities, but almost the entire urban population adopted them."[2] These two cities undoubtedly had an African population that played an important role in everyday life, but it would be a mistake to conclude that because they were in Africa they were only populated by Africans. A significant part of the population of these two cities, and perhaps even the majority of Cyrene's population, was non-African. However, according to the *Encyclopaedia Britannica*, in the city of Cyrene "there was more intermarriage between Greek men and non-Greek women than was usual in Greek colonies".[3] Who were these non-Greeks in the region of Cyrene? According to Maffre, they were the "*Tjehenu*, brown-skinned people with long, black hair, and the *Tjemehu*, fair-skinned people with blond hair and blue eyes, and finally the *Libu*, from which we get the name 'Libyan'".[4] We see then that the Greeks of Cyrene intermarried with the local African people from the very beginning of their stay in Africa.

Simon of Cyrene and Lucius of Cyrene

We now come to the discussion of two other Cyrenians. We find Simon of Cyrene in three of the four gospels; he is the one who carried the cross when Jesus could no longer do so. As for Lucius, he was part of the church at Antioch (Acts 13:1), and was one of the leaders, possibly even one of the founders.[5] This may be the same Lucius we see in Romans 16:21 who was Paul's relative.

Taking into consideration what I said earlier about the city of Cyrene, these two men were probably not Africans, but rather Jews who lived in Africa. Cyrene especially had a large Jewish colony. Some biblical reference works call Simon a Jew,[6] but many reference books say he was *probably* a Jew who came to Jerusalem to celebrate the Passover.[7] Yamauchi takes a more definitive stance, saying that, "In the case of Cyrene, the city was a Greek colony;

Simon was *no doubt* a member of the Jewish community there. The native Libyans of the countryside were not blacks, but Berbers" (italics mine).[8] We must remember, of course, that Berbers are Africans even if they are not black.

Some Christian leaders maintain that Simon must have been an African because the Jews considered death on a cross to be a curse (Deuteronomy 21:23, quoted in Galatians 3:13) and therefore a Jew would not have consented to carry a cross destined for that use. But first of all, we need to remember that this verse from the Old Testament says that "anyone who is hung on a tree is under God's curse". It refers to a dead body, a cadaver, which is left hanging on a tree; it does not speak of a living person carrying a cross, nor does it refer to the actual wood of the cross. Hence, there was no legitimate reason based on this verse to refuse to come into contact with Jesus or with the wooden cross. Secondly, even if the Jews considered the cross itself to be a cursed item, it would have been extremely difficult for a common Jew on the side of the road to refuse a direct order given by an armed Roman soldier. One could imagine that perhaps a Pharisee or a chief priest might have argued with a soldier concerning such an order, but it is doubtful that a simple Jewish passer-by could have refused to obey such an order coming from a Roman soldier. Simon's act of kindness does not prove that he was therefore not a Jew but an African.

However, we cannot say with certainty that Simon and/or Lucius were *not* Africans, because some Africans did convert to Judaism (such as Ebed-Melech and the Ethiopian dignitary), and so some men were Jewish by religion and African by ethnicity. But it is impossible to know if Simon and Lucius were among them. One well-known commentator, William Barclay, speaks of Simon as being of African and not Semitic origin, but he bases this on the idea that Simon of Cyrene is the same person as Simeon called Niger (see below). Since he uses words like "maybe" and "it's possible that" in his argument, he more or less admits that his ideas are open to question.[9] Most scholars believe that the majority of Jews in Cyrene were not of African but rather Asian origin, since the Jews were a Semitic people. As we will see below, the Jews from Cyrene even had their own synagogue in Jerusalem.

Nevertheless, it remains clear that Simon, who carried Jesus's cross, was someone who lived in Africa and not in Israel. It is also very likely that this encounter with Jesus changed his life forever. Since the gospel of Mark speaks of Simon of Cyrene as the father of Alexander and Rufus (Mark 15:21), two Christians who may have lived in Rome and who were evidently well known by the readers of that gospel (Romans 16:13), it would seem that Simon converted to Christianity and that at some later date members of his family did the same.

The Freedmen

Acts 6:9 speaks of an argument between Stephen and certain Jews, among whom were those from "the Synagogue of the Freedmen (as it was called)". The French translation *La Bible en français courant* uses the phrase, "the synagogue of the freed slaves", and gives an explanatory note: "The synagogue of the freed slaves (or Freedmen) included descendants of former slaves who had been brought in by the Roman general Pompeii in 63 BC, and then subsequently freed."[10] The *Nouveau dictionnaire biblique révisé* sheds more light on the subject: "It was probably Jews who had been taken prisoner by Pompeii and other Roman generals, deported to Rome and later freed."[11] Because Pompeii's military campaign of 63 BC took place in Palestine, those slaves were probably Jews from Israel.

However, it is possible that some of these freed slaves might have been Africans. We say this not because it is difficult to separate the idea of slavery from African people, but rather because Acts 6:9 indicates a possible link between the Freedmen and those from Alexandria and Cyrene.

So, who were the people arguing with Stephen? The French translation *Segond Révisée* and the King James Version give the impression that there were five groups of people talking with Stephen: the Freedmen/Libertines, the Cyrenians, the Alexandrians, and the people from the provinces of Cilicia and Asia. Other translations, like the *Bible d'étude Semeur 2000* and the New English Bible, say that the Freedmen included people from Cyrene, Alexandria, Cilicia, and Asia. There are divided opinions on this question, and some think there is no clear answer.[12] Regardless of how one chooses to answer this question, it is probable that these freed slaves were Jews from Israel, as implied by the *Nouveau dictionnaire biblique révisé*, and not African Jews, even if some of these Jews lived at that time in the cities of Cyrene or Alexandria.

The Ethiopian eunuch, a high dignitary[13]

Let us go back to Acts 8 where we see the persecution of the church after Stephen's death, which took place sometime between two to five years after the day of Pentecost.[14] This persecution may have caused several African converts (from Acts 2) to return to Egypt and Libya. Other converts were dispersed throughout Judea and Samaria, proclaiming the message of the good news of Jesus (Acts 2:1-4).

But the story at the end of this chapter mentions another African nationality, because the Holy Spirit sent Philip the deacon to talk to an "Ethiopian eunuch". He was a dignitary, an important government official of the queen. Verse 27 says that he was "an important official in charge of all the treasury of Candace, queen of the Ethiopians". A note from the *Bible d'étude Semeur 2000* helps us understand this man's background:

> The men in the service of a queen were often castrated. This term was later applied to various dignitaries in the royal palace. The O.T. announces to *eunuchs*, who were excluded from the assembly of the Lord according to Deuteronomy 23:2, that they will have their place in the Temple of God (Isaiah 56:3-5). In biblical times, the name *Ethiopia* referred to Nubia, present-day Sudan, about 800 kilometres south of Egypt. There were some Jewish colonies in this area, and his contact with them could have taught this high dignitary a knowledge of the Jewish religion.[15]

While eunuchs did not initially have the right to be part of the Jewish people according to Deuteronomy 23:1, by the time of David's reign eunuchs occupied relatively important places among the Jewish people (see 1 Chronicles 28:1, where the Hebrew word for "palace officials" is the same word as "eunuchs"). Later, during Isaiah's time, it was said that foreigners and eunuchs would no longer be excluded from God's people (Isaiah 56:3). Here in Acts 8, which takes place during New Testament times, many believe that this former practice of excluding eunuchs from the body of believers was no longer operational.

This African dignitary had come to Jerusalem to worship God, and on the way home, he was reading the Greek version of Isaiah 53. Considering the regular contact between the Egypt of the Ptolemies and the kingdom of Meroe over the course of several centuries, it is not surprising that an "Ethiopian" would know how to read Greek. But he did not understand clearly to whom the prophet was referring. Because of this, the Holy Spirit sent Philip to this official, to help him understand that the passage spoke of Jesus Christ. Once he understood, he asked Philip to baptize him, which Philip did. Immediately Philip was taken away by the Spirit and the Ethiopian "did not see him again, but went on his way rejoicing" back to Africa (Acts 8:39).

We read nothing further of this man in the New Testament. Did he preach the good news of Jesus in Africa? Was he the founder of a Christian church in Sudan or in Ethiopia? We have no way of knowing for certain. According to Stedman, "tradition reports that many Ethiopians accepted Christ because of his testimony",[16] and Hays explains that "although there is no evidence of a 1st century church in Ethiopia/Cush, several Church Fathers [such as Irenaeus and Eusebius] credit the Ethiopian eunuch as being the first missionary there".[17] But the main point is that someone from Africa had the opportunity to hear the gospel message, as those from Asia and Europe would later have.

Here is what Andrew Walls, a well-known theologian and missiologist, says about this story:

> The whole way the story is framed is a reminder that Africa, the lands beyond the Nile, will have a Christian history too; one that is not yet charted, and one which is distinct from the story of Asia and Europe which is the concern of the Acts of the Apostles. It is distinct, but not entirely separate; the Ethiopian is, after all, an international traveller who knows the highways of the Greco-Roman world. In the Acts story, he comes as a pilgrim, and returns as a Christian. Perhaps it is not too fanciful to take a hint that he, or his spiritual descendants, may one day travel those highways again, as the representatives and bearers of the Christian Gospel.[18]

So we see that the first "foreigner" to receive an explanation of the Good News of Jesus Christ was an African, and that was the direct result of the working of the Holy Spirit.

Candace, the Queen of "Ethiopia"

Candace is also mentioned in the story of the Ethiopian official in Acts 8. Unfortunately, we do not know anything about this woman except that she was a queen of the kingdom called Meroe, situated in southern Nubia. The *Nouveau dictionnaire biblique révisé* says of this queen: "Strabo, Dion Cassius, [and] Pliny all agree that in the first century Meroe was governed by a dynasty of queens who were all called Candace."[19] From this we understand that in Meroe, "Candace" was a title, and not a personal name, similar to the word "Pharaoh" in Egypt or "Caesar" in the Roman Empire. Diop gives us a fuller history of the first Queen Candace, who doubtless lived before the one spoken of in the NT:

> The reign of Queen Candace was truly historic. She was a contemporary of Caesar Augustus at the height of his glory. Caesar, after conquering Egypt, pushed his armies across the Nubian Desert up to the borders of Ethiopia. According to Strabo, they were commanded by General Gaius Petronius. The queen herself took command of her army, and at the head of her troops, charged the Roman soldiers, as Joan of Arc did later against the English army. Losing an eye in battle served only to heighten her courage.

This heroic resistance impressed the whole ancient world, not because she was a [black person], but because she was a woman: the Indo-European world was not yet used to the idea that a woman could play a political and social role . . . This glorious resistance remains etched in Sudanese memory; Candace's prestige was such that all the queens who followed her took the same name.[20]

It is possible that the Candace in Acts was Queen Amanitare, who reigned from AD 25–41. But these dates for her are not universally accepted, as some believe she reigned earlier and that the Candace in the Bible is an unknown queen.[21] Others opt for Queen Nawidemak as the Candace in the Bible.[22]

It is interesting to consider the physical size of these queens. Kendall calls these Meroitic queens:

> powerful figures, enormously fat, covered with jewels and ornament and elaborate fringed and tasselled robes . . . with the decline of Egyptian influence, extreme corpulence had again become the fashion in Sudan, at least among the ladies at court, and a remarkable succession of massive queens and princesses appears in monumental art from the 3rd century BC to the 4th century AD.[23]

Yamauchi also speaks of Meroe, this time addressing the wealth of this powerful kingdom:

> In the excavation of Wadi ben Naqa by Jean Vercoutter from 1958 to 1960 a great store of ivory and ebony was found. The Meroites also had gold, slaves, leopard skins, and incense to offer. Despite the great distances involved, archaeological finds at Meroitic burial sites, even after the inevitable looting by tomb robbers, indicate the presence of fine imported jewellery, vases, and wine from Rhodes, the west coast of Asia Minor, and southern France, and olive oil from North Africa. These objects came from diplomatic and trade missions.[24]

It would be wrong to believe the kingdom of Meroe (with its capital about 140 miles northeast of the city of Khartoum, in present-day Sudan) was a poor area. Like the Cushites before them, the Meroites were a progressive people who had regular contact with the Mediterranean world.

Men from Cyrene

There is one more mention of the city of Cyrene that deserves our attention:

> Now those who had been scattered by the persecution in connection with Stephen travelled as far as Phoenicia, Cyprus and Antioch, telling the message only to Jews. Some of them, however, men from Cyprus and Cyrene, went to Antioch and began to speak to the Greeks also, telling them the good news about the Lord Jesus (Acts 11:19-20).

In my opinion, these two verses are extremely important, because they show that people from Africa took part in the spread of the church through their involvement in missions.

The link to Acts 8 is obvious, because both passages refer to the persecution and dispersion following the death of Stephen. But the difference is that, whereas in Acts 8 the Christians went to Judea and Samaria, here they spread to that zone that is referred to as "the ends of the earth": Phoenicia (present-day Lebanon); Antioch in what we now call Turkey; and Cyprus, which is the same island of Cyprus that we know today. All three were outside the limits of Judea and Samaria. This passage highlights a turning point for the early church – the scope of their mission field broadened considerably.

In Acts 8, it was an African who *received* the message of the gospel. But here, it is people from Africa and Cyprus who are *announcing* the message to others. So we see a second major turning point – the identity of the messengers. Christian missionaries are no longer only people from Israel.

There was also a third turning point. Up to this time, the Christians only proclaimed the message of Jesus to Jews. Even the Ethiopian official, that foreigner from another continent, was most likely a proselyte, that is, a pagan who had become a Jew. He did not have religious barriers between himself and the other Jews with whom he spoke. But here, people from Cyprus and Cyrene made a concerted effort to speak to Greeks, and this is the first time this happens in the New Testament. In addition, according to Hengel, "the term 'Greek' did not refer to a people, but rather to a community of various peoples who spoke the same language and embraced certain aspects of the same culture . . . Eventually, however, the upper class of Romans began to refer to themselves as Greek (*Hellēn*), and the term 'Greek' became connected to the cultural status of the upper class."[25]

Further, these young missionaries set their sights on a vast mission field. They preached the gospel in Antioch, "the capital of the Roman province of Syria [and the] third largest city of the Roman Empire (after Rome and Alexandria)".[26] In Jesus's time the city of Jerusalem only consisted of about 25,000 people,[27] while Antioch had more than 500,000 people living in it at the time of the apostles.[28] In other words, Antioch was 20 times larger than Jerusalem! These men from Cyprus and Cyrene understood that the message of Jesus Christ was not just for the backwater towns of rural Galilee, but also for the great urban centres: cities full of businessmen and merchants, state employees and soldiers, teachers and intellectuals. The gospel changed the lives of these citizens of the great Roman metropolises like it did those of fishermen and labourers in Israel. These missionaries grasped the importance of urban evangelism. That is why this can be considered a fourth major turning point for the gospel.

Let us note in passing that it is possible that the events in this passage precede those of Acts 10:1–11:18, because it begins with the persecution mentioned in Acts 8. Even if this is not the case, Acts 10:1–11:18 speaks of a single person – Peter – who spoke to non-Jews, which does not exactly constitute a concentrated effort by the Jerusalem church. What is more, some members of the Jerusalem church criticised Peter for his efforts to reach non-Jews. In contrast, the believers from Cyrene and Cyrus were well ahead of their brothers in the Jerusalem church in their mission thinking. Instead of ignoring non-Jews in their evangelistic work, they included them in their scope of action. They recognized that the gospel was destined for all the world's peoples and was not the property of one group. So it is not surprising that the church in Antioch became the top missionary sending church of the New Testament.

Why did they experience such success in their missionary efforts? "The Lord's hand was with them, and a great number of people believed and turned to the Lord" (Acts 11:21). "It indicates divine approval and blessing" on these Christians from Cyrene and Cyprus.[29]

But the question remains: were "these men from Cyprus and Cyrene" Africans or not? Once again, it is impossible to give a definitive answer, but I believe we can answer based on probability. As we saw earlier, most of the Jews from Cyrene were of Asian, not African, origin. Despite this, as we have already seen in our discussion of the day of Pentecost, there were also Cyrenians of African origin who became Christians. This conclusion is based on the fact that the disciples were speaking to them in their mother tongues and not in Aramaic or Greek, which means they were probably Africans. In Acts 11:19-20, it is clear that these men were Christians and not Jews, creating this link with the day of Pentecost. It is therefore likely, though not certain, that these men from Cyrene mentioned here were Africans. Whatever the solution, it is referring to men *from Africa* who were at the forefront of the missionary advance in the New Testament, and the hand of the Lord was with them.

Simeon called Niger

We read in Acts 13:1 that "in the church at Antioch there were prophets and teachers". These terms refer to the gifts received by the leaders of the church: prophecy (which often resembled what we call preaching today) and teaching. The clear explanation of God's Word (either from the Old Testament or the revelations that came from the Holy Spirit) and teaching on the meaning and practice of these words were two key responsibilities of the leaders of this young church in Antioch.

One of these leaders was "Simeon called Niger". "Niger" is the Latin word for "black". Simeon is a Hebraic form of the name Simon. Even if Simeon was Jewish before becoming a Christian, he may have been of African origin. (As we have already seen with the Ethiopian official, there were black people who became Jews.) The *Nouveau dictionnaire biblique révisé* says that "he was called Niger, the Black, and so was possibly of African race".[30] The *Dictionnaire biblique pour tous* goes a bit further and says he was "probably African".[31] The fact that his "nickname" was a Latin name instead of a Greek or Hebrew name makes it likely that Simeon came from the part of North Africa that was oriented toward Italy (western Libya, Tunisia/Carthage, or Algeria) instead of from the part of North Africa that was more oriented toward Greece (Cyrene, Alexandria, or the rest of Egypt). It is probable that here we have an example of an African leader in the greatest missionary church of the New Testament.

Given the fact that the church in Antioch was founded "by men from Cyprus and Cyrene", it is interesting to note that the first three leaders mentioned here are Barnabas from Cyprus (Acts 4:36), Simeon called Niger (who was probably African), and Lucius of Cyrene. Even though Barnabas was not among the founders of the Antioch church, he came on the scene early and assumed a leadership role (Acts 11:22-26). We know that Barnabas had a direct influence on the life of the apostle Paul. But the context of the passage leads me to believe that two men from Africa, Simeon and Lucius, also had a positive influence on the life of the greatest Christian missionary of the New Testament.

I would like to end with a word of explanation of the cultural context of this passage. The Greco-Roman world in New Testament times was very familiar with black men. The presence of varying shades of black-skinned Africans was extraordinary throughout this region. Hays, citing Snowden and Thompson, explains that:

> The Roman world encountered Black Ethiopians as merchants and traders, soldiers, slaves, and former slaves who had become freedmen. Indeed, Black Ethiopians appeared in Roman society at all levels: soldiers, slaves, freedmen, officials, nobles. In addition, intermarriage between these Black Africans and the rest of the Greco-Roman Mediterranean world was not only common but rather the norm. Thus these blacks were continually being assimilated into the genetic melting-pot of the Roman world.[32]

Apollos

Apollos is an interesting case, the last I will treat here. We see him for the first time in Acts 18:24-25:

> Meanwhile a Jew named Apollos, a native of Alexandria, came to Ephesus. He was a learned man, with a thorough knowledge of the Scriptures. He had been instructed in the way of the Lord, and he spoke with great fervor and taught about Jesus accurately, though he knew only the baptism of John.

Apollos came from the city of Alexandria, a large city in Egypt (see chapter four) of about 600,000–700,000 people. It had a Jewish quarter, as well as Egyptian, Roman, and Greek quarters. Because Acts 18:24 calls Apollos "a Jew", one could suppose he lived in this Jewish quarter. It would also seem that Apollos was not a recent convert to Judaism, because Luke (the author of the book of Acts) uses the word "Jew" and not "proselyte" as he does elsewhere to speak of those with a pagan background who became Jews (i.e., Acts 2:11; 6:5; 13:43).

But the question remains: Was Apollos from Hebrew or Egyptian descent? Were he and his ancestors among the many Israelite Jews who immigrated to Alexandria? Or was he an Egyptian whose family had converted to Judaism a few generations earlier? The word "native" helps us answer this question. Often the New Testament, when speaking of a birth, uses the Greek word *gennao*. This was true for the birth of Jesus: Jesus was born (*gennao*) in Bethlehem in Judea. It was also true for all of Jesus's genealogy in Matthew 1: Abraham was the father of (*gennao*) Isaac; Isaac was the father of (*gennao*) Jacob . . . But, when it comes to the birth of Apollos, except for a few translations,[33] it does not say that Apollos was born in Alexandria, but rather that he was a "native of Alexandria". A literal translation of the phrase would be that Apollos was an "Alexandrian by race". The Greek word used is the nominative form *genos*, from the verb *ginomai*. It means "race" and not only "birth". It is translated "race" in 1 Peter 2:9 (RSV): "But you are a chosen race, a royal priesthood, a holy nation, God's own people". We also see a similar meaning in Revelation 22:16 where Jesus says he is the "Offspring of David". So, the word *genos* in Acts 18:24 means "race, offspring" and implies not only that Apollos was born in Alexandria, but that Apollos is "Alexandrian by race". This is, in fact, how the wording appears in the literal translation of the Greek Interlinear New Testament.[34]

Also, W. E. Vine's *An Expository Dictionary of New Testament Words* says of the word *genos*: "generation, sort, race; used in the dative with the article to mean 'by race' in Acts 18:2

and 24".[35] Another dictionary, *The New International Dictionary of New Testament Theology,* edited by Colin Brown, says:

> The noun *genos* formed from the same stem and related to the verb *ginomai* (see "birth"), is frequently translated by race (except where it corresponds to the Hebrew *mîn* = "kind" in Genesis 1). Both in the Septuagint and in the New Testament its prime meaning is nation, people or tribe.[36]

While *genos* is obviously synonymous with the word "people", it puts an emphasis upon belonging to a specific ethnic group of people.

Based on these various definitions and the grammatical use of *genos*, my conclusion is that Apollos was a "native" of Alexandria, exactly as translated in most New Testaments, and not merely a Semite born in Alexandria. Acts 18:24 is not speaking only about Apollos's geographical place of birth, but also about his ethnic bloodlines. He was of the Alexandrian race; that is, he came from an Egyptian background, not an Israelite one. He also came from a family of practising Jews – they had probably followed Judaism for many years – and because of that he knew the Scriptures very well.

An interesting possibility appears here: certain scholars think that the author of the book of Hebrews was Apollos. Martin Luther was the first to propose the name of Apollos as the author of this New Testament book. The introduction to Hebrews in the *NIV Study Bible* says that Barnabas and Apollos are the two main candidates for authorship. If this is true – and it is impossible to verify – that means that one of the authors inspired by God to write part of the New Testament was an African.

---

1   John Stott, *The Spirit, the Church and the World: The Message of Acts* (Downers Grove: InterVarsity Press, 1990), 68.

2   Father John Baur, *2000 ans de christianisme en Afrique: une histoire de l'Église africaine*, trans. Yves Morel S. J. (Abidjan: INADES, 1999), 9-10.

3   Jamil M. Abun-Nasr, Michael Brett, Brian H. Warmington, *Encyclopedia Britannica*, s.v. "North Africa: The Greeks in Cyrenaica" (Chicago: Encyclopedia Britannica, 2016). https://www.britannica.com/place/North-Africa (accessed May 7, 2018).

4   Jean-Jacques Maffre, "Cyrène et la Cyrénaïque grecques, aux époques archaïque et classique," *Clio*, last modified April 2002, https://www.clio.fr/BIBLIOTHEQUE/cyrene_et_la_cyrenaique_grecques_aux_epoques_archaique_et_classique.asp.

5   Lucius "taught at Antioch where he was probably one of the first missionaries (Acts 13:1; cf. 11:19ff)." "Lucius," in the *Dictionnaire biblique pour tous* (Valence, France: Éditions LLB, 1994), 323.

6   William L. Bevan, "Simon," in *Smith's Bible Dictionary*, ed. H. B. Hackett (New York: Hurd and Houghton, 1875), 3046; William Hendriksen, *The Gospel of Matthew* (Grand Rapids: Baker, 1973), 963.

7   Walter Wessell and William Lane, "Mark," in the *NIV Study Bible, 10th Anniversary Edition*, ed. Kenneth Barker et al. (Grand Rapids: Zondervan Publishing House, 1995), 1526; C. E. Graham Swift, "Marc," in *Nouveau commentaire biblique* (Saint-Légier: Éditions Émmaüs, 1978), 923.

8   Edwin Yamauchi, *Africa and the Bible* (Grand Rapids: Baker Academic, 2004), 186.

9   William Barclay, *The Gospel of Mark* (Philadelphia: Westminster Press, 1954), 379-380.

10   "Actes," *La Bible en français courant* (Pierrefitte, France: Alliance Biblique Universelle, 1989), 178 (NT).

11   "Affranchis," in the *Nouveau dictionnaire biblique révisé*, ed. René Pache (Saint-Légier, Switzerland: Editions Emmaüs, 1992), 44.

12   G. T. D. Angel, "*libertinos*," in *New International Dictionary of New Testament Theology*, ed. Colin Brown (Grand Rapids: Zondervan, 1975), vol. 3, 598-599. He says that some believe that this verse refers to only one synagogue, while others opt for two and some even five. Angel believes that the natural interpretation here would be one synagogue, but he concludes that the question of who made up the group of Freedmen remains open.

13   This term "high dignitary" or "high Ethiopian dignitary" is used by both the *Bible du Semeur 2000* and the *Parole Vivante* in Acts 8.27 instead of the term "eunuch", referring to his high position as a court official.

14   *La Bible Déchiffrée* gives two or five years as a possibility between Pentecost and Saul's conversion in its chronological chart. Pat Alexander, David Alexander et al, *La Bible Déchiffrée* (Valence: Éditions LLB, 1983), 549. Different chronologies in the *NIV Study Bible* show five years as the time difference between these two events. *NIV Study Bible, 10th Anniversary Edition*, ed. Kenneth Barker et al. (Grand Rapids: Zondervan Publishing House, 1995), n. p., 1480, 1666.

15   Alfred Kuen, Christophe Paya, Jacques Buchhold, "Actes," in the *Bible d'étude Semeur 2000*, ed. Alfred Kuen et al. (Charols, France: Excelsis, 2005), 1651. Compare H. Baltensweiler, "Eunuch," vol. 1, in *The New International Dictionary of New Testament Theology*, ed. Colin Brown (Grand Rapids: Zondervan, 1975), 560. He says that "sometimes when the word 'eunuch' refers to a high court official (cf. Acts 8.27), it is not clear whether we should opt for a literal rendering of the word, or if 'eunuch' was simply a title."

16   Ray Stedman, *Introduction aux livres de la Bible* (Marne-la-Vallée: Farel, 2000), 599.

17   J. Daniel Hays, *From Every People and Nation: A biblical theology of race* (Downers Grove: Inter Varsity Press, 2003), 176.

18   Andrew Walls, "Africa in Christian History: Retrospect and Prospect," *Journal of African Christian Thought* 1, no. 1 (June 1998), 2.

19   "Candace," in the *Nouveau dictionnaire biblique révisé*, ed. René Pache (Saint-Légier, Switzerland: Editions Emmaüs, 1992), 206.

20   Cheikh Anta Diop, *L'Unité culturelle de l'Afrique Noire* (Paris: Présence Africaine, 1959), 54-55.

21   Hays, *From Every People and Nation*, 173.

22   Yamauchi, *Africa and the Bible*, 172.

23   Timothy Kendall, "Ethnoarchaeology in Meroitic Studies," *Studia Meroitica* 10, 655, quoted in Yamauchi, *Africa and the Bible*, 172.

24   Yamauchi, *Africa and the Bible*, 165.

25   M. Hengel, Jews, Greeks, and Barbarians (Philadelphia: Fortress Press, 1980), 55-66, quoted in Hays, *From Every People and Nation*, 143.

26   Kuen, Paya, Buchhold, "Actes," in the *Bible d'étude Semeur 2000*, ed. Alfred Kuen et al. (Charols, France: Excelsis, 2005), 1657.

27   David W. Smith, *Seeking a City with Foundations* (Nottingham: InterVarsity Press, 2011), 187.

28   "Antioche," in the *Nouveau dictionnaire biblique révisé* ed. René Pache (Saint-Légier, Switzerland: Editions Emmaüs, 1992), 85.

29   Lewis Foster, "Acts," in the *NIV Study Bible, 10th Anniversary Edition*, ed. Kenneth Barker et al. (Grand Rapids: Zondervan Publishing House, 1995), 1669.

30   "Siméon," in the *Nouveau dictionnaire biblique révisé*, ed. René Pache (Saint-Légier, Switzerland: Editions Emmaüs, 1992), 1218.

31   "Siméon," in the *Dictionnaire biblique pour tous* (Valence, France: Éditions LLB, 1994), 532.

32   Hays, *From Every People and Nation*, 148-149.

33 The King James Version and Today's English Version both say Apollos was "born in/at Alexandria". The vast majority of translations give a more literal translation of the Greek word *genos*, using "native".

34 Jay P. Green Sr., *Pocket Interlinear New Testament* (Grand Rapids: Baker, 1983), 327.

35 W. E. Vine, *An Expository Dictionary of New Testament Words, vol. 1* (Old Tappan, New Jersey: Fleming H. Revell, 1940), 110.

36 Colin Brown, "Generation," in *The New International Dictionary of New Testament Theology,* vol. 2, ed. Colin Brown (Grand Rapids: Zondervan, 1976), 35.

4

AFRICAN PLACES IN THE BIBLE

Before concluding this study, I would like to draw attention to the geographical places mentioned in the Bible.

Egypt

The country of Egypt is mentioned more than 600 times in the Bible; very important events took place there. The people of Israel spent more than 400 years there. The beginning of their long stay in Africa was peaceful, but they ended up as slaves to the Egyptians. God raised up a prophet, Moses, to lead his people out of Egypt, working all kinds of miracles and signs to convince the Egyptian Pharaoh to give his permission. The greatest miracle of the Old Testament is surely the crossing of the Red Sea (called the Sea of Reeds in some Bibles). This miracle marked the beginning of the Exodus of the people of Israel and served as an enduring reminder to the people of God's faithfulness. But nowadays we often forget that this miracle happened in Africa. In fact, several of God's miracles (the 10 plagues, the Ten Commandments, etc.) took place in Egypt (see the section on the Sinai Peninsula).

Another event we seldom mention is the time Jesus himself spent in Egypt. The prophet Hosea spoke of it 750 years before the fact (Hosea 11:1), and Matthew the evangelist reminds us of it (Matthew 2:15). Just as Israel, the chosen people of God, began their history by a stay in Egypt, Jesus, the Son of God, did so as well. It is impossible to determine how long Jesus stayed in Africa. Several authors, based on the fact that King Herod died in 4 BC, believe that this was also the year Jesus was born. Even though it seems contradictory to say Jesus was born in the year 4 "before Christ," the problem is actually with the medieval calendars that were mistaken on the dates of certain events. In adjusting for these errors, many set the year of Christ's birth between 6 and 4 BC. It seems clear that Joseph and Mary took Jesus and fled from Herod as soon as the angel warned them. Also, historians more or less agree that Herod died a few months later. So Jesus spent several months of his life in Egypt, perhaps as long as a year, but probably not more than that. Did Jesus learn to talk in Africa? Did he learn to walk in Africa? We cannot answer these questions with any certainty.

The wealth of Egypt

In the Bible, Egypt is generally seen as a place of abundance. For example, in Genesis 13:10 we see that the land of Egypt is compared to the garden of the Lord, that is, the Garden of Eden. The version *La Bible en français courant* translates this verse "it was like paradise, like the valley of the Nile". A note in the *NIV Study Bible* says, "Because of its abundant and dependable water supply, Egypt came the closest to matching Eden's ideal conditions."[1] This shows to what extent Egypt was considered a rich and comfortable place. This verse, when paired with Genesis 2:13, explains why certain scholars say that the Garden of Eden was in Africa and not in Asia, as is commonly believed.

Archaeology finds this argument fairly plausible since eastern Africa is often considered the cradle of humanity. Many theologians, however, do not accept this view, since the Bible speaks of the Tigris and Euphrates Rivers as flowing out of the Garden of Eden, and these two rivers are in Asia, in modern-day Iraq. Still, the idea of associating the Gihon River with the Nile is interesting, especially if one maintains that the Cush of Genesis 2:13 is Ethiopia (as does the *Bible d'étude Semeur 2000*) and not a region in Mesopotamia. The river Pishon, which is associated with the land of Havilah (Genesis 2:11), could be in Africa, because a descendant of Cush is named Havilah (Genesis 10:7). But a descendant of Shem is also named Havilah (Genesis 10:29), and it is possible that the verse in Genesis 2 is speaking of him instead.

Yamauchi speaks of the possible association of the Gihon and Pishon rivers with the dry riverbeds in the region of Shatt al-Arab (modern-day Kuwait, southern Iraq, and western Iran), based on the work of a geologist, Carol Hill, who used satellite photos as evidence.[2]

The *New Living Translation Illustrated Study Bible* speaks of either the Pishon or the Gihon rivers as possibly being the Nile River. Biblical support for the former can be found in Genesis 2:11, where the land of Havilah could conceivably be on the African coast (Genesis 10:7; 25:18; 1 Samuel 15:7),[3] and support for the latter is found in the Septuagint version of Jeremiah 2:18 and in Josephus's book, *Antiquities* (1.1.3).[4] Whether the hypothesis is based on archaeology, geology, or biblical exegesis, all three are impossible to prove definitively with regard to the location of the Garden of Eden.

Returning to the idea of Egyptian abundance, Genesis 41:49 tells us that "Joseph stored up huge quantities of grain, like the sand of the sea; it was so much that he stopped keeping records because it was beyond measure." This verse shows that Egypt was a horn of plenty for the whole region when its harvests were good.

A similar idea is found in Numbers 11:5, when the people of Israel were complaining about their food in the desert. They remembered what they ate in Egypt: "We remember the fish we ate in Egypt at no cost – also the cucumbers, melons, leeks, onions and garlic." Again, Egypt is portrayed as a land of abundance.

Speaking of fish, Isaiah 19:8 comments on how the fishermen of Egypt will groan and lament because of the misfortune that God will bring upon that land. The fishing industry was very prominent in Egypt, providing significant revenue to its people. One author says:

> The Egyptians consumed enormous quantities of fish, which they obtained
> from the teeming waters of the Nile, and the canals that irrigated the
> land. So important was the traffic in fish that at one time the royal profits

from Lake Moeris amounted to a talent of silver a day, which today would probably be close to five-million dollars a year. (Lake Moeris was an ancient lake that was fed by the Nile and once occupied a large area of the al-Fayyum depression in Egypt – it is now represented by the much smaller Lake Qarun.) Large quantities of fish were salted, and many were simply dried in the sun.[5]

We see in 1 Kings 10:26-29, as well as in the parallel passage in 2 Chronicles 1:14-17, that King Solomon imported horses and chariots from Egypt in great numbers. This shows once again the commercial wealth of Egypt in Old Testament times. However, according to a note in the *Bible d'étude Semeur 2000*, we read: "Instead of Egypt (Hebrew *mizraim*), it could be referring to Muzur, a region in Cilicia. The same goes for verse 29. The Musrites had settled in Cilicia and were very invested in raising horses."[6] Whether Solomon imported horses and chariots, or only chariots, from Egypt, in either case Egypt served as a commercial powerhouse for the region. About 250 years later, an Assyrian spokesman reproached the king of Israel for putting his confidence in Egypt because of its chariots and horsemen (2 Kings 18:24).

Proverbs 7:16 says, "I have covered my bed with colored linens from Egypt." The *Bible d'étude Semeur 2000* translates this verse as, "I decorated my bed with blankets, with cloth embroidered with Egyptian thread." Then it gives a note which says, "Egyptian linen was highly prized and expensive (Isaiah 19:9; Ezekiel 27:7); it was a sign of wealth (Proverbs 31:22)."[7] The verse mentioned in Isaiah speaks of "those who work with combed flax and the weavers of fine linen"; the verse in Ezekiel speaks of "fine embroidered linen from Egypt". These verses show that the Egyptians were skilled in embroidery and in the production of fine linen.

Another important verse is found in Daniel 11:43. This verse speaks of "the treasures of gold and silver and all the riches of Egypt". This shows once again the great wealth of Egypt. However, it is found in a passage that speaks of the "last times". Most commentators consider the events in this chapter as things that have not yet happened. If that is true, that means that Egypt will once again become a rich country, up until the time when it will suffer a significant attack from the Antichrist.

Finally, Hebrews 11:26 tells of Moses, how "he regarded disgrace for the sake of Christ as of greater value than the treasures of Egypt". At the time of Moses, there was no wealthier place than Egypt because the other great empires (Greek, Roman, Persian, etc.) had not yet come on the scene. For the authors of the Old Testament, Egypt represented the epitome of wealth, and it did so for well over 1,000 years.

The Sinai Peninsula

We have already pointed out that important events took place in Africa – such as the miracle of crossing the Red Sea – even if the people concerned were not themselves Africans. But God did not limit himself to just one miracle in Africa. After crossing the Red Sea, the Hebrew people spent 40 years in the desert, or rather, several deserts (Shur, Zin, and Paran). All these deserts were in the Sinai Peninsula. During this time, God did many miracles for his people:

- He led the people of Israel by a pillar of cloud and a pillar of fire (Exodus 13) which later stayed over the tabernacle day and night (Exodus 40).

- He gave them manna for food (Exodus 16).

- He brought forth water from the rock (Exodus 17).

- He gave them his law, written by God's own hand on tablets of stone (Exodus 20).

- He filled the tabernacle with his glory (Exodus 40).

- He gave them quail (meat) to eat for a month (Numbers 11)

- He split open the earth to put an end to the revolt of Korah, Dathan, and Abiram (Numbers 16).

- He caused the rod of Aaron to bud (Numbers 17).

In Numbers 20, the people of Israel arrived at the desert of Zin, a place considered to be the border between Africa and Asia. So we see that all the miracles mentioned above – including some of God's greatest displays of power – took place in Africa, because the Sinai Peninsula is part of Africa. This fact is often forgotten by those who read the Bible. When God wrote his laws on the stone tablets on Mount Sinai, his people were still in Africa.

The deserts

Several deserts are mentioned in the Bible. After crossing the Red Sea, the people of Israel began their Exodus by passing through the desert of Shur. Then they went through the desert of Zin, the desert of Sinai, and the desert of Paran. These were inhospitable places where it was hard to find water and the climate was sometimes unbearable. The Lord used such circumstances to show his power and love to his people.

Often the desert where the people of Israel wandered is not specified. Due to the people's rebellion and their desire to return to Egypt, God had the Hebrew people turn away from entering the Promised Land, telling them to "turn back tomorrow and set out toward the desert along the route to the Red Sea" (Numbers 14:25). This began their 40 years of wandering in the desert. While it is not always clear if they were in the desert of Paran, Sinai, Sin, or Zin during those years of wandering, it seems certain that they turned away from the land of Canaan and headed back toward Africa.

The Bible mentions other African places with little commentary. Such is the case for Egyptian cities like Succoth, Migdol, Pelusium, Bubastis, Zoan, Ramesses, Pithom, Pathros, On, Tahpanhes, and Aswan, or for settlements in the Sinai Peninsula like Etham, Pi Hahiroth, Baal Zephon, and Rephidim, places located in mainland Egypt or on the Sinai Peninsula. A few of the settlements are described, however. For example, the settlement of Marah is known for the fact that the water was bitter (Exodus 15:23). On the other hand, the settlement of Elim is known for its 12 springs of water and 70 palm trees, a real oasis (Exodus 15:27).

Goshen

Goshen is a region of Egypt located in the Nile delta, a few kilometres north-east of the city of On/Heliopolis. This area was suitable for small and large animal farming and was considered "the best part of the land", according to the Pharaoh at the time of Joseph (Genesis 47:6). One note in the *Bible d'étude Semeur 2000* explains that "Goshen is a very fertile region suitable for cattle."[8] That is why the Pharaoh called it "the best of the land of Egypt [where] you can enjoy the fat of the land" (Genesis 45:18).

The Nile

It is no exaggeration to say that Egypt depended on the Nile for its existence. Without this river, Egypt would never have become a world power. The *Nouveau dictionnaire biblique revisé* says:

> The Nile covered such a vast area, especially during floods, that it sometimes took the name of "sea" (Isaiah 18:2; Nahum 3:8 KJV). In addition, the Arabic name for the Nile, el Bahr, means "the sea". The waters that feed Lake Victoria-Nyanza constitute the ultimate sources of the Nile, which is 6,500 kilometres long . . . As the river follows its winding course through arid lands, great amounts of water are lost through evaporation, infiltration, and especially through a vast system of irrigation canals, indispensable to the agriculture of the region.
>
> The well-known annual swelling of the Nile, which would fertilize the areas receiving little rainfall, remained a mystery to the ancients (Herodotus 2.19-25) . . . Without the annual flood, the country would be devoid of vegetation. According to Herodotus's famous quote, "Egypt is a gift from the Nile." The rising of the Blue Nile and Atbara rivers are the cause of the flooding; the river slowly grows wider from the first of June, then much more quickly in mid-July. By the end of September the water stops rising and stays for 20 to 30 days at the same level. In October, the swelling resumes and attains its maximum output (100,000 m^3/second). After that, the water level begins to drop: by the end of December the river is back within its riverbed. In January, February, and March the fields gradually dry. The flood has loosened and fertilized the soil . . . The ancient Egyptians regularly recorded the water levels in different places. During the time of the Pharaohs, the Egyptian agricultural year was divided into three seasons: inundation (end of June to end of October); cultivation (end of October to end of February); finally harvest (end of February to end of June).
>
> . . . The length of the region watered by the Nile, from the sea to the first cataract, was roughly 835 kilometres; its width measured an average of 20 kilometres. The arable part, from the first cataract to the sea, consists of an estimated 33,668 km^2; it equals approximately the same area as the country of the Netherlands. Ancient Egypt was a small country, but it was proportionately the longest one in the world.[9]

So we can see why this river was so important for the Egyptians. Their agriculture, their business, and even their lives depended on it.

This great river is mentioned by name 32 times in the Old Testament (in the NIV; 47 times in the NASB).[10] It is also the setting for two of God's miracles: God changed the water of the Nile to blood (Exodus 7) and then made the river swarm with frogs (Exodus 8). It is not surprising that when God wanted to get the Egyptians' attention, he began by striking the Nile, because it was so important as the source of life. In Jeremiah 2:18 there is a reference to "Shihor", which is most likely one of the Nile's branches, perhaps an eastern one.

"Egypt my people"

The prophets of the Old Testament often told the kings of Israel not to put their trust in the Pharaohs of Egypt, but in the Lord (Isaiah 20; 30–31; Jeremiah 42–43; Ezekiel 29–32). The prophet Isaiah used considerable irony to remind the people how useless it is to trust in Egypt instead of God: "the envoys carry their riches . . . to that unprofitable nation, to Egypt, whose help is utterly useless. Therefore I call her Rahab the Do-Nothing" (Isaiah 30:6-7).

Still, not everything the prophets said about Egypt was negative. In Isaiah 19:1-17, we see Egypt's total confusion when confronted with God's power. But starting with verse 18, the chapter ends with a promise that Egypt will be part of God's people! Isaiah 19:19-21, 25 says:

> There will be an altar to the Lord in the heart of Egypt . . . It will be a sign and witness to the Lord Almighty in the land of Egypt . . . So the Lord will make himself known to the Egyptians, and in that day they will acknowledge the Lord . . . The Lord Almighty will bless them, saying, "Blessed be Egypt my people".

Throughout this passage Isaiah uses the name Yahweh for God (Lord = Yahweh) emphasizing that he is the covenant God of Israel. Israel's covenant God calls Egypt "my people". In this part of the prophecy, which is a promise not yet fulfilled, "here a relationship between Egypt and Israel is envisioned in which the two are part of the same covenant relationship with God".[11] We must admit that there is no such promise in the Bible concerning Europe or America.

Other promises about Egypt

We see this same kind of promise in Psalm 68:31 as well, where King David prophesies that "nobles shall come from Egypt; Cush shall hasten to stretch out her hands to God" (ESV). The preceding verse gives a metaphorical description of Pharaoh (without specifying which one), calling him "the beast among the reeds" (the *Bible d'étude Semeur 2000* uses "the crocodile lurking in the rushes"). The whole psalm speaks of "the glorious and triumphant rule of Israel's God",[12] and ends with this reference to Egypt, Cush, and the kingdoms of the earth (Psalm 68:31-32). Some rabbis give a messianic interpretation to this passage, thereby indicating that Egyptians and Cushites will be included among the Lord's disciples.[13]

In the same vein, Psalm 87:4 speaks of Egypt (Rahab), Cush, and other traditional enemies of Israel as "those who acknowledge me". Like the verse we just discussed, the context of this one is describing the day when all the nations will acknowledge the glory of Zion.[14]

Isaiah 11:11 also speaks of the way in which "the Lord will reach out his hand a second time to reclaim the remnant that is left of his people from Assyria, from Lower Egypt, from Upper Egypt, from Cush". The context of this passage is the "messianic era", that is, the time when Jesus Christ will return to reign on the earth. According to several commentators, this verse is not only alluding to the Jews who lived in these countries at the time of the exile, but also to those who will be gathered at Jesus's return.[15] This means, therefore, that at the return of Christ, the people of God will have been well established in Africa. This seems clear today, but when Isaiah wrote these words 2,700 years ago, it was not at all obvious.

Some African cities

Several cities on the African continent had worldwide importance and influence – Cyrene in Libya as well as Alexandria, Memphis, Heliopolis, and Thebes in Egypt. Alexandria and Cyrene were both founded by the Greeks, but both certainly had a significant African population. People from Cyrene and Alexandria argued with Stephen about Jesus of Nazareth (Acts 6:9). Apollos was a native of Alexandria (Acts 18:24). Also, Acts 27:6 and 28:11 both speak of an Alexandrian ship, which indicates that this city was well known for its shipbuilding. Memphis, Heliopolis, and Thebes were founded by the Egyptians and, according to the archaeological finds in these cities, the prophets were justified in warning Israel about the abundance and wealth of Egypt.

In the sections that follow, I quote what the *Nouveau dictionnaire biblique révisé* says about these five cities. My own comments are interspersed throughout.

Alexandria

Alexander the Great founded this city in 332 BC, on the northern coast of Egypt, and wanted to make it the capital city of the Greek world. He chose a favourable site west of the mouth of the Nile. The Mediterranean currents from the West swept away the silt from the river and kept this build-up away from the port. The city, built on a strip of land between the Mediterranean and Lake Mareotis, was linked by a causeway to the Pharos island, with its famous lighthouse. Alexandria's wonderful setting surely helped expand its commercial interests. The city of Alexandria became the major port for the export of Egyptian wheat. Cargo for Rome could be transported directly to Puteoli, as long as unfavourable winds did not force the ships to sail along the coast of Asia Minor. It was also the centre of trade between East and West.

The city prospered under the Ptolemies; later, under Roman rule, it grew to almost 25 km wide along the coast and 2 km deep inland. Alexandria, with its 600,000–700,000 inhabitants, was the second greatest city in the Roman Empire. The Ptolemies founded a museum which included the famous library with hundreds of thousands of volumes. Greeks, Egyptians, Jews, and Romans spoke Greek there. The different races generally lived in different quarters. The Jews lived in the north-east, enjoyed the same rights as other citizens, and had their own leaders.

The translation of the Scriptures from Hebrew into Greek was begun in the 3rd century BC, in Egypt, probably in Alexandria, and was finished in the 2nd [century]. It was also in this city that Judaism became heavily influenced by the spirit of Greek philosophers. This community produced exegetes like Philo, who allegorized the Scriptures in an exaggerated way. Alexandrian Jews even had their own synagogue in Jerusalem; they were some of Stephen's persecutors. But the teaching of John the Baptist and the knowledge of Jesus made their way into Alexandria, and God raised up men there like Apollos. Tradition attributes the birth of the church in this city to Mark the evangelist. At the time of the early church, Alexandria had a famous catechism school, with teachers like Clement and Origen.[16]

Father John Baur gives a few more details about the founding of the Christian church in Alexandria, saying:

> A group of Jewish Christians living in Jewish communities between 50 and 100 AD are the link between the Egyptian church and the apostles. Egyptian tradition unanimously reveres Saint Mark as the founder of the apostolic seat in Alexandria; he is said to have ordained Annianas in the year 62, as the first bishop of this great metropolis. Historians often reject this claim because it is only found in *Ecclesiastical History* by Eusebius of Caesarea (320), and not in the earlier writings of Clement and Origen, which are more voluminous and less historical. But the authenticity of this tradition is corroborated by the fact that Mark assisted Peter when he was sent to the Jews. Alexandria was home to the largest Jewish diaspora; why would it not have been visited by Peter and his spiritual son (1 Peter 5:1)? We can then, with good reason, refer to the year 62 AD as the date of the founding of the first Christian church in Africa.[17]

To conclude this section, the reader should note the influence that this city has had on the world. Thomas Oden argues that Alexandria came to represent all of Africa, even though some (see chapter one) have tried to separate Egypt from Africa.

> Each of these three land masses [the continents of Europe, Africa, and Asia] was symbolized by a leading city in the maps of late antiquity. The three great cities that pointed beyond themselves to these three continents were Rome, Alexandria, and Antioch.

> At its zenith the Afro-Hellenic city of Alexandria was larger than either Rome or Antioch, and of far more importance in the world of ideas, literature, and learning. Alexandria stood for centuries as one of the three leading cities of the ancient world. It should not be surprising that the Christian leader of Alexandria came to represent all Christians on the continent [of Africa] in terms of ecclesiastical organization . . . In this way the whole of the vast and largely unknown continent of Africa became symbolized by the largest city in the ancient world, Alexandria. This is why Alexandria cannot be detached from Africa.[18]

Noph/Moph/Memphis

Memphis was a very important Egyptian city:

> According to Herodotus, its founder was the first king in the history of Egypt, Menes, who built on land snatched from the Nile by draining. Memphis rose from the plain, on the western bank of the Nile, at about 25 kilometres upstream from the ancient head of the delta. Manetho (Egyptian

priest and historian of the 3rd century BC) says it was the capital of Lower Egypt under the 3rd, 4th, 5th, 7th and 8th dynasties. The god Ptah was worshipped there. When Thebes became the capital, Memphis continued to flourish; it did not begin to decline until the founding of Alexandria.

The Hebrews knew this city as Noph or Moph (Hosea 9:6 in Hebrew). After the fall of Jerusalem and the assassination of Gedaliah, the Jews fled to Egypt; and some of them settled at Noph (Memphis, Jeremiah 44:1). Jeremiah and Ezekiel foretold their judgment. A large part of Memphis still existed in the Middle Ages, but building materials were constantly being taken from there to Cairo. There are only two Arab villages on the original site of Memphis, but in the area 20 pyramids (the ancient city of the dead) and the famous Sphinx nobly attest to its former glory.[19]

On/Heliopolis

In the ancient world, [On was] a famous city of Lower Egypt, several kilometres from the Nile, in the delta, and about 30 kilometres away from Memphis. On was the main centre for the worship of the sun, and was called Heliopolis by the Greeks and Beth-shemesh (KJV) by Jeremiah. It seems that Isaiah also mentions this city (Isaiah 19:18). A slight change in the first letter of the name changes the meaning from "City of the Sun" to "City of Destruction". If we accept this reading, as proposed by many interpreters, the passage means that the worship of the sun will give way to the worship of the true God, after the idols are destroyed. In this city the priests and doctors had schools which were related to the temple dedicated to the sun. Greek philosophers came to study there. At the time of Herodotus, the priests of On were the best historians in all Egypt (Herodotus 2:3). Pharaoh gave Joseph the daughter of a priest of On as a wife.[20]

No/Thebes

The name No designates the Egyptian city of Thebes. Herodotus says he reached it after traveling nine days up the Nile from On. Ahmose drove the Hyksos rulers from Egypt, then reorganized and developed the empire. He made Thebes his capital city, enlarging and beautifying it. Homer speaks of its 100 city gates (*Iliad* 9.381). Amon was the guardian deity of this city; the high priest of Amon was second only to the king. Thebes was the centre of Egyptian civilization until two invasions occurred: 1) Esarhaddon, king of Assyria, conquered Egypt in 671 BC; 2) Ashurbanipal, his son and successor, began a new campaign in 667 BC, and the Assyrians reached Thebes. During a second expedition in 663 BC, Ashurbanipal looted the city. Despite this disaster, the city retained its importance for a long time. Cornelius Gallus destroyed Thebes because it had joined Upper Egypt, from 30–29 BC, in revolting against Roman acts of violence.

Splendid remains of the city, temples, obelisks, sphinxes, etc. can still be seen at Luxor and Karnak (names of modern-day cities nearby), on the right bank of the Nile. Others can be seen at Qurneh and Medinet Habu, on the left bank. In a gorge to the west of the ancient city, the famous Valley of the Kings was discovered, cut into the limestone rock. The ruins at Thebes are undoubtedly the most remarkable remains along the Nile valley, except for the pyramids at Giza. The temple at Karnak is a wonder, and its architecture represents a marvel of mechanical skill. Its large Hypostyle Hall has 134 massive columns: the largest are 23 metres high and 3.65 metres in diameter. The hall itself measures 100 metres long and 54 metres wide. There are so many inscriptions there that it is said, "Each stone is itself a book and each column a library."[21]

Cyrene

An important city in a Greek colony in northern Africa, Cyrene was magnificently located on a plateau 600 metres high, approximately 16 kilometres from the Mediterranean Sea. This city was one of five Greek cities known as the Pentapolis, located in Libyan Cyrenaica . . . It is thought that Cyrene was founded by Dorian Greeks around 632 BC. Under the reign of the Ptolemies, in the 3rd century BC, a large number of Jews lived in Cyrene. Simon, who was forced to carry the cross of Christ, seems to have been a Jew from Cyrene.[22]

Concerning this same city, the author Philip Ward says: "Cyrene is the Athens of Africa. So too it excelled all African cities except Alexandria in the number and greatness of its ancient writers and scientists."[23] We must not forget, however, as already mentioned in chapter three, that even though Cyrene was a Greek colony, there were a significant number of mixed marriages between Greeks and the local indigenous population in the region surrounding Cyrene. Therefore, it is impossible to determine the ethnic origin of someone who is simply described as "of Cyrene."

In reading everything that the *Nouveau dictionnaire biblique révisé* and other works say about these five cities and the Nile River, it is easy to understand why Egypt and its surrounding area were seen as regions of abundance and wealth during both Old and New Testament times.

Libya and Put

Several times the Bible mentions people who come from regions which are probably located in modern-day Libya (see chapter two, section C), but it does not describe these places in detail. Other than the fact that Libyans were known as warriors, the Bible does not say anything about the country itself. This is also true for the region known as "Put". Put may be in either Libya or Somalia, but one cannot say with certainty if it is one or the other, since the Bible does not specify the region's geography, climate, or riches.

Pul

Isaiah 66:19 speaks of Libyans ("Pul" in Hebrew) as one of the regions in the world which will receive some of God's envoys, and these envoys will proclaim God's glory to different nations. Certain versions of the Bible say that Pul is the same as Put. Just about every version of the Bible says that Pul is to be found in Africa. The *Bible d'étude Semeur 2000* study Bible and the French edition of the Thompson Study Bible say that Pul is in present-day Somalia. *La Bible en français courant* says: "Pul (or Put): a region of Africa which is a neighbour to Ethiopia, possibly Eritrea; according to others, it is in Libya."[24] Whether Pul's location is to be found in Somalia, Eritrea, or Libya, this region is in Africa. Its people, along with those from Tarshish and Lud (NIV – Lydians) are said to be "famous as archers" (NIV), or "skilled bowmen" (TEV).

Promises concerning Libyans (Pul) and Lydians (Lud)

In Isaiah 66:19 we see one of God's promises concerning the "great final gathering", to quote the title given to this section by *La Bible en français courant*. According to this passage, at the end of time all the nations will honour the Lord, and in order to bring this about, God will send his envoys to far-off regions as missionaries. Two of these far-off regions are Pul and Lud (in Hebrew), to the Libyans and Lydians, according to the NIV. Some commentators speak of Lud/Lydians as a part of Asia Minor, but other Bibles and Bible commentaries speak of "Pul and Lud" as both being in Africa without, however, specifying their location.[25] In such a case, Lud is generally considered to be west of Egypt. As mentioned above, some see Pul as being the same as Put, thereby locating it in Libya, Eritrea, or Somalia. A note in the French edition of the Thompson Study Bible says that Pul is "probably the Put of Genesis 10:6, the Punt of the Egyptians, that is, Somalia".[26]

This verse indicates that missionaries will be sent as God's envoys to declare his glory among the nations that do not yet know him, and these regions of Africa will be part of that group of nations. It is understood that these peoples from Africa and elsewhere who turn to God and join the faithful worshipers of the Messiah will thereby be partakers of the eternal salvation God offers to these men and women.

Cush/"Ethiopia"

The Bible mentions Cush/"Ethiopia" (the region which includes southern Egypt and northern Sudan) several times, as we have said earlier, but it gives very few details about this region. We know that Cush was generally located from the Nile's first cataract in southern Egypt down to the region of the fourth cataract in northern Sudan. This area was also called Wawat, Meroe, and Nubia (a term dating from the Roman era). Hays explains that "the northernmost area (between the first and fourth cataracts) was called Wawat, and the southernmost area (above the fourth cataract) was called Cush . . . [With time] the terms soon became interchangeable. The southern area became more powerful and dominant, and thus the name Cush became the common term used in Egyptian texts for the entire region."[27]

It appears that initially the Egyptians called the region Ta-sety, the "Land of the Bow", referring either to the great bend in the Nile in that area, or to the weapon the Cushites used with such skill.[28] Many scholars opt for this latter interpretation.

Isaiah 18:2 speaks of Cush/Ethiopia as a land "divided by rivers", a land which "sends envoys by sea in papyrus boats over the water". As noted above in the section on the Nile River, this verse refers to the Nile as a "sea" due to its vast size, especially during flooding. The preceding verse calls this area "the land of whirring wings along the rivers of Cush". The rivers which cross the region of Cush are the Blue Nile, the White Nile, and the Atbara. It is possible that the Cushites were very skilled in the art of navigating the Nile. But it must be admitted that this verse is not an easy one to interpret. Scholars interpret the expression "land of whirring wings" to refer to either the insects (either mosquitos or beetles) in that area,[29] Cush's numerous and active people,[30] the armada of Cushite boats that often had two sails,[31] the Egyptian armies,[32] or Egypt's patron god of the sun as represented by a disc with outstretched wings.[33] So it is anyone's guess as to whether this verse is talking about Cush's flora and fauna, its economic activity, its military strength, or Egypt's religion adopted by the Cushites. The greatest number of commentators seems to opt for the meaning involving the insects in the area.

One of the rare references to Cush's natural resources is found in Job 28:19, where we read of "the topaz of Cush", which indicates that this region was well known for this particular gem. Cush was known not only for its precious gems, but also for its natural resources in minerals. Regarding Cush's culture and riches, Hays says:

> Kerma became the capital city, and prospered from 2500 to 1500 BC This culture excelled in art as well as in the manufacture of bronze items, especially weapons. These people were famous especially for their ceramics, producing some of the most advanced pottery of that period.
>
> Perhaps the most important commodity in Cush was gold. Gadd writes that this region was "the general gold-mine of the ancient world". This wealth was quite a temptation to the Cushites' powerful neighbour Egypt to the north.[34]

Cush's wealth from its gold is confirmed by Yamauchi, who says, "Between 1901 and 1903 British geologists identified 85 ancient gold-mining sites in what was then the Anglo-Egyptian Sudan. Between 1989 and 1994 German investigators identified more than a hundred additional sites."[35]

Like Egypt, "Ethiopia" (Cush or Meroe) was considered by other ancient civilizations to be a land of abundance. We already saw earlier (chapter one, section A) that around 650 BC people spoke of the "boundless strength" of Cush (Nahum 3:9). This shows that the power and wealth of Cush were not simply a temporary phenomenon. Yamauchi adds that the Cushite king Taharqa (Tirhakah in the Bible) "built on a lavish scale in Egypt, especially in Memphis and Thebes . . . The sack of Thebes by the Assyrians in 663 was a memorable event. Massive booty was taken from Thebes, including 'silver, gold, gems, costumes, chattels, and even obelisks!'"[36] Hays assesses that the Cushite civilization lasted for roughly 3,000 years, from 2500 BC to AD 400,[37] although it was most powerful for the first 1,000 years and then began slowly declining.

Promises concerning Cush/"Ethiopia"

In Psalm 68:31 we see a promise that applies both to Egypt and to Cush/Ethiopia: "Nobles shall come from Egypt; Cush shall hasten to stretch out her hands to God" (ESV). This is also true for Psalm 87:4: "I will record Rahab [Egypt] and Babylon among those who acknowledge me . . . along with Cush". These verses show that Cushites/Sudanese/"Ethiopians" will be among those who are the Lord's disciples, a promise which began to be fulfilled with Ebed-Melech (if not before him) and continued with the conversion of the "Ethiopian eunuch", who might be better referred to as the court official from Sudan. This promise has yet to be fully fulfilled.

In Psalm 72:10 we read that the kings of "Seba will present him gifts". We remember from our discussion in chapter two about the Queen of Sheba that Seba is a descendant of Cush who most likely lived in North Africa, and is not to be confused with Sheba (also mentioned in this same verse) which is probably a region of southwestern Arabia. This psalm was considered Messianic by both the later Jewish tradition and by the early church.[38] In reading this psalm, we note that the subject gradually shifts from the king to God, from the local to the universal. Therefore there are two different meanings to this psalm, one that applies to the actual king of Israel and one that applies to the future, ideal King of Israel. The kings of Sheba (Arabia) and Seba (Africa) most likely appeared before King Solomon to present him with gifts. But in the future, kings/leaders coming from Arabia and Africa will bow down before the Messiah to worship him, and all nations will serve him (Psalm 72:11). Africa will not be excluded from God's glorious future kingdom.[39]

In an earlier section we saw that Isaiah 11:11 also speaks of how "the Lord will reach out his hand a second time to reclaim the remnant that is left of his people from Assyria, from Lower Egypt, from Upper Egypt, from Cush". This event will probably occur during the time of the Messiah, that is, when Jesus will return to reign on earth and, according to some commentators, this event does not only concern the Jews.[40]

Let us return to Isaiah 18, since it also speaks of the future of Cush. In this passage the prophet Isaiah warns King Hezekiah to not trust in the power of Cush, but rather to trust in the Lord. "At that time gifts will be brought to the Lord Almighty from a people tall and smooth-skinned, from a people feared far and wide, an aggressive nation of strange speech, whose land is divided by rivers – the gifts will be brought to Mount Zion, the place of the Name of the Lord Almighty" (Isaiah 18:7). As is the case for many prophetic verses, this verse (which as we will see resembles Zephaniah 3:9) was fulfilled in the near future in Isaiah's time, and will also be fulfilled more fully at a future time. According to 2 Chronicles 32:23, with the defeat of the Assyrians, "many brought offerings to Jerusalem for the Lord and valuable gifts for Hezekiah king of Judah. From then on he was highly regarded by all the nations." This was the more immediate fulfilment of Isaiah 18:7. It is assumed that Cushite emissaries were also among the people coming from "all the nations" to thank Hezekiah.

At the same time, some scholars see an even greater event in this prophecy, a time when Cush will regularly come and bring offerings to the Lord. The *Bible Knowledge Commentary* says that "possibly Isaiah was speaking of the millennial kingdom when peoples from around the world will worship the Lord".[41] Likewise, a note on this verse in the *Nouveau commentaire biblique* says:

> The final verse [Isaiah 18:7] seems to look beyond the immediate crisis of the Assyrian aggression, which had led the envoys all the way to Jerusalem. Isaiah now sees these travellers as part of a new day, as the first of many who will come to Zion to pay homage . . . This perspective, glimpsed in 2:3 and 11:10, will be more fully developed in chapters 60–62; it is expressed with delight in Psalm 68:30-31 and 87:4.[42]

In other words, this new day of worship will include many Cushites/Sudanese.

One last passage which speaks of a promise for Cush/"Ethiopia" is Zephaniah 3:9-12. "Then I will purify the lips of the peoples, that all of them may call on the name of the Lord and serve him shoulder to shoulder. From beyond the rivers of Cush my worshipers, my scattered people, will bring me offerings" (Zephaniah 3:9-10). As we saw above, the rivers of Cush are the Blue Nile, the White Nile, and the Atbara. A note in the *NIV Study Bible* says that these verses refer to "the most distant area imaginable".[43] These verses imply, therefore, that peoples coming from other parts of Africa – from "the heart of Africa" according to Hays[44] – will be true worshipers of the Lord. Hays adds:

> Thus, for Zephaniah, Cush becomes a paradigm for the inclusion of foreign people into the people of God. The mixing of Black Africans shoulder to shoulder with the remnant of Israel in worship of Yahweh is at the core of the prophetic imagery regarding the fulfilment of God's great salvific plan for the ages.[45]

This is a promise that pertains to all of sub-Saharan Africa, a promise whose fulfilment we are seeing today.

---

1   Ronald Youngblood, "Genesis," in the *NIV Study Bible, 10th Anniversary Edition*, ed. Kenneth Barker et al. (Grand Rapids: Zondervan Publishing House, 1995), 26.

2   Edwin Yamauchi, *Africa and the Bible* (Grand Rapids: Baker Academic, 2004), 38.

3   Alan Ross, "Genesis," *NLT Illustrated Study Bible*, ed. Sean Harrison (Carol Stream, IL: Tyndale House Publishers, 2015), 27.

4   Ross, "Genesis, 28.

5   James Freeman, "Isaiah 19:8 Egyptian Fishing" in *The New Manner and Customs of the Bible* (Gainesville, Florida: Bridge-Logos Publishers, 1998), 353.

6   Alfred Kuen, Hubert Goudineau, Sylvain Romerowski, "1 Rois," in the *Bible d'étude Semeur 2000*, ed. Alfred Kuen et al. (Charols, France: Excelsis, 2005), 482

7   Alfred Kuen, Hubert Goudineau, Sylvain Romerowski, "Proverbes," in the *Bible d'étude Semeur 2000*, ed. Alfred Kuen et al. (Charols, France: Excelsis, 2005), 888.

8   Alfred Kuen, Christophe Paya, Hubert Goudineau, Sylvain Romerowski, "Genèse," in the *Bible d'étude Semeur 2000*, ed. Alfred Kuen et al. (Charols, France: Excelsis, 2005), 75.

9   "Nil," in the *Nouveau dictionnaire biblique révisé*, ed. René Pache (Saint-Légier, Switzerland: Editions Emmaüs, 1992), 905-907; "Egypte," in the *Nouveau dictionnaire biblique révisé*, 384.

10 In Hebrew, the proper name "Nile" does not exist; it is always "the river" that is used, and that is how the KJV translates it each time.

11 James Hoffmeier, "Egypt," page 567 in vol. 4 of *New International Dictionary of Old Testament Theology and Exegesis (NIDOTTE)*, ed. Willem VanGemeren (Grand Rapids: Zondervan, 1997).

12 John H. Stek, "Psalms," in the *NIV Study Bible, 10th Anniversary Edition*, ed. Kenneth Barker et al. (Grand Rapids: Zondervan Publishing House, 1995), 846.

13 Colin Brown, "Incense, Myrrh," in *The New International Dictionary of New Testament Theology*, vol. 2, ed. Colin Brown (Grand Rapids, MI: Zondervan, 1976), 294. He is referring to comments made by H. L. Strack and P. Billerbeck in the *Kommentar zum Neuen Testament aus Talmud und Midrasch*, vol. 1 (Munich: Beck, 1922-1961), 83 f.

14 Mark Phelps, "רחב (rhb)" page 1065 in vol. 3 of *New International Dictionary of Old Testament Theology and Exegesis (NIDOTTE)*, ed. Willem VanGemeren (Grand Rapids: Zondervan, 1997).

15   See Alfred Kuen, Hubert Goudineau, Sylvain Romerowski, "Esaïe," in the *Bible d'étude Semeur 2000*, ed. Alfred Kuen et al. (Charols, France: Excelsis, 2005), 977, where the title of this chapter is "Le Roi et le règne à venir" [The King and his coming reign.] Herbert Wolf and John Stek, "Isaiah," in the *NIV Study Bible, 10th Anniversary Edition*, ed. Kenneth Barker et al. (Grand Rapids: Zondervan Publishing House, 1995), 1027, say that some interpreted the phrase "a second time" as referring to the return of Jesus Christ. Additionally, LaSor, Hubbard, and Bush maintain that this passage refers to the "messianic kingdom", saying that "the kingdom to be established in the latter days is to be 'forever and ever.' It includes the nations (or gentiles) and extends to the ends of the earth." William LaSor, David Hubbard, and Frederic Bush, *Old Testament Survey* (Grand Rapids, MI: Eerdmans, 1982), 401.

16   "Alexandrie," in the *Nouveau dictionnaire biblique révisé*, ed. René Pache (Saint-Légier, Switzerland: Editions Emmaüs, 1992), 56-57.

17   Father John Baur, *2000 ans de christianisme en Afrique : une histoire de l'Église africaine*, trans. Yves Morel S. J. (Abidjan: INADES, 1999), 9.

18   Thomas Oden, *How Africa Shaped the Christian Mind* (Downers Grove: InterVarsity Press, 2007), 17-18.

19   "Memphis," in the *Nouveau dictionnaire biblique révisé*, ed. René Pache (Saint-Légier, Switzerland: Editions Emmaüs, 1992), 838-839.

20   "On," in the *Nouveau dictionnaire biblique révisé*, 932.

21   "Amôn de No," in the *Nouveau dictionnaire biblique révisé*, 66.

22   "Cyrène," in the *Nouveau dictionnaire biblique révisé*, 309.

23   Philip Ward, *Touring Libya: The Southern Provinces* (London: Faber & Faber, 1968), 57, quoted in Yamauchi, *Africa and the Bible*, 191.

24   "Esaïe," *La Bible en français courant* (Pierrefitte, France: Alliance Biblique Universelle, 1989), 970.

25   While some Bibles in English locate Lud in Asia Minor, the majority of French Bibles maintain it is in Africa: Pul and Lud are two peoples from Africa (Somalia and Libya) (*Bible d'étude Semeur 2000*); Lud is "maybe Libya" (*Bible Thompson*); Put and Lud are "undoubtedly African peoples along the Red Sea" (*TOB*); "'Pul' and 'Lud' [are] in North Africa" (*Sainte Bible*); Lud is a "region neighbouring Egypt, but unidentified" (*La Bible en français courant*); Lud is a "region near Egypt" (Parole de Vie).

Kuen, Goudineau, and Romerowski, "Esaïe," in the *Bible d'étude Semeur 2000*, 1056; Thompson, "Esaïe," in *La Bible Thompson avec chaîne de références* (Miami: Editions Vida, 1990), 849; "Esaïe," *Traduction Œcuménique de la Bible* (Paris: Société Biblique Française/Éditions du Cerf, 1975), 543 ; "Esaïe," in the *Sainte Bible avec commentaires de John MacArthur* (Geneva: Société Biblique de Genève, 2006), 1056; "Esaïe," *La Bible en français courant*, 970; "Esaïe," in *La Bible: Ancien Testament et Nouveau Testament: Parole de Vie* (Villiers-le-Bel, France : Société Biblique Française, 2000), 906.

26   Thompson, "Esaïe," in *La Bible Thompson*, 849.

27   J. Daniel Hays, "The Cushites: A Black Nation in Ancient History," *Bibliotheca Sacra 153*, no. 611 (July-September 1996), 271.

28   Hays, "The Cushites: A Black Nation in Ancient History," 270.

29   Kuen, Goudineau, and Romerowski, "Esaïe," in the *Bible d'étude Semeur 2000*, 986; "Esaïe," *La Bible en français courant*, 904; Thompson, "Esaïe," in *La Bible Thompson*, 789; Wolf and Stek, "Isaiah," in the *NIV Study Bible*, 1035.

30   Kuen, Goudineau, and Romerowski, "Esaïe," in the *Bible d'étude Semeur 2000*, 986.

31   MacArthur, "Esaïe," in the *Sainte Bible*, 986.

32   Kuen, Goudineau, and Romerowski, "Esaïe," in the *Bible d'étude Semeur 2000*, 986; Wolf and Stek, "Isaiah," in the *NIV Study Bible*, 1035.

33   Thompson, "Esaïe," in *La Bible Thompson*, 789.

34 Hays, "The Cushites: A Black Nation in Ancient History," 275.

35 Yamauchi, *Africa and the Bible*, 53-54.

36 Yamauchi, *Africa and the Bible*, 133, 140.

37 J. Daniel Hays, "Black Soldiers in the Ancient Near East", *Bible Review 14* (August 1998), 31. The reader will note that Hays seems to extend the length of the Cushite civilization here in this article written in 1998. In a 1996 article, "The Cushites: A Black Nation in Ancient History," he spoke of more than 2500 years for the length of this same civilization.

38 John Stek, "Psalms," in the *NIV Study Bible, 10th Anniversary Edition*, ed. Kenneth Barker et al. (Grand Rapids: Zondervan Publishing House, 1995), 852.

39 We note here that certain writers, such as David Adamo, use this passage, along with others, to maintain that one of the Magi (or even all of them) from Matthew 2 was an African. Such an interpretation seems to be a gross exaggeration, in my opinion, for it does not respect the normal principles of exegesis for either Psalm 72 or Matthew 2. To understand his position, see David Adamo, *Africa and Africans in the New Testament* (Lanham: University Press of America, 2006), 52-55.

40 See the previous sections on "Egypt my people" and "Promises about Egypt" along with the corresponding endnotes.

41 John A. Martin, "Isaiah," in the *Bible Knowledge Commentary*, ed. John F. Walvoord, Roy B. Zuck et al. (Colorado Springs, CO: Victor Books/Scripture Press, 1985), 1065.

42 Derek Kidner, "Esaïe," *Nouveau commentaire biblique* (Saint-Légier: Éditions Émmaüs, 1978), p. 623.

43 Roland K. Harrison, "Zephaniah," in the *NIV Study Bible, 10th Anniversary Edition*, ed. Kenneth Barker et al. (Grand Rapids: Zondervan Publishing House, 1995), 1391.

44 J. Daniel Hays, "The Cushites: A Black Nation in the Bible," *Bibliotheca Sacra 153*, no. 612 (October-December 1996), 406.

45 J. Daniel Hays, *From Every People and Nation: A biblical theology of race* (Downers Grove: InterVarsity Press, 2003), 129-130.

5

CONCLUSION

The biblical references to Africans and Africa are more numerous than one thinks. These references can be found from Genesis to Revelation, and the appendices at the end of this book clearly show the abundant number of references. Of the 66 books of the Bible, 47 of them contain a reference to an African place or person. If I have counted correctly, there are 1,253 references to African places and 1,440 references to African people, for a total of 2,693 references in 1,325 biblical verses.

However, it is not just the sheer number of Bible references which makes for a strong link between Christianity and Africa. Rather, it is what the Bible actually says about Africa that is important. As David Adamo says, "Africans and Africa have participated fully in the drama of redemption and they are not latecomers in the preaching of the Gospel. They have contributed socially, economically, and religiously to the life of the people in the biblical period."[1]

Africa was involved when God was preparing his people during the Old Testament period for the coming of his Messiah, Jesus Christ. We see the warm welcome the Egyptian Pharaoh gave the people of Israel during the time of Joseph. Such a welcome was granted by other Pharaohs as well (such as the Pharaoh during the time of Abraham and the Pharaoh married to Queen Tahpenes) throughout the history of Israel. Another African Pharaoh, Siamen, went even further, concluding an alliance with Solomon and giving his daughter in marriage to the king of Israel. That demonstrates the privileged relationship that existed between Egypt and Israel, at least for a certain period of time. Other African kings came to the aid of Israel militarily, such as So and Tirhakah. God even used certain kings, such as Neco II and Shishak, to serve as his spokesman to Israel, but God's people would not listen.

Other African Pharaohs were enemies of the people of Israel, and as such they refused to listen to the Lord. The Pharaoh who drove Moses out of Egypt, or the one who reigned during the time of the Exodus are two classic examples of kings who opposed the will of God. Pharaoh Hophra was also an example of a proud and haughty king.

The African women in the Bible are generally seen in a positive light by the biblical writers. With the exception of Potiphar's wife, who is an excellent example of bad behaviour, we see the bravery demonstrated by Shiphrah and Puah when they stood before the Pharaoh, as well as the audacity of that same Pharaoh's daughter to adopt a Hebrew baby as her own. We should not forget, either, the faith shown by Bithiah and the courage of Hagar.

Speaking of courage, one of the best examples of a courageous person can be found in the person of Ebed-Melech, the Cushite who saved the life of Jeremiah the prophet. This important court official bravely trusted in the Lord and received God's blessing as a result. Another Cushite who serves as a good example is the Cushite in Joab's service, for he was a man who did his duty promptly and faithfully. We cannot forget the zeal with which Phinehas served the Lord, putting an end to the plague which resulted from the Israelites' idolatry. Afterwards he became the high priest, the person who served as mediator between God and the people of Israel on the Day of Atonement. It would not be an exaggeration to say that Phinehas is the most important African in the whole Bible.

We also see that Africa – its cities, its regions, its commerce – is generally seen in a very positive light in the biblical texts. The people of Israel saw Africa as a region of wealth and abundance. That is why the Old Testament prophets warned the kings of Israel over and over again to not trust in Egypt, but rather to trust in the Lord.

We see that God himself worked a lot of miracles on African soil. The crossing of the Red Sea, considered to be the greatest miracle in the Old Testament, occurred in Egypt. But other great miracles also took place in Africa, such as writing the Ten Commandments on tablets of stone, or guiding the people of Israel by a pillar of fire at night and a pillar of cloud in the day.

During New Testament times, God continued to work in Africa and among Africans. Jesus himself spent a part of his early childhood in Africa. According to the biblical evidence, there were Africans (Cyrenians and Egyptians) who followed Jesus Christ starting from the day of Pentecost, the day the Christian church was born. Another person, the "Ethiopian eunuch" (or "Sudanese dignitary"), was the object of the Holy Spirit's missionary work. There were also Africans who taught in the early church (Simeon called Niger and men of Cyrene) and who, afterwards, took part in sending others out for cross-cultural mission. One other African, Apollos, became a well-known servant of God.

Finally, certain promises in the Bible indicate that God has not yet finished being involved with the peoples of Africa, and that the fulfilments of these promises will still occur in the future. The relationship between God and Africa continues.

All of these biblical examples of Africans show us that Africans can be recipients of God's blessing as well as his wrath. Certain ones obtained positions of great responsibility alongside a prophet (such as Ebed-Melech) or in the church (such as Simeon called Niger). Others were responsible for the death of a person whom God had sent, such as the men of Cyrene and Alexandria who argued with Stephen and took part in instigating his death. At times God used Africans to bless his people, whether Israel or the church (such as the Pharaohs at the time of Abraham and Joseph, Phinehas, and Apollos), and at times God used Africans to chastise his people (Shishak). But in both cases, they are quite involved in the story of God's relationship with his people, from the beginning to the end, whether it be Israel or the church. Therefore, it can be concluded that Africans are not recent recipients of the gospel message; rather, they are an integral part of that message. Based on these scriptural facts, Christians in Africa can legitimately claim Christianity as an African religion, in the same way that many animists claim different traditional religions as African religions.

Scottish mission historian Andrew Walls agrees with this conclusion. In challenging the view that the early history of Christianity in North Africa has nothing to do with the contemporary history of Christianity in sub-Saharan Africa, Walls comments on the use of the word "Ethiopian" in church names during the last century to denote churches that were free from missionary control and to assert their "Africanness". He comments:

> I suggest that this Ethiopian consciousness should be taken seriously as representing an important instinct that many simple people have identified when more sophisticated people have missed it. "Ethiopian" stands for Africa indigenously Christian, Africa *primordially* Christian; for a Christianity that was established in Africa not only before the white people came, but before Islam came; for a Christianity that has been continuously in Africa for far longer than it has in Scotland, and infinitely longer than it has in the United States. African Christians today can assert their right to the *whole* history of Christianity in Africa, stretching back almost to the apostolic age (emphasis in original).[2]

But we should be careful – Christianity is not exclusively African by any means! Asian Christians can also claim Christianity as an Asian religion since the Bible clearly speaks of numerous Asian countries. After all, Israel is in Asia. Many Asians play an important role in the Scriptures. The same can be said for people from Europe and countries in Europe, especially with regard to the New Testament. It is therefore false to consider Christianity as a white man's religion. Based on its history and its geography, Christianity belongs to all the peoples of the world. No single people, ethnic group, or nationality has the copyright to the biblical message.

* *

What importance can be attributed to the fact that Africans are part of the Christian message from start to finish? I see several practical ramifications for the Church in Africa.

1. It is clear in the Bible that Canaan and not Ham was the one cursed by Noah (Genesis 9:25). Ham received, in fact, not Noah's curse but rather his blessing (9:1). That means that there is no legitimate biblical basis for saying that Africans, as descendants of Ham, were to be slaves for centuries because of some supposed curse from God. Those who see slavery as a part of God's will for Africa are looking for a pretext to relegate blacks to an inferior social position. In doing so they are ignoring the true meaning of the Christian message. Their argument is baseless, since Genesis 9 has nothing to do with the enslavement of Africans. Rather, it specifically concerns the conquest of Canaan by the Israelites during the time of Moses and Joshua. Because of the Canaanite people's abominable practices by which they defiled themselves, God gave the Promised Land over to the Israelites (Leviticus 18:24-25; 20:23; Deuteronomy 9:4-5). The result of the curse of Canaan was the conquest of the land of Canaan and not the enslavement of Africans in America nearly 4,000 years later.

2. God is not racist in his dealings with humankind. He does not favour one people over another, "For God does not show favoritism" (Romans 2:11). We have already seen that God blesses those who obey him and chastises those who disobey him. He is very concerned about how people respond to his commandments; he is not

concerned at all about their skin colour. That means that an African who repents of his sins and believes in Jesus does not have to adopt American or European religious practices. All he has to do is put his faith into practice. As professor Lamin Sanneh says, "Christianity helped Africans to become renewed Africans, not remade Europeans."[3] Every culture, without exception, should respect biblical teaching. If that happens, God will not prefer one culture over another one. Sanneh goes on to say, "No culture is so advanced and so superior that it can claim exclusive access or advantage to the truth of God, and none so marginal or inferior that it can be excluded. All have merit".[4] Well-known biblical passages such as Genesis 12:3, Isaiah 49:6, Matthew 28:19-20, and Revelation 7:9 demonstrate that, from start to finish, God has equal love for all peoples of the earth whether they are specifically named in the Bible or not. God sent Jesus into the world to bring people from every nation into a relationship with him, a relationship built on love and trust, not on culture.

3. All these references to Africans in the Bible show that God has not forgotten the people of Africa. They are the object of some of his great promises (Isaiah 11; 19; Psalms 68; 87; Zephaniah 3). Christianity has deep roots in African soil. No African need therefore apologize for being a Christian, as if he or she were somehow betraying their ancestral religion. Certain African ancestors were already following the Lord God more than 3,000 years ago. As a result, each African Christian should seek to spread the gospel message so that the African continent will become even more permeated with a deep and intimate knowledge of Jesus Christ.

4. Another logical consequence of all these biblical references to Africa is that the church in Africa should take the Word of God all the more seriously. Africa should feel truly motivated and also challenged by what the Bible says. Today there are local churches where the pastor only has a very superficial knowledge of the Scriptures. Some pastors even prefer to pray and say they are led by the Spirit rather than spending an adequate amount of time seriously meditating on and studying the Bible. They forget that the Spirit of God works in conjunction with the Word of God. Other Christian leaders say that certain Bible passages do not apply to African Christians, as if it were white missionaries in the 19th century who had written the biblical texts prior to coming to Africa. Conceivably, a person from China or Korea could say that the Scriptures do not apply to them, since the Bible says nothing about the Far East. The same would be true for Canadians and Americans. But an African does not have this option: the 2,693 Bible references to Africa or Africans show how much God is interested in this continent and its peoples. If there are so many references to Africa in the Word of God, from start to finish, Africans should consider themselves to be implicated in and concerned with its message. The church in Africa must take the Bible seriously; otherwise it will experience problems of syncretism and spiritual shallowness. If it does not seek to listen to the Lord through his Word, it will consist of many nominal converts but few committed disciples. I want to encourage us to follow the example of the Sudanese dignitary who was reading the Scriptures and sincerely seeking to understand their meaning. May we imitate Apollos who "was a learned man, with a thorough knowledge of the Scriptures . . . [He] taught about Jesus accurately" (Acts 18:24-25). Let us refuse to accept a superficial understanding of the Bible message. The Word of God is an inestimable treasure for all nations, including those on the African continent, provided that we take the time to dig deep and to obey what God says.

5. A fifth ramification of all these verses that speak of Africa is that the African church needs to launch out once again into mission. Africans were on the front line of mission in Acts 11 and 13; they were so again during the time of Tertullian and Augustine. The 21st century could signal yet again a time when the church in Africa is mobilized to proclaim the message of Jesus Christ throughout the entire world. The African church has experienced a certain kind of life and vitality, both at the beginning of Christianity and in the modern era, that the average church in Europe and America has not known for a long time. Hence, it is her job to launch out in mission, a job that will only be finished when there is a great gathering around the throne of the Lamb, a gathering that will include "a great multitude that no one could count, from every nation, tribe, people and language" (Revelation 7:9). That is the mission awaiting the church in Africa.

6. Finally, I believe that it is time for the church in Africa to recognize its very rich biblical heritage. When Martin Luther recognized the importance of the idea that "the righteous will live by faith" (Romans 1:17), it marked the beginning of the Reformation. The biblical truth that "Abraham believed God, and it was credited to him as righteousness" (Romans 4:3) occupies a very important place in the history of Christianity. In the same way, it is important to recognize the contribution made by Phinehas, an African leader of God's people. In the Bible we read of his zealous love for the Lord, his close relationship with God, and his decisive actions which resulted from those two foundations. The result was that "this was credited to him as righteousness for endless generations to come" (Psalm 106:31). Abraham and Phinehas are the only two people about whom the Bible speaks in this way, using the phrase "credited to him as righteousness". Abraham's faith and Phinehas's deeds were credited to them as righteousness. It goes without saying that Abraham's faith was accompanied by deeds, and Phinehas's deeds were founded on his faith. When Luther understood the importance of faith being credited as righteousness, it launched the Protestant Reformation. When the African church understands the importance of good works based on living faith, it could also set off an "African Reformation", that is, a movement where the African church:

- understands the presence and the importance of Africans and Africa in the Bible, and

- aims for spiritual maturity by putting the Word of God into practice through discipleship, following the example of those Africans about whom the Bible speaks. Such an "African Reformation" could silence the critics of the church who say that Christianity in Africa is a mile wide but only an inch deep.

Africans are not late recipients of the gospel message; they are truly a part of the Christian message, and that can be seen through their history, their ethnicity, and their geography, for all three can be traced through the Scriptures. There are many links, many connections, and many commonalities between the history and culture found in the Bible and those found in Africa. The Ghanaian theologian, Kwame Bediako, wrote a book entitled *Christianity in Africa: The Renewal of a Non-Western Religion*. In discussing the links between Africa and biblical theology, he says:

> After nearly two decades of investigations into the primal religions and spiritualities of numerous African societies, often with authors studying their own particular peoples, Africa's theologians came to a virtual consensus on a matter of prime concern: recognising "the radical quality

of God's self revelation in Jesus Christ" – they were nonetheless convinced that "this knowledge of God was not totally discontinuous with African peoples' previous traditional knowledge of him".[5]

Or to say it in a different way, God had prepared Africa for the message of Jesus Christ well before the arrival of Western missionaries in the 19th century, and all these Bible references concerning Africa were a part of that preparation.

Referring to the well-known African theologian, John Mbiti, Bediako goes on to say: "At least one prominent African theologian has written that 'Christianity in Africa can rightly be described as an indigenous, traditional, and African religion.'"[6]

Today, Christians in Africa do not need to consider Christianity as some kind of foreign religion. They can legitimately claim it as an "African religion" which dates back to 2,000 years ago, and they can do so without fear of betraying their own history or culture.

---

1   David Adamo, *Africa and Africans in the New Testament*, p. 118.

2   Andrew Walls, *The Cross-Cultural Process in Christian History* (Maryknoll, NY: Orbis, 2002), 91.

3   Lamin Sanneh, *Whose Religion Is Christianity?: The Gospel beyond the West* (Grand Rapids MI: Eerdmans, 2003), 43.

4   Sanneh, *Whose Religion Is Christianity?*, 106.

5   Kwame Bediako, *Christianity in Africa: The Renewal of a Non-Western Religion* (Edinburgh: Edinburgh University Press, 1995), 177.

6   Bediako, *Christianity in Africa*, 179, quoting John Mbiti, *African Religions and Philosophy* (London: Heinemann, 1969), 229.

THE COLOUR OF CHRISTIANITY

Many people in Africa see Christianity as a "white man's religion", and they do so primarily because people from Western Europe or North America brought the gospel message to their country most recently. While it is understandable to so categorize Christianity for that reason, we need to understand that in many countries around the world, Christianity was first introduced by other sources. Let's investigate what some biblical texts say about this matter.

In we go back to Acts 2, it is clear that men from Asia, Africa, and Europe took part in the celebration of Pentecost when the Christian church was born. Fifteen people groups are listed in that chapter: 11 from Asia, two from Africa, and two from Europe. While the two from Europe could be considered to be white, most of those attending would today be classified as brown, coming from Turkey, Iran, Iraq, Egypt, Libya, and Jordan (and perhaps Saudi Arabia). Some scholars maintain that all those present were members of the Jewish diaspora who had returned to Jerusalem for the feast of Pentecost, and therefore were ethnic Jews. That is undoubtedly true for some of them, since Luke calls them "Jews" in verse 5, which is primarily a reference to ethnic Israelites from Judah.[1] However, the same verse also relates that Jews "from every nation under heaven", hyperbole for the 15 people groups listed in verses 9 to 11, were staying in Jerusalem. The question must therefore be asked: Are all of these people at Pentecost ethnic Jews from Israel who had simply migrated from Israel to these other lands? Or do they include Jewish proselytes, that is, indigenous people from those 15 other lands who had turned to the God of Israel and, as non-Israelites, are worshiping in Jerusalem, much as the Ethiopian eunuch would do later in Acts 8?

The answer can be found in the biblical text itself. First of all, verse 10 refers to "proselytes" who were in attendance at Pentecost, and a proselyte is defined in the New Testament as "a Gentile who, through conversion, committed himself/herself to the practice of the Jewish law".[2] People who were not Israelite Jews were, in fact, in attendance at Pentecost, and it is a matter of interpretation as to whether the word "proselyte" only refers to those coming from Rome in verse 10, or from all of the groups listed in verses 9 and 10. If the latter, then the number of proselytes is even greater. Verse 8, as well as the overall context of chapter 2, supports a large number of proselytes, not a small number.

Secondly, and more importantly, those peoples attending the feast of Pentecost say they heard the Galilean disciples speaking in their "native language" (Acts 2:8) and in their "own tongues" (2:11), *dialektos* in both verses. The miracle of Pentecost would not make any sense, however, if all of those in attendance were Israelite Jews, since their "own tongue" would have been the same language as that spoken by the disciples. There would have been no need whatsoever for a miraculous intervention by the Holy Spirit if they all already spoke the same "native language." As both the Bible and history books confirm, Jews do not readily forget their mother tongue. If other languages were deemed necessary by God at Pentecost, it is because other people groups from around the world were present, people who understood their "own tongues" better than the Aramaic Hebrew of Palestine.

Thirdly, Peter addresses himself in verse 14 to "Men of Judea *and . . .*" or to "Fellow Jews *and . . .*". He recognizes two different groups of people at Pentecost: those from Judea (ethnic Israelites) and those from elsewhere who were staying temporarily in Jerusalem, as mentioned in verse 5. This latter group needed to hear the gospel message in their "native language", as mentioned in verse 8. Thus, many brown people from Asia and Africa participated in the birth of the Christian church, along with their Israelite counterparts, who were probably far more brown than ethnic Jews from Israel today. Men from Asia and Africa were undoubtedly a minority of those attending the feast, but they seem to have been a significant minority.

In Acts 8 the first black man came to know Jesus Christ. The "Ethiopian eunuch" should more properly be called the "Sudanese dignitary", since he was from the region known as Meroe, which today would be part of north-eastern Sudan. Some scholars debate whether the term "eunuch" had kept its technical meaning of a castrated man in New Testament times, or if it had evolved to mean a person serving as a high dignitary.[3] But whatever his physical state, his spiritual state changed completely when he heard the good news of Jesus Christ. He then "went on his way rejoicing" (Acts 8:39) back to his home in Africa. The early Church Father, Irenaeus, asserts that this African convert went home, where he became a missionary to his own people.[4] Bible scholar Craig Keener states, "This African court official was the first non-Jewish Christian. Such information may be helpful in establishing that Christianity is not only not a western religion, but that after its Jewish origins it was first of all an African faith."[5] Such comments indicate that Christianity had a significant and very early impact in black Africa.

These passages in Acts 2 and 8 make clear that Christianity was initially a religion of brown and black people, although evangelism among white people would start in Acts 10 with Cornelius and then continue with Paul's missionary journey into Greece in Acts 16. Jesus's command to make disciples of all nations included all the continents of the world, and the three known continents at that time were Africa, Asia, and Europe. Interestingly, in Acts 8 someone from Africa turns to Christ: the "Ethiopian eunuch." In Acts 9 someone from Asia turns to Christ: Saul of Tarsus (in present-day Turkey, previously known as Asia Minor). In Acts 10 someone from Europe turns to Christ: Cornelius, who was a member of the "Italian Regiment". Luke seems to foreshadow that the whole world will become Christian.

Acts 11:19-21 provides yet another interesting insight into the colour of Christianity. There we see that the persecution connected with Stephen's death caused believers to scatter, and some scattered as far as Phoenicia (present-day Lebanon), Cyprus, and the city of Antioch (then in Syria but today the southern-most city in Turkey). This is the first instance in the book of Acts where Christians go beyond Jerusalem, Judea, and Samaria and cross into that zone known as "the ends of the earth" (Acts 1:8).

Some of these believers would only talk to Jews about Jesus, but men from Cyprus (in Asia) and Cyrene (in Africa) took the bold measure of speaking directly to Greeks. They may have been astute theologians, anticipating the debate at the Jerusalem council in Acts 15 and concluding, before Paul and Peter did, that Gentiles did not first have to become Jews before they could become Christians. But a more likely supposition is that, because "the hand of the Lord was with them" (verse 21), these "brown missionaries" were simply sensitive to what the Holy Spirit wanted them to do. It should be noted that not only is this the first time in the book of Acts that missionaries cross over into "the ends of the earth" – and going from Libya to Syria would make them the first cross-cultural missionaries in the New Testament – but it is also the first time in Acts that the messengers of the gospel are not Israelite men, and it is the first time in Acts that the hearers are not linked to Judaism. A new zone, a new messenger, a new audience – these are three reasons why this passage is a crucial turning point in Christian history!

Not surprisingly, the church founded in Antioch by these brown missionaries became the missionary church par excellence in the New Testament. Acts 13:1 says this church's leaders were Barnabas, Simeon called Niger, Lucius of Cyrene, Manaen, and Saul. Here we see that two of the five leaders had lived in Africa. Cyrene was a large city in Libya, and it is where Lucius had lived at one time. However, it must be noted that Cyrene was a large Greek colony, and it had a substantial Jewish population as well. So even though it was in Africa, everyone who lived there was not ethnically African. It seems probable, based on his name, that Lucius was a Jew who was born in Cyrene but who later migrated to Antioch, perhaps as one of the missionaries who evangelized the Greeks there. But most likely he was not a proselyte. Nonetheless, he was known as Lucius "of Cyrene", showing that his African heritage remained with him wherever he went.

Another church leader was Simeon called Niger. "Niger" is the Latin word for "black". Many commentators hold that Simeon was a black man from Africa who had migrated to Antioch. Since his nickname was a Latin and not a Greek word, a plausible explanation is that he came from Latin-speaking North Africa (present-day Tunisia or Algeria) rather than Greek-speaking North Africa (Egypt and Libya). The presence of Lucius and Simeon as prophets and teachers in the Antioch church demonstrates that men from Africa had an influential role in church leadership, and as foreigners they may have played a major role in the missionary emphasis for which their church became known.

These biblical texts show that brown or black men 1) were present the day the Christian church was born; 2) were involved in church-planting and cross-cultural mission; and 3) were leaders in a large urban church. All of this does not depict some kind of later developmental stage in church history; rather, it all pre-dates Paul's first missionary journey! Church history only reinforces what the biblical text began, showing how Christianity's roots go deep in African and Asian soil. The many-hued colours of the Global South have played a more significant role in the origin of our faith, our church, and our mission than many of us realize.

TIM WELCH

[This article is a revision of Tim Welch's article "The Color of Christianity," in the *Encyclopedia of Christianity in the Global South*, ed. Mark Lamport (Lanham, MD: Rowman & Littlefield, 2018). All rights reserved.]

---

1   We need to remember that modern Israelis are far more "white" than their first-century counterparts, since numerous Jews from Europe and North America returned to Israel after 1948.

2   P. Trebilco and R. A. Stewart, "Proselyte" in the *New Bible Dictionary, Third edition* (Downers Grove: IVP Academic, 1996), 976.

3   See H. Baltensweiler, "Eunuch", in *The New International Dictionary of New Testament Theology*, vol. 1, ed. Colin Brown (Grand Rapids, MI: Zondervan, 1975), 560, where he says that "sometimes when the word 'eunuch' refers to a high court official (cf. Acts 8.27), it is not clear whether we should opt for a literal rendering of the word, or if 'eunuch' was simply a title."

4   J. Unger, OFM Cap, *Saint Irenaeus of Lyons: Against the Heresies* (New York/Mahwah, NJ: Newman Press, 2012), 64–65.

5   Craig Keener, "Philip preaches to the Ethiopian eunuch in Acts 8:26-27" August 29, 2011 in http://www.craigkeener.com/philip-preaches-to-the-ethiopian-eunuch-in-acts-826-27/

APPENDIX 1

VERSES WHICH REFER TO AFRICA (BY ORDER OF APPEARANCE)

This first appendix is the most extensive, as it lists all the references (both direct and indirect) to African people or places in the Bible. They are listed in order of appearance in the Scriptures. I have done my best to ensure the accuracy of those references, but I admit that an error may have crept in here and there, especially since I used several French Bibles as the initial sources for this list. Any such errors in this or the other appendices should be brought to the attention of the author.

GENESIS

1	2:13	Cush
2	10:6	Cush, Mizraim, Put
3	10:7	Cush, Seba
4	10:8	Cush
5	10:13	Mizraim, Ludites, Anamites, Lehabites, Naphtuhites
6	10:14	Pathrusites, Casluhites
7	12:10	Egypt
8	12:11	Egypt
9	12:12	Egyptians
10	12:14	Egypt, Egyptians
11	12:15	Pharaoh during the time of Abraham, his officials
12	12:16	Pharaoh during the time of Abraham
13	12:17	Pharaoh during the time of Abraham, his household
14	12:18	Pharaoh during the time of Abraham
15	12:19	Pharaoh during the time of Abraham
16	12:20	Pharaoh during the time of Abraham
17	13:1	Egypt
18	13:10	Egypt
19	15:18	Egypt
20	16:1	Hagar, Egyptian
21	16:2	Hagar
22	16:3	Hagar, Egyptian
23	16:4	Hagar
24	16:5	Hagar
25	16:6	Hagar
26	16:7	Hagar, Desert of Shur
27	16:8	Hagar
28	16:9	Hagar
29	16:11	Hagar
30	16:13	Hagar

	GENESIS (cont.)	
31	16:15	Hagar
32	16:16	Hagar
33	20:1	Shur
34	21:9	Hagar, Egyptian
35	21:10	Hagar
36	21:12	Hagar
37	21:13	Hagar
38	21:14	Hagar
39	21:15	Hagar
40	21:16	Hagar
41	21:17	Hagar
42	21:19	Hagar
43	21:21	Hagar, Ishmael's wife, Egypt, Desert of Paran
44	25:12	Hagar, Egyptian
45	25:18	Shur, Egypt
46	26:2	Egypt
47	37:25	Egypt
48	37:28	Egypt
49	37:36	Egypt, Potiphar, Pharaoh during the time of Joseph
50	39:1	Egypt, Potiphar, Pharaoh during the time of Joseph, Egyptian
51	39:2	Potiphar, Egyptian
52	39:3	Potiphar
53	39:4	Potiphar
54	39:5	Potiphar, Egyptian
55	39:6	Potiphar
56	39:7	Potiphar's wife, Potiphar
57	39:8	Potiphar's wife, Potiphar
58	39:9	Potiphar's wife, Potiphar
59	39:10	Potiphar's wife
60	39:11	Household servants
61	39:12	Potiphar's wife
62	39:13	Potiphar's wife
63	39:14	Potiphar's wife
64	39:15	Potiphar's wife
65	39:16	Potiphar's wife, Potiphar
66	39:17	Potiphar's wife, Potiphar
67	39:18	Potiphar's wife
68	39:19	Potiphar's wife, Potiphar
69	39:20	Potiphar
70	39:21	Prison warden
71	39:22	Prison warden
72	39:23	Prison warden
73	40:1	Cupbearer, baker, king of Egypt
74	40:2	Pharaoh during the time of Joseph, cupbearer, baker
75	40:3	Cupbearer, baker, captain of the guard
76	40:4	Captain of the guard, cupbearer, baker
77	40:5	Cupbearer, baker, king of Egypt
78	40:6	Cupbearer, baker
79	40:7	Cupbearer, baker, Pharaoh during the time of Joseph
80	40:8	Cupbearer, baker
81	40:9	Cupbearer
82	40:11	Pharaoh during the time of Joseph, cupbearer
83	40:12	Cupbearer
84	40:13	Pharaoh during the time of Joseph, cupbearer
85	40:14	Cupbearer, Pharaoh during the time of Joseph
86	40:16	Baker
87	40:17	Pharaoh during the time of Joseph, baker
88	40:19	Pharaoh during the time of Joseph, baker
89	40:20	Pharaoh during the time of Joseph, his officials, cupbearer, baker
90	40:21	Pharaoh during the time of Joseph, cupbearer
91	40:22	Pharaoh during the time of Joseph, baker

92	40:23	Cupbearer
93	41:1	Pharaoh during the time of Joseph, Nile
94	41:2	River (Nile)
95	41:3	Nile
96	41:4	Pharaoh during the time of Joseph
97	41:5	Pharaoh during the time of Joseph
98	41:7	Pharaoh during the time of Joseph
99	41:8	Pharaoh during the time of Joseph, the magicians and wise men, Egypt
100	41:9	Cupbearer, Pharaoh during the time of Joseph
101	41:10	Pharaoh during the time of Joseph, cupbearer, baker, captain of the guard
102	41:11	Cupbearer, baker
103	41:12	Cupbearer, baker, captain of the guard
104	41:13	Cupbearer, baker
105	41:14	Pharaoh during the time of Joseph
106	41:15	Pharaoh during the time of Joseph
107	41:16	Pharaoh during the time of Joseph
108	41:17	Pharaoh during the time of Joseph, Nile
109	41:18	River (Nile)
110	41:19	Egypt, Pharaoh during the time of Joseph
111	41:21	Pharaoh during the time of Joseph
112	41:22	Pharaoh during the time of Joseph
113	41:24	Pharaoh during the time of Joseph, magicians
114	41:25	Pharaoh during the time of Joseph
115	41:28	Pharaoh during the time of Joseph
116	41:29	Egypt
117	41:30	Egypt
118	41:31	Land (of Egypt)
119	41:32	Pharaoh during the time of Joseph
120	41:33	Pharaoh during the time of Joseph, Egypt
121	41:34	Pharaoh during the time of Joseph, Egypt
122	41:35	Pharaoh during the time of Joseph
123	41:36	Egypt
124	41:37	Pharaoh during the time of Joseph, his officials
125	41:38	Pharaoh during the time of Joseph, his officials
126	41:39	Pharaoh during the time of Joseph
127	41:40	Pharaoh during the time of Joseph, people in his palace
128	41:41	Pharaoh during the time of Joseph, Egypt
129	41:42	Pharaoh during the time of Joseph
130	41:43	Pharaoh during the time of Joseph, Egypt
131	41:44	Pharaoh during the time of Joseph, Egypt
132	41:45	Pharaoh during the time of Joseph, Asenath, Potiphera, On, Egypt
133	41:46	Pharaoh during the time of Joseph, Egypt
134	41:48	Egypt
135	41:50	Asenath, Potiphera, On
136	41:52	Land (of Joseph's suffering - Egypt)
137	41:53	Egypt
138	41:54	Egypt

GENESIS (Cont.)

139	41:55	Egypt, Pharaoh during the time of Joseph, Egyptians
140	41:56	Egyptians, Egypt
141	41:57	Egypt
142	42:1	Egypt
143	42:2	Egypt
144	42:3	Egypt
145	42:6	Land (of Egypt)
146	42:9	Land (of Egypt)
147	42:12	Land (of Egypt)
148	42:15	Pharaoh during the time of Joseph
149	42:16	Pharaoh during the time of Joseph
150	42:30	Land (of Egypt)
151	42:33	Land (of Egypt)
152	42:34	Land (of Egypt)
153	43:2	Egypt
154	43:15	Egypt
155	43:32	Egyptians
156	44:18	Pharaoh during the time of Joseph
157	45:2	Egyptians, Pharaoh during the time of Joseph, his household
158	45:4	Egypt
159	45:6	Land (of Egypt)
160	45:8	Pharaoh during the time of Joseph, Egypt
161	45:9	Egypt
162	45:10	Goshen
163	45:13	Egypt
164	45:16	Pharaoh during the time of Joseph, his officials
165	45:17	Pharaoh during the time of Joseph
166	45:18	Egypt, Pharaoh during the time of Joseph
167	45:19	Egypt
168	45:20	Egypt
169	45:21	Pharaoh during the time of Joseph
170	45:23	Egypt
171	45:25	Egypt
172	45:26	Egypt
173	46:3	Egypt
174	46:4	Egypt
175	46:5	Pharaoh during the time of Joseph
176	46:6	Egypt
177	46:7	Egypt
178	46:8	Egypt
179	46:20	Egypt, Asenath, Potiphera, On
180	46:26	Egypt
181	46:27	Egypt
182	46:28	Goshen
183	46:29	Goshen
184	46:31	Pharaoh during the time of Joseph
185	46:33	Pharaoh during the time of Joseph
186	46:34	Goshen, Egyptians
187	47:1	Pharaoh during the time of Joseph, Goshen
188	47:2	Pharaoh during the time of Joseph
189	47:3	Pharaoh during the time of Joseph
190	47:4	Pharaoh during the time of Joseph, Goshen
191	47:5	Pharaoh during the time of Joseph
192	47:6	Egypt, Goshen
193	47:7	Pharaoh during the time of Joseph
194	47:8	Pharaoh during the time of Joseph
195	47:9	Pharaoh during the time of Joseph
196	47:10	Pharaoh during the time of Joseph

197	47:11	Egypt, Rameses, Pharaoh during the time of Joseph
198	47:13	Egypt
199	47:14	Egypt, Pharaoh during the time of Joseph
200	47:15	Egypt, Egyptians
201	47:16	Egyptians
202	47:17	Egyptians
203	47:18	Egyptians
204	47:19	Egyptians, Pharaoh during the time of Joseph
205	47:20	Egypt, Pharaoh during the time of Joseph, Egyptians
206	47:21	Egyptians, Egypt
207	47:22	Pharaoh during the time of Joseph
208	47:23	Egyptians, Pharaoh during the time of Joseph
209	47:24	Egyptians, Pharaoh during the time of Joseph
210	47:25	Egyptians, Pharaoh during the time of Joseph
211	47:26	Egypt, Pharaoh during the time of Joseph
212	47:27	Egypt, Goshen
213	47:28	Egypt
214	47:29	Egypt
215	47:30	Egypt
216	48:5	Egypt
217	50:2	(Egyptian) Physicians in Joseph's service
218	50:3	Egyptians
219	50:4	Pharaoh during the time of Joseph, his court
220	50:6	Pharaoh during the time of Joseph
221	50:7	Pharaoh during the time of Joseph, his officials, the dignitaries, Egypt
222	50:8	Goshen
223	50:9	Egyptian horsemen
224	50:11	Egyptians

225	50:14	Egypt
226	50:22	Egypt
227	50:26	Egypt, Egyptian physicians

EXODUS

228	1:1	Egypt
229	1:5	Egypt
230	1:7	Land (of Egypt)
231	1:8	Egypt, king/pharaoh after Joseph
232	1:9	Pharaoh after Joseph, Egyptian people
233	1:10	Pharaoh after Joseph, Egyptian people
234	1:11	Pithom, Rameses, Pharaoh after Joseph
235	1:12	Egyptians
236	1:14	Egyptians
237	1:15	King/pharaoh of Egypt
238	1:17	King/pharaoh of Egypt
239	1:18	King/pharaoh of Egypt
240	1:19	Pharaoh after Joseph, Egyptian women
241	1:22	Pharaoh after Joseph, Nile
242	2:3	Nile
243	2:5	Pharaoh's daughter, Nile
244	2:6	Pharaoh's daughter
245	2:7	Pharaoh's daughter
246	2:8	Pharaoh's daughter
247	2:9	Pharaoh's daughter
248	2:10	Pharaoh's daughter
249	2:11	Egyptian
250	2:12	Egyptian
251	2:14	Egyptian
252	2:15	Pharaoh who drove Moses out of Egypt
253	2:19	Egyptian
254	2:23	King/pharaoh who drove Moses out of Egypt
255	3:1	Desert, Mount Horeb

		EXODUS (cont.)
256	3:7	Egypt
257	3:8	Egyptians, Egypt
258	3:9	Egyptians
259	3:10	Pharaoh at the time of the Exodus, Egypt
260	3:11	Pharaoh at the time of the Exodus, Egypt
261	3:12	Egypt, Mount Horeb
262	3:16	Egypt
263	3:17	Egypt
264	3:18	King of Egypt/pharaoh at the time of the Exodus, desert
265	3:19	King of Egypt/pharaoh at the time of the Exodus
266	3:20	Egyptians, Pharaoh at the time of the Exodus
267	3:21	Egyptians
268	3:22	Egyptians
269	4:9	Nile
270	4:18	Egypt
271	4:19	Egypt
272	4:20	Egypt
273	4:21	Egypt, Pharaoh at the time of the Exodus
274	4:22	Pharaoh at the time of the Exodus
275	4:23	Pharaoh at the time of the Exodus
276	4:27	Desert, mountain of God (Horeb)
277	5:1	Pharaoh at the time of the Exodus, desert
278	5:2	Pharaoh at the time of the Exodus
279	5:3	Desert
280	5:4	King of Egypt/pharaoh at the time of the Exodus
281	5:5	Pharaoh at the time of the Exodus, Egypt
282	5:6	Pharaoh at the time of the Exodus, slave drivers
283	5:7	Slave drivers
284	5:10	Pharaoh at the time of the Exodus, slave drivers
285	5:12	Egypt
286	5:13	Slave drivers
287	5:14	Pharaoh at the time of the Exodus, his slave drivers
288	5:15	Pharaoh at the time of the Exodus
289	5:17	Pharaoh at the time of the Exodus
290	5:20	Pharaoh at the time of the Exodus
291	5:21	Pharaoh at the time of the Exodus, his officials
292	5:23	Pharaoh at the time of the Exodus
293	6:1	Pharaoh at the time of the Exodus, country (of Egypt)
294	6:5	Egyptians
295	6:6	Egyptians
296	6:7	Egyptians
297	6:11	King of Egypt/pharaoh at the time of the Exodus, his country (Egypt)
298	6:12	Pharaoh at the time of the Exodus
299	6:13	King of Egypt/pharaoh at the time of the Exodus, Egypt
300	6:25	Putiel, his daughter, Phinehas
301	6:26	Egypt
302	6:27	King of Egypt/pharaoh at the time of the Exodus, Egypt
303	6:28	Egypt
304	6:29	King of Egypt/pharaoh at the time of the Exodus
305	6:30	Pharaoh at the time of the Exodus

306	7:1	Pharaoh at the time of the Exodus
307	7:2	Pharaoh at the time of the Exodus, country (of Egypt)
308	7:3	Pharaoh at the time of the Exodus, Egypt
309	7:4	Pharaoh at the time of the Exodus, Egypt
310	7:5	Egyptians, Egypt
311	7:7	Pharaoh at the time of the Exodus
312	7:9	Pharaoh at the time of the Exodus
313	7:10	Pharaoh at the time of the Exodus, his officials
314	7:11	Pharaoh at the time of the Exodus, his wise men, sorcerers, Egyptian magicians
315	7:12	Sorcerers, Egyptian magicians
316	7:13	Pharaoh at the time of the Exodus
317	7:14	Pharaoh at the time of the Exodus
318	7:15	Pharaoh at the time of the Exodus, Nile
319	7:16	Pharaoh at the time of the Exodus, desert
320	7:17	Nile
321	7:18	Nile, Egyptians
322	7:19	Egyptian streams, canals, ponds and reservoirs, Egypt
323	7:20	Nile, Pharaoh at the time of the Exodus, his officials
324	7:21	Nile, Egyptians, Egypt
325	7:22	Egyptian magicians, Pharaoh at the time of the Exodus
326	7:23	Pharaoh at the time of the Exodus
327	7:24	Egyptians, Nile
328	7:25	Nile
329	8:1	Pharaoh at the time of the Exodus
330	8:2	Pharaoh at the time of the Exodus, country (of Egypt)
331	8:3	Nile, Pharaoh at the time of the Exodus, his officials, his people
332	8:4	Pharaoh at the time of the Exodus, his people, his officials
333	8:5	Streams, canals, ponds (of Egypt), Egypt
334	8:6	Egypt
335	8:7	Magicians, Egypt
336	8:8	Pharaoh at the time of the Exodus, his people
337	8:9	Pharaoh at the time of the Exodus, his officials, his people, Nile
338	8:10	Pharaoh at the time of the Exodus
339	8:11	Pharaoh at the time of the Exodus, his officials, his people, Nile
340	8:12	Pharaoh at the time of the Exodus
341	8:14	Land (of Egypt)
342	8:15	Pharaoh at the time of the Exodus
343	8:16	Egypt
344	8:17	Egypt
345	8:18	Magicians
346	8:19	Magicians, Pharaoh at the time of the Exodus
347	8:20	Pharaoh at the time of the Exodus
348	8:21	Pharaoh at the time of the Exodus, his officials, his people, Egyptians
349	8:22	Goshen

EXODUS (cont.)

350	8:23	Egyptians
351	8:24	Pharaoh at the time of the Exodus, his officials, Egypt
352	8:25	Pharaoh at the time of the Exodus
353	8:26	Egyptians
354	8:27	Desert
355	8:28	Pharaoh at the time of the Exodus, desert
356	8:29	Pharaoh at the time of the Exodus, his officials, his people
357	8:30	Pharaoh at the time of the Exodus
358	8:31	Pharaoh at the time of the Exodus, his officials, his people
359	8:32	Pharaoh at the time of the Exodus
360	9:1	Pharaoh at the time of the Exodus
361	9:2	Pharaoh at the time of the Exodus
362	9:4	Egypt
363	9:5	Land (of Egypt)
364	9:6	Egyptians
365	9:7	Pharaoh at the time of the Exodus
366	9:8	Pharaoh at the time of the Exodus
367	9:9	Egypt
368	9:10	Pharaoh at the time of the Exodus
369	9:11	Magicians, Egyptians
370	9:12	Pharaoh at the time of the Exodus
371	9:13	Pharaoh at the time of the Exodus
372	9:14	Pharaoh at the time of the Exodus, his officials and people
373	9:15	Pharaoh at the time of the Exodus, Egyptians
374	9:16	Pharaoh at the time of the Exodus
375	9:17	Pharaoh at the time of the Exodus
376	9:18	Egypt
377	9:19	Pharaoh at the time of the Exodus, every man (Egyptian)
378	9:20	Pharaoh at the time of the Exodus, his officials
379	9:21	Egyptians
380	9:22	Egyptians, Egypt
381	9:23	Egypt
382	9:24	Egypt
383	9:25	Egypt, Egyptians
384	9:26	Goshen
385	9:27	Pharaoh at the time of the Exodus, Egyptians
386	9:28	Pharaoh at the time of the Exodus
387	9:29	Pharaoh at the time of the Exodus
388	9:30	Pharaoh at the time of the Exodus, his officials
389	9:33	Pharaoh at the time of the Exodus
390	9:34	Pharaoh at the time of the Exodus, Egyptians
391	9:35	Pharaoh at the time of the Exodus
392	10:1	Pharaoh at the time of the Exodus, officials
393	10:2	Egyptians
394	10:3	Pharaoh at the time of the Exodus
395	10:4	Country (of Egypt), Pharaoh at the time of the Exodus

396	10:6	Egyptians, Pharaoh at the time of the Exodus, country (of Egypt)
397	10:7	Pharaoh at the time of the Exodus, his officials, Egypt
398	10:8	Pharaoh at the time of the Exodus
399	10:10	Pharaoh at the time of the Exodus
400	10:11	Pharaoh at the time of the Exodus
401	10:12	Egypt
402	10:13	Egypt
403	10:14	Egypt
404	10:15	Egypt
405	10:16	Pharaoh at the time of the Exodus
406	10:17	Pharaoh at the time of the Exodus
407	10:18	Pharaoh at the time of the Exodus
408	10:19	Red Sea, Egypt
409	10:20	Pharaoh at the time of the Exodus
410	10:21	Egypt
411	10:22	Egypt
412	10:24	Pharaoh at the time of the Exodus
413	10:25	Pharaoh at the time of the Exodus
414	10:27	Pharaoh at the time of the Exodus
415	10:28	Pharaoh at the time of the Exodus
416	10:29	Pharaoh at the time of the Exodus
417	11:1	Pharaoh at the time of the Exodus, Egypt
418	11:3	Egyptians, Egypt, Pharaoh at the time of the Exodus, his officials
419	11:4	Egypt
420	11:5	Egyptians, Egypt, Pharaoh at the time of the Exodus
421	11:6	Egypt
422	11:7	Egypt
423	11:8	Pharaoh at the time of the Exodus, his officials
424	11:9	Pharaoh at the time of the Exodus, Egypt
425	11:10	Pharaoh at the time of the Exodus, country (of Egypt)
426	12:1	Egypt
427	12:12	Egypt, Egyptians
428	12:13	Egypt
429	12:17	Egypt
430	12:23	Land (of Egypt), Egyptians
431	12:27	Egypt, Egyptians
432	12:29	Egyptians, Egypt, Pharaoh at the time of the Exodus
433	12:30	Pharaoh at the time of the Exodus, his officials, Egyptians, Egypt
434	12:31	Pharaoh at the time of the Exodus
435	12:32	Pharaoh at the time of the Exodus
436	12:33	Egyptians, country (of Egypt)
437	12:35	Egyptians
438	12:36	Egyptians
439	12:37	Rameses, Succoth
440	12:39	Egypt
441	12:40	Egypt
442	12:41	Egypt
443	12:42	Egypt
444	12:51	Egypt
445	13:3	Egypt
446	13:8	Egypt
447	13:9	Egypt
448	13:14	Egypt

EXODUS (cont.)

449	13:15	Pharaoh at the time of the Exodus, Egyptians, Egypt
450	13:16	Egypt
451	13:17	Pharaoh at the time of the Exodus, Egypt
452	13:18	Desert, Red Sea, Egypt
453	13:20	Succoth, Etham, desert
454	14:2	Pi Hahiroth, Midgol, Red Sea, Baal Zephon
455	14:3	Pharaoh at the time of the Exodus, desert
456	14:4	Pharaoh at the time of the Exodus, his army, Egyptians
457	14:5	King of Egypt/pharaoh at the time of the Exodus, his officials
458	14:6	Pharaoh at the time of the Exodus, his army
459	14:7	Pharaoh at the time of the Exodus, Egypt, his officers
460	14:8	King of Egypt/pharaoh at the time of the Exodus
461	14:9	Egyptians, Pharaoh at the time of the Exodus, his horsemen and troops, Red Sea, Pi Hahiroth, Baal Zephon
462	14:10	Pharaoh at the time of the Exodus, Egyptians
463	14:11	Egypt, desert
464	14:12	Egypt, Egyptians, desert
465	14:13	Egyptians
466	14:16	Red Sea
467	14:17	Egyptians, Pharaoh at the time of the Exodus, his army/his horsemen
468	14:18	Egyptians, Pharaoh at the time of the Exodus, his horsemen
469	14:20	Armies of Egypt
470	14:21	Red Sea
471	14:22	Red Sea
472	14:23	Egyptians, Pharaoh at the time of the Exodus, his horsemen, Red Sea
473	14:24	Egyptian army
474	14:25	Egyptian (army)
475	14:26	Red Sea, Egyptians, the horsemen
476	14:27	Red Sea, Egyptian (army)
477	14:28	Pharaoh's horsemen/army, Pharaoh at the time of the Exodus, Red Sea
478	14:29	Red Sea
479	14:30	Egyptians
480	14:31	Egyptians
481	15:1	Red Sea, rider
482	15:4	Red Sea, Pharaoh at the time of the Exodus, his officers
483	15:5	Red Sea, Egyptian army
484	15:8	Red Sea
485	15:10	Red Sea
486	15:19	Pharaoh at the time of the Exodus, his horsemen, Red Sea
487	15:21	Red Sea, rider
488	15:22	Red Sea, desert of Shur
489	15:23	Marah
490	15:26	Egyptians
491	15:27	Elim
492	16:1	Elim, desert of Sin, Sinai, Egypt
493	16:2	Desert of Sin
494	16:3	Egypt, desert of Sin
495	16:6	Egypt
496	16:10	Desert of Sin
497	16:14	Desert of Sin
498	16:32	Egypt, desert of Sin
499	17:1	Desert of Sin, Rephidim
500	17:3	Egypt
501	17:5	Nile

502	17:6	Horeb
503	17:7	Massah/Meribah
504	17:8	Rephidim
505	18:1	Egypt
506	18:4	Pharaoh who drove Moses from Egypt
507	18:5	Desert and mountain of Horeb
508	18:8	Pharaoh at the time of the Exodus, Egyptians
509	18:9	Egyptians
510	18:10	Egyptians, Pharaoh at the time of the Exodus
511	19:1	Egypt, desert of Sinai
512	19:2	Rephidim, desert of Sinai, Mount Sinai
513	19:3	Mount Sinai
514	19:4	Egypt
515	19:11	Mount Sinai
516	19:12	Mount Sinai
517	19:13	Mount Sinai
518	19:14	Mount Sinai
519	19:16	Mount Sinai
520	19:17	Mount Sinai
521	19:18	Mount Sinai
522	19:20	Mount Sinai
523	19:23	Mount Sinai
524	20:2	Egypt
525	20:18	Mount Sinai
526	22:21	Egypt
527	23:9	Egypt
528	23:15	Egypt
529	23:31	Red Sea
530	24:4	Mount Sinai
531	24:12	Mount Sinai
532	24:13	Mount Sinai
533	24:15	Mount Sinai
534	24:16	Mount Sinai
535	24:17	Mount Sinai
536	24:18	Mount Sinai
537	25:40	Mount Sinai
538	26:30	Mount Sinai
539	27:8	Mount Sinai
540	29:46	Egypt
541	31:18	Mount Sinai
542	32:1	Mount Sinai, Egypt
543	32:4	Egypt
544	32:7	Egypt
545	32:8	Egypt
546	32:11	Egypt
547	32:12	Egyptians
548	32:15	Mount Sinai
549	32:19	Mount Sinai
550	32:23	Egypt
551	33:1	Egypt
552	33:6	Mount Horeb
553	34:2	Mount Sinai
554	34:3	Mount Sinai
555	34:4	Mount Sinai
556	34:18	Egypt
557	34:29	Mount Sinai
558	34:32	Mount Sinai

LEVITICUS

559	7:38	Mount Sinai, desert of Sinai
560	11:45	Egypt
561	18:3	Egypt
562	19:34	Egypt
563	19:36	Egypt
564	22:33	Egypt
565	23:43	Egypt
566	24:10	Egyptian (father)
567	25:1	Mount Sinai
568	25:38	Egypt
569	25:42	Egypt
570	25:55	Egypt
571	26:13	Egypt, Egyptians
572	26:45	Egypt
573	26:46	Mount Sinai

574	27:34	Mount Sinai

NUMBERS

575	1:1	Desert of Sinai, Egypt
576	1:19	Desert of Sinai
577	3:1	Mount Sinai
578	3:4	Desert of Sinai
579	3:13	Egypt, firstborn (Egyptians)
580	3:14	Desert of Sinai
581	8:17	Egypt, firstborn (Egyptians)
582	9:1	Desert of Sinai, Egypt
583	9:5	Desert of Sinai
584	10:12	Desert of Sinai, desert of Paran
585	10:31	Desert of Paran
586	10:33	Mount Sinai
587	11:3	Taberah
588	11:5	Egypt
589	11:18	Egypt
590	11:20	Egypt
591	11:34	Kibroth Hattaavah
592	11:35	Kibroth Hattaavah, Hazeroth
593	12:1	Cushite (wife)
594	12:16	Hazeroth, desert of Paran
595	13:3	Desert of Paran
596	13:22	Zoan, Egypt
597	13:26	Desert of Paran
598	14:2	Egypt
599	14:3	Egypt
600	14:4	Egypt
601	14:13	Egyptians
602	14:19	Egypt
603	14:22	Egypt, desert
604	14:25	Desert, Red Sea
605	14:29	Desert
606	14:32	Desert
607	14:33	Desert
608	14:35	Desert
609	15:41	Egypt
610	16:13	Desert
611	20:5	Egypt
612	20:15	Egypt, Egyptians
613	20:16	Egypt
614	21:4	Red Sea
615	21:5	Egypt
616	22:5	Egypt
617	22:11	Egypt
618	23:22	Egypt
619	24:8	Egypt
620	25:7	Phinehas
621	25:8	Phinehas
622	25:11	Phinehas
623	25:12	Phinehas
624	25:13	Phinehas
625	26:4	Egypt
626	26:59	Egypt
627	26:64	Desert of Sinai
628	28:6	Mount Sinai
629	31:6	Phinehas
630	32:11	Egypt
631	32:13	Desert
632	33:1	Egypt
633	33:3	Rameses, Egyptians
634	33:4	Egyptians, firstborn
635	33:5	Rameses, Succoth
636	33:6	Succoth, Etham, desert
637	33:7	Etham, Pi Hahiroth, Baal Zephon, Midgol
638	33:8	Pi Hahiroth, Red Sea, desert of Etham, Marah
639	33:9	Marah, Elim
640	33:10	Elim, Red Sea
641	33:11	Red Sea, desert of Sin
642	33:12	Desert of Sin, Dophkah
643	33:13	Dophkah, Alush
644	33:14	Alush, Rephidim
645	33:15	Rephidim, desert of Sinai

646	33:16	Desert of Sinai, Kibroth Hattaavah
647	33:17	Kibroth Hattaavah, Hazeroth
648	33:18	Hazeroth, Rithmah
649	33:19	Rithmah, Rimmon Perez
650	33:20	Rimmon Perez, Libnah
651	33:21	Libnah, Rissah
652	33:22	Rissah, Kehelathah
653	33:23	Kehelathah, Mount Shepher
654	33:24	Mount Shepher, Haradah
655	33:25	Haradah, Makheloth
656	33:26	Makheloth, Tahath
657	33:27	Tahath, Terah
658	33:28	Terah, Mithcah
659	33:29	Mithcah, Hashmonah
660	33:30	Hashmonah, Moseroth
661	33:31	Moseroth, Bene Jaakan
662	33:32	Bene Jaakan, Hor Haggidgad
663	33:33	Hor Haggidgad, Jotbathah
664	33:34	Jotbathah, Abronah
665	33:35	Abronah
666	33:38	Egypt
667	34:5	Egypt

DEUTERONOMY

668	1:2	Mount Horeb
669	1:6	Mount Horeb
670	1:19	Mount Horeb
671	1:27	Egypt
672	1:30	Egypt
673	1:31	Desert
674	1:40	Red Sea, desert (of Paran)
675	2:1	Red Sea
676	2:7	Desert
677	4:10	Mount Horeb
678	4:11	Mount Horeb
679	4:15	Mount Horeb
680	4:20	Egypt

681	4:34	Egypt
682	4:37	Egypt
683	4:45	Egypt
684	4:46	Egypt
685	5:2	Mount Horeb
686	5:4	Mount Horeb
687	5:5	Mount Horeb
688	5:6	Egypt
689	5:15	Egypt
690	5:22	Mount Horeb
691	5:23	Mount Horeb
692	6:12	Egypt
693	6:16	Massah
694	6:21	Pharaoh at the time of the Exodus, Egypt
695	6:22	Egypt, Pharaoh at the time of the Exodus
696	7:8	Pharaoh at the time of the Exodus/king of Egypt
697	7:15	Egypt
698	7:18	Pharaoh at the time of the Exodus, Egypt
699	8:2	Desert
700	8:14	Egypt
701	8:15	Desert
702	8:16	Desert
703	9:7	Desert, Egypt
704	9:8	Mount Horeb
705	9:9	Mount Horeb
706	9:10	Mount Horeb
707	9:12	Egypt
708	9:15	Mount Horeb
709	9:21	Mount Horeb
710	9:22	Taberah, Massah, Kibroth Hattaavah
711	9:26	Egypt
712	9:28	Desert
713	10:1	Mount Horeb
714	10:3	Mount Horeb
715	10:4	Mount Horeb

	DEUTERONOMY (cont.)	
716	10:5	Mount Horeb
717	10:6	Wells of the Jaakanites, Moserah
718	10:7	Gudgodah, Jotbathah
719	10:10	Mount Horeb
720	10:19	Egypt
721	10:22	Egypt
722	11:3	Egypt, Pharaoh/king of Egypt
723	11:4	Egyptian army, Red Sea
724	11:5	Desert
725	11:10	Egypt
726	13:5	Egypt
727	13:10	Egypt
728	15:15	Egypt
729	16:1	Egypt
730	16:3	Egypt
731	16:6	Egypt
732	16:12	Egypt
733	17:16	Egypt
734	18:16	Mount Horeb
735	20:1	Egypt
736	23:4	Egypt
737	23:7	Egyptian, country (of Egypt)
738	23:8	Egyptians
739	24:9	Egypt
740	24:18	Egypt
741	24:22	Egypt
742	25:17	Egypt
743	26:5	Egypt
744	26:6	Egyptians
745	26:8	Egypt
746	28:27	Egypt
747	28:60	Egypt
748	28:68	Egypt
749	29:1	Mount Horeb
750	29:2	Egypt, Pharaoh at the time of the Exodus, his oficials, land (of Egypt)

751	29:5	Desert
752	29:16	Egypt
753	29:25	Egypt
754	33:2	Sinai, Mount Paran
755	33:8	Massah, Meribah
756	34:11	Egypt, Pharaoh at the time of the Exodus, his officials, land (of Egypt)
	JOSHUA	
757	2:10	Egypt, Red Sea
758	4:23	Red Sea
759	5:4	Egypt, desert
760	5:5	Egypt, desert
761	5:6	Desert, Egypt
762	5:9	Egypt
763	9:9	Egypt
764	13:3	Egypt
765	15:4	Egypt
766	15:47	Egypt
767	22:13	Phinehas
768	22:14	Phinehas
769	22:30	Phinehas
770	22:31	Phinehas
771	22:32	Phinehas
772	24:4	Egypt
773	24:5	Egyptians
774	24:6	Egypt, Red Sea, Egyptians, horsemen
775	24:7	Egyptians, Red Sea, desert
776	24:14	Egypt
777	24:17	Egypt
778	24:32	Egypt
779	24:33	Phinehas
	JUDGES	
780	2:1	Egypt
781	2:12	Egypt
782	5:5	Mount Sinai
783	6:8	Egypt
784	6:9	Egypt

785	6:13	Egypt
786	10:11	Egyptians
787	11:13	Egypt
788	11:16	Egypt, Red Sea, desert
789	19:30	Egypt
790	20:28	Phinehas

1 SAMUEL

791	2:27	Egypt, Pharaoh at the time of the Exodus
792	4:8	Egyptians, desert
793	6:6	Egyptians, Pharaoh at the time of the Exodus
794	8:8	Egypt
795	10:18	Egypt
796	12:6	Egypt
797	12:8	Egypt
798	15:2	Egypt
799	15:6	Egypt
800	15:7	Shur, Egypt
801	27:8	Shur, Egypt
802	30:11	Egyptian
803	30:12	Egyptian
804	30:13	Egyptian
805	30:15	Egyptian
806	30:16	Egyptian

2 SAMUEL

807	7:6	Egypt
808	7:23	Egypt
809	18:21	A Cushite
810	18:22	A Cushite
811	18:23	A Cushite
812	18:26	A Cushite
813	18:29	A Cushite
814	18:31	A Cushite
815	18:32	A Cushite
816	23:21	Egyptian

1 KINGS

817	3:1	Pharaoh/king of Egypt at the time of Solomon, Pharaoh's daughter
818	4:21	Egypt
819	4:30	Egypt
820	6:1	Egypt
821	7:8	Pharaoh's daughter at the time of Solomon
822	8:9	Mount Horeb, Egypt
823	8:16	Egypt
824	8:21	Egypt
825	8:51	Egypt
826	8:53	Egypt
827	8:65	Egypt
828	9:9	Egypt
829	9:16	Pharaoh/king of Egypt at the time of Solomon, Pharaoh's daughter
830	9:24	Pharaoh's daughter at the time of Solomon
831	9:26	Red Sea
832	10:28	Egypt
833	10:29	Egypt
834	11:1	Pharaoh's daughter at the time of Solomon
835	11:17	Egypt
836	11:18	Paran, Egypt, Pharaoh husband of Queen Tahpenes
837	11:19	Pharaoh husband of Tahpenes, Queen Tahpenes, her sister
838	11:20	Tahpenes, her sister, Pharaoh husband of Tahpenes
839	11:21	Egypt, Pharaoh husband of Tahpenes
840	11:22	Pharaoh husband of Tahpenes
841	11:40	Egypt, Shishak
842	12:2	Egypt
843	12:28	Egypt
844	14:25	Shishak, Egypt
845	14:26	Shishak
846	19:8	Mount Horeb

2 KINGS

847	7:6	Egyptian kings
848	17:4	(Pharaoh) So, Egypt
849	17:7	Egypt, Pharaoh at the time of the Exodus
850	17:36	Egypt
851	18:21	Egypt, (Pharaoh) Tirhakah
852	18:24	Egypt, its horsemen
853	19:9	(Pharaoh) Tirhakah, Cushite, Egypt
854	21:15	Egypt
855	23:29	Pharaoh Neco, Egypt
856	23:33	Pharaoh Neco
857	23:34	Pharaoh Neco, Egypt
858	23:35	Pharaoh Neco
859	24:7	Pharaoh Neco, Egypt
860	25:26	Egypt

1 CHRONICLES

861	1:8	Cush, Mizraim, Put
862	1:9	Cush, Seba
863	1:10	Cush
864	1:11	Mizraim, Ludites, Anamites, Lehabites, Naphtuhites
865	1:12	Pathrusites, Casluhites
866	2:34	Egyptian, Jarha
867	2:35	Jarha
868	4:18	Bithiah, Pharaoh father of Bithiah
869	6:4	Phinehas
870	6:50	Phinehas
871	9:20	Phinehas
872	11:23	Egyptian
873	13:5	Egypt
874	17:21	Egypt
875	21:29	Desert

2 CHRONICLES

876	1:3	Desert
877	1:16	Egypt
878	1:17	Egypt
879	5:10	(Mount) Horeb, Egypt
880	6:5	Egypt
881	7:8	Egypt
882	7:22	Egypt
883	8:11	Pharaoh's daughter at the time of Solomon
884	9:26	Egypt
885	9:28	Egypt
886	10:2	Egypt
887	12:2	Shishak, Egypt
888	12:3	Shishak, horsemen, Egypt, Libyans, Sukkites, Cushites
889	12:4	Shishak
890	12:5	Shishak
891	12:7	Shishak
892	12:8	Shishak
893	12:9	Shishak, Egypt
894	14:9	Zerah, Cushite, his army
895	14:10	Zerah
896	14:11	Cushite army
897	14:12	Cushites
898	14:13	Cushites
899	16:8	Cushites, Libyans, horsemen
900	20:10	Egypt
901	21:16	Cushites
902	26:8	Egypt
903	35:20	Pharaoh Neco, Egypt
904	35:21	Pharaoh Neco
905	35:22	Pharaoh Neco
906	36:3	Pharaoh Neco, Egypt
907	36:4	Pharaoh Neco, Egypt

EZRA

908	7:5	Phinehas
909	9:1	Egyptians

NEHEMIAH

910	9:9	Egypt, Red Sea

911	9:10	Pharaoh at the time of the Exodus, his officials, his people, land (Egypt), Egyptians
912	9:13	Mount Sinai
913	9:18	Egypt
914	9:19	Desert
915	9:21	Desert

ESTHER

916	1:1	Cush
917	8:9	Cush

JOB

918	28:19	Cush

PSALMS

919	68:8	Sinai
920	68:17	Sinai
921	68:30	Egypt (beast among the reeds)
922	68:31	Egypt, Cush
923	72:10	Seba
924	78:12	Egypt, Zoan
925	78:15	Desert
926	78:17	Desert
927	78:19	Desert
928	78:40	Desert
929	78:43	Egypt, Zoan
930	78:51	Egypt
931	78:52	Desert
932	78:53	Red Sea
933	80:8	Egypt
934	81:5	Egypt
935	81:7	Meribah
936	81:10	Egypt
937	87:4	Rahab (Egypt), Cush
938	89:10	Rahab (Egypt)
939	95:8	Meribah, Massah, desert
940	105:23	Egypt (land of Ham)
941	105:27	Egypt (land of Ham)
942	105:38	Egypt

943	106:7	Egypt, Red Sea
944	106:9	Red Sea
945	106:14	Desert
946	106:19	Horeb
947	106:21	Egypt
948	106:22	Egypt (land of Ham), Red Sea
949	106:26	Desert
950	106:30	Phinehas
951	106:31	Phinehas
952	106:32	Meribah
953	114:1	Egypt
954	114:3	Red Sea
955	114:5	Red Sea
956	114:8	(Sinai desert)
957	135:8	Egypt, firstborn (Egyptians)
958	135:9	Egypt, Pharaoh at the time of the Exodus, his servants
959	136:10	Egypt, firstborn (Egyptians)
960	136:11	Egyptians
961	136:13	Red Sea
962	136:14	Red Sea
963	136:15	Pharaoh at the time of the Exodus, his army, Red Sea
964	136:16	Desert

PROVERBS

965	7:16	Egypt

SONG OF SONGS

966	1:9	Pharaoh at the time of Solomon

ISAIAH

967	7:18	Distant streams of Egypt (Nile)
968	10:24	Egypt
969	10:26	Waters (Red Sea), Egypt
970	11:11	Lower Egypt, Upper Egypt, Cush

ISAIAH (cont.)

971	11:15	Egyptian sea (Red Sea)
972	11:16	Egypt
973	18:1	Cush, its rivers (Nile)
974	18:2	Cush, its rivers (Nile), Cushites
975	18:7	Cush, its rivers (Nile), Cushites
976	19:1	Egypt, Egyptians
977	19:2	Egyptian
978	19:3	Egyptians, its mediums and spiritists
979	19:4	Egyptians
980	19:5	River (Nile)
981	19:6	Canals, streams (Nile), Egypt
982	19:7	Nile, river
983	19:8	Nile, Egyptian fishermen
984	19:9	Egyptian weavers
985	19:10	Egyptian cloth workers
986	19:11	Zoan, Pharaoh (Shabaka, Shebitku or Tirhakah), his officials, his counselors
987	19:12	Wise men, Egypt
988	19:13	Officials of Zoan, leaders of Memphis, Egypt
989	19:14	Egyptians, Egypt
990	19:15	Egypt
991	19:16	Egyptians
992	19:17	Egyptians
993	19:18	Egypt, City of Destruction (Heliopolis)
994	19:19	Egypt
995	19:20	Egypt, Egyptians
996	19:21	Egyptians
997	19:22	Egypt, Egyptians
998	19:23	Egypt, Egyptians
999	19:24	Egypt
1000	19:25	Egypt
1001	20:3	Egypt, Cush
1002	20:4	Egyptian captives, Cushite exiles, Egypt
1003	20:5	Cush, Egypt
1004	23:3	Nile
1005	23:5	Egypt
1006	23:10	Nile
1007	27:12	Egypt
1008	27:13	Egypt
1009	30:2	Egypt, Pharaoh (Shabaka, Shebitku or Tirhakah)
1010	30:3	Pharaoh (Shabaka, Shebitku or Tirhakah), Egypt
1011	30:4	Zoan, Hanes
1012	30:6	Egypt
1013	30:7	Egypt
1014	31:1	Egypt, its horsemen
1015	31:3	Egyptians
1016	36:6	Egypt, Pharaoh/king of Egypt (Tirhakah)
1017	36:9	Egypt, its horsemen
1018	37:9	Tirhakah, Cushite, Egypt
1019	43:3	Egypt, Cush, Seba
1020	45:14	Egypt, Cush, Sabeans
1021	49:12	Aswan
1022	50:2	Red Sea
1023	51:9	Rahab (Egypt)
1024	51:10	Red Sea
1025	52:4	Egypt
1026	66:19	Libyans, Lydians

JEREMIAH

1027	2:6	Egypt, desert
1028	2:16	Memphis, Tahpanhes
1029	2:18	Egypt, Shihor (Nile)
1030	2:36	Egypt
1031	7:22	Egypt
1032	7:25	Egypt
1033	9:26	Egypt
1034	11:4	Egypt
1035	11:7	Egypt

1036	13:23	Ethiopian
1037	16:14	Egypt
1038	23:7	Egypt
1039	24:8	Egypt
1040	25:19	Pharaoh (Neco), Egypt, his officials, his people
1041	26:21	Egypt
1042	26:22	Egypt
1043	26:23	Egypt
1044	31:32	Egypt
1045	32:20	Egypt
1046	32:21	Egypt
1047	34:13	Egypt
1048	36:14	Cushi
1049	37:5	Pharaoh (Hophra), his army, Egypt
1050	37:7	Pharaoh (Hophra), his army, Egypt
1051	37:11	Pharaoh (Hophra), his army
1052	38:7	Ebed-Melech, Cushite
1053	38:8	Ebed-Melech
1054	38:10	Ebed-Melech, Cushite
1055	38:11	Ebed-Melech
1056	38:12	Ebed-Melech, Cushite
1057	39:16	Ebed-Melech, Cushite
1058	39:17	Ebed-Melech
1059	39:18	Ebed-Melech
1060	41:17	Egypt
1061	42:14	Egypt
1062	42:15	Egypt
1063	42:16	Egypt
1064	42:17	Egypt
1065	42:18	Egypt
1066	42:19	Egypt
1067	42:22	Egypt
1068	43:2	Egypt
1069	43:7	Egypt, Tahpanhes
1070	43:8	Tahpanhes
1071	43:9	Pharaoh (Hophra), Tahpanhes

1072	43:11	Egypt
1073	43:12	Egypt
1074	43:13	Temple of the sun, Egypt
1075	44:1	Lower Egypt, Migdol, Tahpanhes, Memphis, Upper Egypt
1076	44:8	Egypt
1077	44:12	Egypt
1078	44:13	Egypt
1079	44:14	Egypt
1080	44:15	Lower and Upper Egypt
1081	44:24	Egypt
1082	44:26	Egypt
1083	44:27	Egypt
1084	44:28	Egypt
1085	44:30	Pharaoh Hophra, Egypt
1086	46:2	Egypt, Pharaoh Neco, his army
1087	46:4	Horsemen of Egypt
1088	46:5	Horsemen of Egypt
1089	46:6	Horsemen of Egypt
1090	46:7	Nile
1091	46:8	Egypt, Nile
1092	46:9	Charioteers, warriors, men of Cush, Put, men of Lydia
1093	46:10	(Egyptian) foes
1094	46:11	Egypt
1095	46:12	Egyptian army
1096	46:13	Egypt
1097	46:14	Egypt, Migdol, Memphis, Tahpanhes
1098	46:15	Egyptian army
1099	46:16	Egyptian army
1100	46:17	Pharaoh (Neco or Hophra), Egypt
1101	46:19	Egypt, Memphis
1102	46:20	Egypt
1103	46:21	Egyptian army
1104	46:24	Egypt

1105	46:25	Thebes, Pharaoh (Neco or Hophra), Egypt
1106	47:1	Pharaoh (Neco or Hophra)
1107	49:21	Red Sea

LAMENTATIONS

1108	5:6	Egypt

EZEKIEL

1109	16:26	Egyptians
1110	17:7	(Pharaoh Hophra)
1111	17:15	Egypt
1112	17:17	Pharaoh (Hophra), his army
1113	19:4	Egypt
1114	20:5	Egypt
1115	20:6	Egypt
1116	20:7	Egypt
1117	20:8	Egypt
1118	20:9	Egypt
1119	20:10	Egypt, desert
1120	20:13	Desert
1121	20:15	Desert
1122	20:17	Desert
1123	20:18	Desert
1124	20:21	Desert
1125	20:23	Desert
1126	20:36	Desert, Egypt
1127	23:3	Egypt
1128	23:8	Egypt
1129	23:19	Egypt
1130	23:21	Egypt
1131	23:27	Egypt
1132	23:42	Sabeans
1133	27:7	Egypt
1134	27:10	Lydia, Put
1135	29:2	Pharaoh (Hophra), Egypt
1136	29:3	Pharaoh (Hophra), Egypt, Nile
1137	29:4	(Pharaoh Hophra), streams (of Egypt)
1138	29:5	(Pharaoh Hophra), desert, streams (of Egypt)
1139	29:6	(Pharaoh Hophra) Egypt
1140	29:7	(Pharaoh Hophra)
1141	29:8	(Pharaoh Hophra), his (Egyptian) men
1142	29:9	Egypt, (Pharaoh Hophra), Nile
1143	29:10	(Pharaoh Hophra), streams (of Egypt), Migdol, Aswan, Cush
1144	29:12	Egypt, Egyptians
1145	29:13	Egyptians
1146	29:14	Upper Egypt, Egyptians
1147	29:16	Egypt
1148	29:19	Egypt
1149	29:20	Egypt
1150	30:4	Egypt, Cush
1151	30:5	Cush, Put, Lydia, Libya (Cub), Egypt
1152	30:6	Egypt, Migdol, Aswan
1153	30:8	Egypt
1154	30:9	Cush, Egypt, Cushites
1155	30:10	Egypt
1156	30:11	Egypt
1157	30:12	Nile, land (of Egypt)
1158	30:13	Memphis, Egypt
1159	30:14	Upper Egypt, Zoan, Thebes
1160	30:15	Pelusium, Egypt, Thebes
1161	30:16	Egypt, Pelusium, Thebes, Memphis
1162	30:17	Heliopolis, Bubastis
1163	30:18	Tahpanhes, Egypt
1164	30:19	Egypt
1165	30:21	Pharaoh (Hophra), Egypt
1166	30:22	Pharaoh (Hophra), Egypt
1167	30:23	Egyptians
1168	30:24	Pharaoh (Hophra)
1169	30:25	Pharaoh (Hophra), Egypt

1170	30:26	Egyptians
1171	31:2	Pharaoh (Hophra), Egypt, his hordes
1172	31:18	Pharaoh (Hophra), his hordes
1173	32:2	Pharaoh (Hophra), Egypt, streams (of Egypt)
1174	32:3	(Pharaoh Hophra)
1175	32:4	(Pharaoh Hophra)
1176	32:5	(Pharaoh Hophra)
1177	32:6	(Pharaoh Hophra)
1178	32:7	(Pharaoh Hophra)
1179	32:8	(Pharaoh Hophra), land (of Egypt)
1180	32:9	Pharaoh (Hophra)
1181	32:10	Pharaoh (Hophra)
1182	32:11	Pharaoh (Hophra)
1183	32:12	Pharaoh (Hophra), Egypt, her hordes
1184	32:13	Abundant waters (of Egypt)
1185	32:14	Streams (of Egypt)
1186	32:15	Egypt, Egyptians
1187	32:16	Egypt, her hordes
1188	32:18	Egypt, her hordes
1189	32:19	Egypt, her hordes
1190	32:20	Egypt, its army, her hordes
1191	32:21	Egypt, its army
1192	32:28	Pharaoh (Hophra), Egyptians
1193	32:31	Pharaoh (Hophra), his army
1194	32:32	Pharaoh (Hophra), his hordes
1195	38:5	Cush, Put

DANIEL

1196	9:15	Egypt
1197	11:8	Egypt
1198	11:42	Egypt
1199	11:43	Egypt, Libyans, Nubians

HOSEA

1200	2:15	Egypt
1201	7:11	Egypt
1202	7:16	Egypt
1203	8:13	Egypt
1204	9:3	Egypt
1205	9:6	Egypt, Memphis
1206	11:1	Egypt
1207	11:5	Egypt
1208	11:11	Egypt
1209	12:1	Egypt
1210	12:9	Egypt
1211	12:13	Egypt
1212	13:4	Egypt
1213	13:5	Desert

JOEL

1214	3:19	Egypt

AMOS

1215	2:10	Egypt, desert
1216	3:1	Egypt
1217	3:9	Egypt
1218	4:10	Egypt
1219	5:25	Desert
1220	8:8	Nile, Egypt
1221	9:5	Nile, Egypt
1222	9:7	Cushites, Egypt

MICAH

1223	6:4	Egypt
1224	7:12	Egypt
1225	7:15	Egypt

NAHUM

1226	3:8	Thebes, Nile
1227	3:9	Cush, Egypt, Put, Libya

HABAKKUK

1228	3:3	Mount Paran

ZEPHANIAH

1229	1:1	Cushi
1230	2:12	Cushites

1231	3:10	Rivers of Cush, sub-Saharan Africans

HAGGAI

1232	2:5	Egypt

ZECHARIAH

1233	10:10	Egypt
1234	10:11	Nile, Egypt, Red Sea
1235	14:18	Egyptian people
1236	14:19	Egypt

MALACHI

1237	2:4	Phinehas
1238	2:5	Phinehas
1239	2:6	Phinehas
1240	2:8	Phinehas
1241	4:4	(Mount) Horeb

MATTHEW

1242	2:13	Egypt
1243	2:14	Egypt
1244	2:15	Egypt
1245	2:19	Egypt
1246	27:32	Cyrene

MARK

1247	15:21	Cyrene

LUKE

1248	23:26	Cyrene

JOHN

1249	6:31	Desert
1250	6:49	Desert

ACTS

1251	2:9	Residents of Egypt and Libya/Cyrene
1252	2:10	Egypt, Libya, Cyrene
1253	6:9	Cyrene, Alexandria
1254	7:9	Egypt
1255	7:10	Pharaoh during the time of Joseph, Egypt
1256	7:11	Egypt
1257	7:12	Egypt
1258	7:13	Pharaoh during the time of Joseph

1259	7:15	Egypt
1260	7:17	Egypt
1261	7:18	Pharaoh after the death of Joseph, Egypt
1262	7:19	Pharaoh after the death of Joseph
1263	7:21	Pharaoh's daughter
1264	7:22	Egyptians
1265	7:24	Egyptian
1266	7:28	Egyptian
1267	7:30	Desert, Mount Sinai
1268	7:34	Egypt
1269	7:36	Egypt, Red Sea, desert
1270	7:38	Desert, Mount Sinai
1271	7:39	Egypt
1272	7:40	Egypt
1273	7:42	Desert
1274	7:44	Desert
1275	8:27	Ethiopian eunuch, Candace, Ethiopians
1276	8:28	Ethiopian eunuch
1277	8:30	Ethiopian eunuch
1278	8:31	Ethiopian eunuch
1279	8:32	Ethiopian eunuch
1280	8:34	Ethiopian eunuch
1281	8:35	Ethiopian eunuch
1282	8:36	Ethiopian eunuch
1283	8:38	Ethiopian eunuch
1284	8:39	Ethiopian eunuch
1285	11:20	Cyrene
1286	13:1	Simeon called Niger, Cyrene
1287	13:17	Egypt
1288	13:18	Desert
1289	18:24	Apollos, Alexandria
1290	18:25	Apollos
1291	18:26	Apollos
1292	18:27	Apollos
1293	18:28	Apollos
1294	19:1	Apollos

1295	21:38	Egyptian
1296	27:6	Alexandrian
1297	28:11	Alexandrian

ROMANS

1298	9:17	Pharaoh at the time of the Exodus

1 CORINTHIANS

1299	1:12	Apollos
1300	3:4	Apollos
1301	3:5	Apollos
1302	3:6	Apollos
1303	3:22	Apollos
1304	4:6	Apollos
1305	10:1	Red Sea
1306	10:2	Red Sea
1307	10:5	Desert
1308	16:12	Apollos

GALATIANS

1309	4:22	Slave woman (Hagar)
1310	4:23	Slave woman (Hagar)
1311	4:24	Mount Sinai, Hagar
1312	4:25	Hagar, Mount Sinai

TITUS

1313	3:13	Apollos

HEBREWS

1314	3:8	Desert
1315	3:16	Egypt
1316	3:17	Desert
1317	8:9	Egypt
1318	11:22	Egypt
1319	11:23	Pharaoh after the death of Joseph
1320	11:24	Pharaoh's daughter after the death of Joseph
1321	11:26	Egypt
1322	11:27	Egypt, Pharaoh at the time of the Exodus
1323	11:29	Red Sea, Egyptians

JUDE

1324	5	Egypt

REVELATION

1325	11:8	Egypt

APPENDIX 2

BIBLE REFERENCES TO AFRICANS AND PEOPLE OF PROBABLE AFRICAN ORIGIN

This appendix covers all the Bible references to African people that I could find. Finding and classifying all of the Bible references was an arduous task, and it is quite possible that I have left some references out or made a mistake in listing others. Remember, however, that one version of the Bible does not always number verses in the same way as another version. Again, I have opted for the numbering used by the NIV.

Note on how to read this list of verses:

A Bible reference *not* in parentheses indicates a verse where the person's proper name is used in the text. If the person's name is mentioned more than once, the reference is followed by 2x, 3x, etc. Bible references *in* parentheses refer to verses which allude to an African person indirectly, that is, the person's name is not found in the verse. A number in parentheses after a verse indicates the number of indirect references to that person in the verse.

For example, for Hagar, there are 61 references to Hagar found in 28 verses. Of those references, 15 are direct references where her name is used, and 46 are indirect references where a pronoun is used. Genesis 16:1 names her one time; Genesis 16:2 refers to her two times but without naming her; Genesis 16:3 names her one time and speaks of her using a pronoun one time; Genesis 21:17 names her twice and speaks of her indirectly one other time.

These figures are based on the number of times names and references appear in the NIV Bible.

Africans (sub-Sahran)
(1 indirect ref. in 1 verse)
Zeph 3:10

Anamites
(2 ref. in 2 verses)
Gen 10:13
1 Chr 1:11

Apollos
(29 ref. in 14 verses: 11 direct ref. and 18 indirect ref.)

Acts 18:24 (1)
(Acts 18:25) (3)
(Acts 18:26) (4)
Acts 18:27 (3)
(Acts 18:28)
Acts 19:1
1 Cor 1:12
1 Cor 3:4
1 Cor 3:5
1 Cor 3:6
1 Cor 3:22
1 Cor 4:6
1 Cor 16:12 (4)
Titus 3:13 (2)

Asenath
(6 ref. in 3 verses: 3 direct ref. and 3 indirect ref.)
Gen 41:45 (1)
Gen 41:50 (1)
Gen 46:20 (1)

Bithiah
(1 ref. in 1 verse)
1 Chr 4:18

Candace
(1 ref. in 1 verse)
Acts 8:27

Captain of the guard
(4 ref. in 4 verses)
Gen 40:3
Gen 40:4
Gen 41:10

Gen 41:12

Casluhites
(2 ref. in 2 verses)
Gen 10:14
1 Chr 1:12

Chief baker
(31 ref. in 17 verses: 7 direct ref. and 24 indirect ref.)
Gen 40:1
Gen 40:2 (1)
(Gen 40:3)
(Gen 40:4) (3)
(Gen 40:5) (1)
(Gen 40:6) (2)
(Gen 40:7)
(Gen 40:8) (3)
(Gen 40:17)
(Gen 40:19)
Gen 40:20
Gen 40:22 (1)
Gen 41:10
(Gen 41:11)
(Gen 41:12) (4)
(Gen 41:13) (2)

Chief cupbearer
(42 ref. in 22 verses: 9 direct ref. and 33 indirect ref.)
Gen 40:1
Gen 40:2 (1)
(Gen 40:3)
(Gen 40:4) (3)
(Gen 40:5) (1)
(Gen 40:6) (2)
(Gen 40:7)
(Gen 40:8) (3)
Gen 40:9 (3)
(Gen 40:10)
(Gen 40:11)
(Gen 40:12)
Gen 40:13 (4)
(Gen 40:14)
Gen 40:20
Gen 40:21 (1)

Gen 40:23 (1)
Gen 41:9 (1)
(Gen 41:10)
(Gen 41:11)
(Gen 41:12) (3)
(Gen 41:13) (2)

Cush
(6 ref. in 6 verses)
Gen 10:6
Gen 10:7
Gen 10:8
1 Chr 1:8
1 Chr 1:9
1 Chr 1:10

Cushi
(2 ref. in 2 verses)
Jer 36:14
Zeph 1:1

**Cushite(s)/Ethiopian(s)/
Nubians (see also
"Ethiopian eunuch")**
(44 ref. in 30 verses: 29 direct ref. and 15 indirect ref.)
Num 12:1 – 2x
2 Sam 18:21 – 2x
2 Sam 18:22
2 Sam 18:23
(2 Sam 18:26) (3)
(2 Sam 18:29)
2 Sam 18:31
2 Sam 18:32 – 2x
2 Kings 19:9
2 Chr 12:3
2 Chr 14:9
2 Chr 14:12 – 2x
2 Chr 14:13 (3)
2 Chr 16:8 (1)
2 Chr 21:16
(Isa 18:2) (2)
(Isa 18:7) (2)
Isa 20:4
Isa 37:9
Jer 13:23

Ex 32:12
Lev 24:10
Lev 26:13
(Num 3:13)
(Num 8:17)
Num 14:13
Num 20:15
Num 33:3
(Num 33:4)
Deut 23:7
(Deut 23:8)
Deut 26:6
Josh 24:5
Josh 24:6
Josh 24:7 – 2x, (2)
Judg 10:11
1 Sam 4:8
1 Sam 6:6 (2)
1 Sam 30:11 (2)
(1 Sam 30:12) (2)
1 Sam 30:13 (6)
(1 Sam 30:14) (2)
(1 Sam 30:15) (7)
(1 Sam 30:16)
2 Sam 23:21 – 3x, (2)
2 Kings 7:6
1 Chr 2:34
1 Chr 11:23 – 3x, (2)
Ezra 9:1
Neh 9:10 (2)
(Ps 135:8) (2)
(Ps 136:10)
(Ps 136:11)
Isa 19:1 (1)
Isa 19:2 – 2x
Isa 19:3 (1)
Isa 19:4 (1)
(Isa 19:8) (3)
(Isa 19:9) (2)
(Isa 19:10) (2)
Isa 19:16 (2)
Isa 19:17
(Isa 19:20) (3)
Isa 19:21 (3)

(Isa 19:22) (4)
Isa 19:23 – 2x
(Isa 19:25)
Isa 20:4
(Isa 23:5)
Isa 31:3
(Jer 25:19) (3)
Ezek 16:26 (1)
(Ezek 29:8)
Ezek 29:12 (1)
Ezek 29:13 (1)
(Ezek 29:14) (3)
Ezek 30:23 (1)
Ezek 30:26 (2)
(Ezek 32:15) (2)
Zech 14:18 (2)
(Acts 2:9/10)
Acts 7:22
Acts 7:24 – 2x
Acts 7:28
Acts 21:38
Heb 11:29 (1)

Egyptian army/horsemen
(84 ref. in 52 verses: 28
direct ref. and 56 indirect
ref.)
Gen 50:9
Ex 14:4
Ex 14:6
Ex 14:7
Ex 14:9
Ex 14:17 (1)
Ex 14:18
Ex 14:20 (2)
Ex 14:23
Ex 14:24 (1)
(Ex 14:25)
Ex 14:26
(Ex 14:27)
Ex 14:28 – 2x
(Ex 15:1)
Ex 15:4 – 2x
(Ex 15:5) (2)
Ex 15:19 (1)

(Ex 15:21)
Deut 11:4 (4)
Josh 24:6
2 Kings 18:24
2 Chron 12:3
Isa 31:1
Isa 36:9
Jer 37:5 (1)
Jer 37:7
Jer 37:11
Jer 46:2 (1)
(Jer 46:3)
(Jer 46:4)
(Jer 46:5) (4)
(Jer 46:6) (3)
(Jer 46:9)
(Jer 46:10)
(Jer 46:12)
(Jer 46:15) (3)
(Jer 46:16) (3)
(Jer 46:17)
(Jer 46:21) (5)
Ezek 17:17 (1)
(Ezek 31:2)
(Ezek 31:18)
(Ezek 32:12) (2)
(Ezek 32:16)
(Ezek 32:18)
(Ezek 32:19)
(Ezek 32:20) (2)
(Ezek 32:21) (2)
(Ezek 32:28)
Ezek 32:31 (1)
(Ezek 32:32)

Egyptian physicians
(3 ref. in 2 verses; 2 direct
ref. and 1 indirect ref.)
Gen 50:2 – 2x
(Gen 50:26)

Ethiopian army/horsemen
(4 ref. in 3 verses: 2 direct
ref. and 2 indirect ref.)
2 Chr 14:9
(2 Chr 14:11)

2 Chr 16:8 (1)

Ethiopian eunuch

(23 ref. in 9 verses: 6 direct ref. and 17 indirect ref.)

Acts 8:27 (1)

(Acts 8:30) (3)

(Acts 8:31) (5)

Acts 8:32

Acts 8:34 (1)

(Acts 8:35)

Acts 8:36 (3)

Acts 8:38 (2)

Acts 8:39 (1)

Hagar

(66 ref. in 28 verses: 15 direct ref. and 51 indirect ref.)

Gen 16:1 (1)

(Gen 16:2) (2)

Gen 16:3 (1)

Gen 16:4 (4)

(Gen 16:5) (4)

Gen 16:6 (3)

Gen 16:7

Gen 16:8 (5)

(Gen 16:9)

(Gen 16:11) (4)

(Gen 16:13) (6)

Gen 16:15 (1)

Gen 16:16

Gen 21:9

(Gen 21:10) (2)

(Gen 21:12)

(Gen 21:13)

Gen 21:14 (2)

(Gen 21:15)

(Gen 21:16) (5)

Gen 21:17 - 2x, (1)

(Gen 21:19) (3)

(Gen 21:21)

Gen 25:12

(Gal 4:22)

(Gal 4:23)

Gal 4:24

Gal 4:25

Hophra

(71 ref. in 38 verses: 1 direct ref. and 70 indirect ref., including 5 indirect ref. where the identity cannot be confirmed)

(Jer 37:5)

(Jer 37:7)

(Jer 37:11)

(Jer 43:9)

Jer 44:30

(Jer 46:17) (2) ?

(Jer 46:25) (2) ?

(Jer 47:1) ?

(Ezek 17:7)

(Ezek 17:17)

(Ezek 29:2) (2)

(Ezek 29:3) (6)

(Ezek 29:4)

(Ezek 29:5) (4)

(Ezek 29:6)

(Ezek 29:7) (5)

(Ezek 29:8)

(Ezek 29:9) (2)

(Ezek 29:10)

(Ezek 30:21)

(Ezek 30:22)

(Ezek 30:24) (2)

(Ezek 30:25)

(Ezek 31:2) (2)

(Ezek 31:18) (4)

(Ezek 32:2) (4)

(Ezek 32:3) (2)

(Ezek 32:4) (4)

(Ezek 32:5)

(Ezek 32:6)

(Ezek 32:7)

(Ezek 32:8)

(Ezek 32:9)

(Ezek 32:10) (2)

(Ezek 32:11)

(Ezek 32:28) (2)

(Ezek 32:31) (3)

(Ezek 32:32) (2)

Ishmael's Egyptian wife

(1 ref. in 1 verse)

Gen 21:21

Jarha

(2 ref. in 2 verses)

1 Chr 2:34

1 Chr 2:35

Lehabites

(2 ref. in 2 verses)

Gen 10:13

1 Chr 1:11

Libyans/Lydians/Ludites/ Cyrenians (see also "Put/ those from Put")

(8 ref. in 7 verses: 6 direct ref. and 2 indirect ref.)

Gen 10:13

1 Chr 1:11

2 Chr 12:3

2 Chr 16:8 (1)

Isa 66:19 – 2x

Dan 11:43

(Acts 2:9, 10)

Magicians of Egypt

(16 ref. in 10 verses: 9 direct ref. and 7 indirect ref.)

Gen 41:8 (1)

Gen 41:24

Ex 7:11 – 2x

(Ex 7:12)

Ex 7:22

Ex 8:7 (1)

Ex 8:18 (1)

Ex 8:19

Ex 9:11 (1)

(Isa 19:3) (2)

Mizraim

(4 ref. in 4 verses)

Gen 10:6

Gen 10:13

1 Chr 1:8

1 Chr 1:11

Moses's Cushite wife

(2 ref. in 1 verse)

Num 12:1 – 2x

Naphtuhites

(2 ref. in 2 verses)

Gen 10:13

1 Chr 1:11

Neco II

(32 ref. in 15 verses: 10 direct ref. and 22 indirect ref., including 5 indirect ref. where the identity cannot be confirmed)

2 Kings 23:29 – 2x, (1)

2 Kings 23:33 (1)

2 Kings 23:34 (1)

2 Kings 23:35 (1)

(2 Kings 24:7)

2 Chr 35:20 (1)

2 Chr 35:21 (5)

2 Chr 35:22 (3)

(2 Chr 36:3)

2 Chr 36:4 (1)

(Jer 25:19)

Jer 46:2

(Jer 46:17) (2) ?

(Jer 46:25) (2) ?

(Jer 47:1) ?

Officials/dignitaries/ counsellors of Pharaoh

(55 ref. in 41 verses: 39 direct ref. and 16 indirect ref.)

Gen 12:15

(Gen 12:20)

Gen 40:20 – 2x

Gen 41:37

(Gen 41:38)

(Gen 41:40)

(Gen 45:2)

(Gen 45:16)

Gen 50:7 – 3x

Ex 5:21

Ex 7:10

Ex 7:20

Ex 8:3

Ex 8:4

Ex 8:9

Ex 8:11

Ex 8:21

Ex 8:24

Ex 8:29

Ex 8:31

Ex 9:14

Ex 9:20

(Ex 9:21)

Ex 9:30

Ex 9:34

Ex 10:1 (1)

Ex 10:6

Ex 10:7 (1)

Ex 11:3

Ex 11:8

Ex 12:30

Ex 14:5 (2)

Deut 29:2

Deut 34:11

Neh 9:10

(Ps 135:9)

Isa 19:11 – 2x, (1)

(Isa 19:12) (1)

Isa 19:13 – 3x

(Isa 19:14) (2)

Jer 25:19 (1)

Pathrusites

(2 ref. in 2 verses)

Gen 10:14

1 Chr 1:12

Pharaoh/King of Egypt at the time of Abraham

(10 ref. in 6 verses: 5 direct ref. and 5 indirect ref.)

Gen 12:15 – 2x

(Gen 12:16)

Gen 12:17

Gen 12:18 (3)

(Gen 12:19)

Gen 12:20

Pharaoh/King of Egypt at the time of Joseph

(118 ref. in 81 verses: 89 direct ref. and 29 indirect ref.)

Gen 37:36

Gen 39:1

Gen 40:1 – 2x

Gen 40:2

Gen 40:5

Gen 40:7

Gen 40:11 – 2x

Gen 40:13 – 2x

Gen 40:14

Gen 40:17

Gen 40:19

Gen 40:20 (2)

Gen 40:21 (1)

(Gen 40:22)

Gen 41:1 (1)

Gen 41:4

(Gen 41:5)

Gen 41:7

Gen 41:8 (2)

Gen 41:9

Gen 41:10 (1)

Gen 41:14 – 2x

Gen 41:15 (2)

Gen 41:16 – 2x

Gen 41:17 (1)

(Gen 41:19)

(Gen 41:21)

(Gen 41:22)

(Gen 41:24) (2)

Gen 41:25 – 3x

Gen 41:28 – 2x

Gen 41:32

Gen 41:33

Gen 41:34

Gen 41:35

Gen 41:37

Gen 41:38

Gen 41:39

(Gen 41:40)

Gen 41:41 (1)

Gen 41:42 (1)

(Gen 41:43) (2)

Gen 41:44 – 2x, (1)

Gen 41:45

Gen 41:46 – 2x

Gen 41:55 – 2x

Gen 42:15

Gen 42:16

Gen 44:18

Gen 45:2

Gen 45:8

Gen 45:16 – 2x

Gen 45:17

(Gen 45:18) (2)

Gen 45:21

Gen 46:5

Gen 46:31 (1)

Gen 46:33

Gen 47:1

Gen 47:2

Gen 47:3 – 2x

(Gen 47:4)

Gen 47:5

Gen 47:7 – 2x

Gen 47:8

Gen 47:9

Gen 47:10

Gen 47:11

Gen 47:14

Gen 47:19

Gen 47:20 – 2x

Gen 47:22 – 2x

Gen 47:23

Gen 47:24

Gen 47:25

Gen 47:26 – 2x

Gen 50:4 – 2x, (1)

Gen 50:6

Gen 50:7

Acts 7:10 (1)

Acts 7:13

Pharaoh/King of Egypt after Joseph's death

(18 ref. in 18 verses: 15 direct ref. and 3 indirect ref.)

Ex 1:8

(Ex 1:9)

(Ex 1:10)

Ex 1:11

Ex 1:15

Ex 1:17

Ex 1:18

Ex 1:19

Ex 1:22

Ex 2:5

Ex 2:7

Ex 2:9

Ex 2:10

Acts 7:18

(Acts 7:19)

Acts 7:21

Heb 11:23

Heb 11:24

Pharaoh/King of Egypt who drove Moses from Egypt

(4 ref. in 3 verses)

Ex 2:15 – 2x

Ex 2:23

Ex 18:4

Pharaoh/King of Egypt at the time of the Exodus

(236 ref. in 144 verses: 124 direct ref. and 112 indirect ref.)

Ex 3:10

Ex 3:11

Ex 3:18 (1)

Ex 3:19 (1)

(Ex 3:20)

Ex 4:21 (1)

Ex 4:22

(Ex 4:23) (2)

Ex 5:1

Ex 5:2 (3)

Ex 5:4

Ex 5:5

Ex 5:6

Ex 5:10 (1)

Ex 5:14

Ex 5:15 (1)

Ex 5:17

Ex 5:20

Ex 5:21

Ex 5:23 (1)

Ex 6:1 (2)

Ex 6:11

Ex 6:12

Ex 6:13

Ex 6:27

Ex 6:29

Ex 6:30

Ex 7:1

Ex 7:2

Ex 7:3

(Ex 7:4)

Ex 7:7

Ex 7:9 – 2x

Ex 7:10 – 2x

Ex 7:11

Ex 7:13 (1)

Ex 7:14 (1)

Ex 7:15 (2)

(Ex 7:16) (3)

Ex 7:20

Ex 7:22 (1)

(Ex 7:23)

Ex 8:1 (1)

(Ex 8:2)

(Ex 8:3) (6)

(Ex 8:4)

Ex 8:8 (2)

Ex 8:9 (3)

Ex 8:10 (2)

(Ex 8:11)

Ex 8:12 – 2x

Ex 8:15 (1)

Ex 8:19 – 2x, (1)

Ex 8:20 (2)

(Ex 8:21) (5)

(Ex 8:22)

Ex 8:24

Ex 8:25

Ex 8:28 (2)

Ex 8:29 – 2x, (1)

Ex 8:30

Ex 8:31

Ex 8:32

Ex 9:1 (1)

(Ex 9:2)

Ex 9:7 (1)

Ex 9:8

Ex 9:10

Ex 9:12 (1)

Ex 9:13 (1)

(Ex 9:14) (2)

(Ex 9:15) (2)

(Ex 9:16) (2)

(Ex 9:17)

(Ex 9:19)

Ex 9:20

Ex 9:27 (3)

(Ex 9:28)

(Ex 9:29)

(Ex 9:30)

Ex 9:33

Ex 9:34 (2)

Ex 9:35 (1)

Ex 10:1

Ex 10:3 (3)

(Ex 10:4)

(Ex 10:5)

Ex 10:6 (4)

Ex 10:7 (2)

Ex 10:8 (1)

Ex 10:10 (1)

Ex 10:11

Ex 10:16 (1)

(Ex 10:17)

Ex 10:18

Ex 10:20 (1)

Ex 10:24

(Ex 10:25)

Ex 10:27 (1)

Ex 10:28 (1)

(Ex 10:29) (2)

Ex 11:1 (3)

Ex 11:3

Ex 11:5

Ex 11:8

Ex 11:9

Ex 11:10 – 2x, (1)

Ex 12:29

Ex 12:30

Ex 12:31

(Ex 12:32)

Ex 13:15

Ex 13:17

Ex 14:3

Ex 14:4 – 2x, (1)

Ex 14:5 – 2x

(Ex 14:6) (2)

(Ex 14:7)

Ex 14:8 (1)

Ex 14:9

Ex 14:10

Ex 14:17

Ex 14:18

Ex 14:23

Ex 14:28

Ex 15:4 – 2x

Ex 15:19

Ex 18:8

Ex 18:10

Deut 6:21

Deut 6:22

Deut 7:8

Deut 7:18

Deut 11:3

Deut 29:2

Deut 34:11

1 Sam 2:27

1 Sam 6:6

2 Kings 17:7

Neh 9:10

Ps 135:9

Ps 136:15

Rom 9:17 (2)

(Heb 11:27)

**Pharaoh/King of Egypt at
the time of Solomon**

(9 ref. in 7 verses: 7 direct
ref. and 2 indirect ref.)

1 Kings 3:1

1 Kings 7:8

1 Kings 9:16 (2)

1 Kings 9:24

1 Kings 11:1

2 Chr 8:11

Song 1:9

**Pharaoh/King of Egypt
father of Bithiah**

(1 ref. in 1 verse)

1 Chr 4:18

**Pharaoh/King of Egypt
Hophra**

(71 ref. in 38 verses: 1
direct ref. and 70 indirect
ref., including 5 indirect ref.
where the identity cannot be
confirmed)

(Jer 37:5)

(Jer 37:7)

(Jer 37:11)

(Jer 43:9)

Jer 44:30

(Jer 46:17) (2) ?

(Jer 46:25) (2) ?

(Jer 47:1) ?

(Ezek 17:7)

(Ezek 17:17)

(Ezek 29:2) (2)

(Ezek 29:3) (6)

(Ezek 29:4)

(Ezek 29:5) (4)

(Ezek 29:6)

(Ezek 29:7) (5)

(Ezek 29:8)

(Ezek 29:9) (2)

(Ezek 29:10)

(Ezek 30:21)

(Ezek 30:22)

(Ezek 30:24) (2)

(Ezek 30:25)

(Ezek 31:2) (2)

(Ezek 31:18) (4)

(Ezek 32:2) (4)

(Ezek 32:3) (2)

(Ezek 32:4) (4)

(Ezek 32:5)

(Ezek 32:6)

(Ezek 32:7)

(Ezek 32:8)

(Ezek 32:9)

(Ezek 32:10) (2)

(Ezek 32:11)

(Ezek 32:28) (2)

(Ezek 32:31) (3)

(Ezek 32:32) (2)

**Pharaoh/King of Egypt
Husband of Queen Tahpenes**

(6 ref. in 5 verses: 5 direct
ref. and 1 indirect ref.)

1 Kings 11:18

1 Kings 11:19 (1)

1 Kings 11:20

1 Kings 11:21

1 Kings 11:22

**Pharaoh/King of Egypt
Neco II**

(32 ref. in 15 verses: 10
direct ref. and 22 indirect
ref., including 5 indirect ref.
where the identity cannot be
confirmed)

2 Kings 23:29 – 2x, (1)

2 Kings 23:33 (1)

2 Kings 23:34 (1)

2 Kings 23:35 (1)

(2 Kings 24:7)

2 Chr 35:20 (1)

2 Chr 35:21 (5)

2 Chr 35:22 (3)

(2 Chr 36:3)

2 Chr 36:4 (1)

(Jer 25:19)

Jer 46:2

(Jer 46:17) (2) ?

(Jer 46:25) (2) ?

(Jer 47:1) ?

**Pharaoh/King of Egypt
Shabaka, Shebitku, or
Tirhakah?**

(4 indirect ref. in 3 verses)

(Isa 19:11) (2)

(Isa 30:2)

(Isa 30:3)

**Pharaoh/King of Egypt
Shishak**

(14 ref. in 10 verses: 7 direct
ref. and 7 indirect ref.)

1 Kings 11:40

1 Kings 14:25

(1 Kings 14:26) (2)

2 Chr 12:2

(2 Chr 12:3)

(2 Chr 12:4)

2 Chr 12:5 - 2x

2 Chr 12:7

(2 Chr 12:8)

2 Chr 12:9 (2)

Pharaoh/King of Egypt So

(1 ref. in 1 verse)

2 Kings 17:4

**Pharaoh/King of Egypt
Tirhakah**

(6 ref. in 4 verses: 2 direct
ref. and 4 indirect ref.)

(2 Kings 18:21) (2)

2 Kings 19:9

(Isa 36:6) (2)

Isa 37:9

**Pharaoh's daughter who
adopted Moses**

(16 ref. in 8 verses: 6 direct
ref. and 10 indirect ref.)

Ex 2:5 (1)

(Ex 2:6) (3)

Ex 2:7 (1)

(Ex 2:8)

Ex 2:9 (2)

Ex 2:10 (2)

Acts 7:21

Heb 11:24

**Pharaoh's daughter who
married King Solomon**

(10 ref. in 6 verses: 6 direct
ref. and 4 indirect ref.)

1 Kings 3:1 (1)

1 Kings 7:8

1 Kings 9:16

1 Kings 9:24 (1)

1 Kings 11:1

2 Chr 8:11 (2)

**Pharaoh's daughter Bithiah,
who married Mered**

(1 ref. in 1 verse)

1 Chr 4:18

Phinehas

(33 ref. in 24 verses: 16
direct ref. and 17 indirect
ref.)

Ex 6:25

Num 25:7 (1)

(Num 25:8)

Num 25:11 (1)

(Num 25:12) (2)

(Num 25:13) (2)

Num 31:6 (1)

Josh 22:13

(Josh 22:14)

Josh 22:30

Josh 22:31

Josh 22:32

Josh 24:33

Judg 20:28

1 Chr 6:4 – 2x

1 Chr 6:50

1 Chr 9:20 (1)

Ezra 7:5

Ps 106:30

(Ps 106:31)

(Mal 2:4)

(Mal 2:5) (3)

(Mal 2:6)

(Mal 2:8)

Potiphar

(30 ref. in 14 verses: 4 direct ref. and 26 indirect ref.)

Gen 37:36 (1)

Gen 39:1 (1)

(Gen 39:2)

(Gen 39:3)

Gen 39:4 (2)

Gen 39:5 (3)

(Gen 39:6) (4)

(Gen 39:7)

(Gen 39:8) (4)

(Gen 39:9)

(Gen 39:16)

(Gen 39:17) (2)

(Gen 39:19) (3)

(Gen 39:20)

Potiphar's wife

(27 ref. in 12 verses: 4 direct ref. and 23 indirect ref.)

Gen 39:7 (1)

Gen 39:8

Gen 39:9 (2)

(Gen 39:10) (3)

(Gen 39:12) (2)

(Gen 39:13)

(Gen 39:14) (4)

(Gen 39:15) (2)

(Gen 39:16) (2)

(Gen 39:17) (3)

(Gen 39:18) (2)

Gen 39:19 (1)

Potiphera

(3 ref. in 3 verses)

Gen 41:45

Gen 41:50

Gen 46:20

Prison warden

(3 ref. in 3 verses)

Gen 39:21

Gen 39:22

Gen 39:23

Put/men from Put

(7 ref. in 5 verses: 5 direct ref. and 2 indirect ref.)

Gen 10:6

1 Chr 1:8

Jer 46:9

Ezek 27:10 (2)

Ezek 38:5

Putiel

(1 ref. in 1 verse)

Ex 6:25

Putiel's daughter

(2 ref. in 1 verse: 1 direct ref. and 1 indirect ref.)

Ex 6:25 (1)

Seba/Sabeans

(9 ref. in 6 verses: 6 direct ref. and 3 indirect ref.)

Gen 10:7

1 Chr 1:9

Psalm 72:10

Isa 43:3

Isa 45:14 (3)

Ezek 23:42

Shabaka, Shebitku, or Tirhakah?

(4 indirect ref. in 3 verses)

(Isa 19:11) (2)

(Isa 30:2)

(Isa 30:3)

Shishak

(14 ref. in 10 verses: 7 direct ref. and 7 indirect ref.)

1 Kings 11:40

1 Kings 14:25

(1 Kings 14:26) (2)

2 Chr 12:2

(2 Chr 12:3)

(2 Chr 12:4)

2 Chr 12:5 - 2x

2 Chr 12:7

(2 Chr 12:8)

2 Chr 12:9 (2)

Simeon called Niger

(1 ref. in 1 verse)

Acts 13:1

So

(1 ref. in 1 verse)

2 Kings 17:4

Sukkites

(1 ref. in 1 verse)

2 Chr 12:3

Tahpenes, Queen and her sister

(6 ref. in 2 verses: 5 direct ref. and 1 indirect ref.)

1 Kings 11:19 - 2x, (1)

1 Kings 11:20 - 3x

Tirhakah

(6 ref. in 4 verses: 2 direct ref. and 4 indirect ref.)

(2 Kings 18:21) (2)

2 Kings 19:9

(Isa 36:6) (2)

Isa 37:9

Zerah

(2 ref. in 2 verses: 1 direct ref. and 1 indirect ref.)

2 Chr 14:9

(2 Chr 14:10)

APPENDIX 3

BIBLE REFERENCES TO AFRICAN PLACES

This appendix covers all the Bible references to African places that I could find. Finding and classifying all of the Bible references was an arduous task, and it is quite possible that I have left some references out or made a mistake in listing others. Remember, however, that one version of the Bible does not always number verses in the same way as another version. Again, I have opted for the numbering used by the NIV.

Note on how to read this list of verses:

A Bible reference *not* in parentheses indicates a verse where an African place name is used in the text. If the place's name is mentioned more than once, the reference is followed by 2x, 3x, etc. Bible references *in* parentheses refer to verses which allude to an African place indirectly, that is, the place's proper name is not found in the verse. A number in parentheses after a verse indicates the number of indirect references to that place in the verse.

For example, for the land of Goshen, there are 15 references to Goshen found in 11 verses. Of those references, 12 are direct references where its name is used, and 3 are indirect references where another word is used. Genesis 45:10 speaks of Goshen by name; Genesis 46:28 refers to it by name two times; Genesis 47:6 uses the name Goshen one time and speaks of that same region another time without using its proper name.

These figures are based on the number of times names and references appear in the NIV Bible.

Acts 7:38
Acts 7:42
Acts 7:44
Acts 13:18
1 Cor 10:5
Heb 3:8
Heb 3:17

Dophkah

(2 ref. in 2 verses)
Num 33:12
Num 33:13

Egypt (see also "Pathros")

(686 ref. in 592 verses: 603
direct ref. and 83 indirect
ref.)

Gen 12:10
Gen 12:11
Gen 12:14
Gen 13:1
Gen 13:10
Gen 15:18
Gen 21:21
Gen 25:18
Gen 26:2
Gen 37:25
Gen 37:28
Gen 37:36
Gen 39:1
Gen 40:1 – 2x
Gen 40:5
Gen 41:8
Gen 41:19
Gen 41:29
Gen 41:30 (1)
(Gen 41:31)
Gen 41:33
Gen 41:34 (1)
Gen 41:36 (2)
Gen 41:41
Gen 41:43
Gen 41:44
Gen 41:45
Gen 41:46 – 2x
Gen 41:48
(Gen 41:52)
Gen 41:53
Gen 41:54

Gen 41:55
Gen 41:56 (1)
Gen 41:57
Gen 42:1
Gen 42:2
Gen 42:3
(Gen 42:6)
(Gen 42:9)
(Gen 42:12)
(Gen 42:30) (2)
(Gen 42:33)
(Gen 42:34)
Gen 43:2
Gen 43:15
Gen 45:4
(Gen 45:6)
Gen 45:8
Gen 45:9
Gen 45:13
Gen 45:18 (1)
Gen 45:19
Gen 45:20
Gen 45:23
Gen 45:25
Gen 45:26
Gen 46:3 (1)
Gen 46:4
Gen 46:6
Gen 46:7
Gen 46:8
Gen 46:20
Gen 46:26
Gen 46:27 – 2x
Gen 47:6 (1)
Gen 47:11 (1)
Gen 47:13
Gen 47:14
Gen 47:15 – 2x
Gen 47:20
Gen 47:21
Gen 47:26
Gen 47:27
Gen 47:28
Gen 47:29
Gen 47:30
Gen 48:5
Gen 50:7
Gen 50:14

Gen 50:22
Gen 50:26
Ex 1:1
Ex 1:5
(Ex 1:7)
Ex 1:8
(Ex 1:10)
Ex 1:15
Ex 1:17
Ex 1:18
Ex 2:23
Ex 3:7
(Ex 3:8)
Ex 3:10
Ex 3:11
Ex 3:12
Ex 3:16
Ex 3:17
Ex 3:18
Ex 3:19
Ex 4:18
Ex 4:19
Ex 4:20
Ex 4:21
Ex 5:4
(Ex 5:5)
Ex 5:12
(Ex 6:1)
Ex 6:11 (1)
Ex 6:13 – 2x
Ex 6:26
Ex 6:27 – 2x
Ex 6:28
Ex 6:29
(Ex 7:2)
Ex 7:3
Ex 7:4
Ex 7:5
Ex 7:19 – 2x
Ex 7:21
Ex 8:5
(Ex 8:6)
Ex 8:7
Ex 8:16
Ex 8:17
(Ex 8:18)
Ex 8:24
Ex 9:4

(Ex 9:5)
Ex 9:9 (1)
Ex 9:18
Ex 9:22 – 2x
Ex 9:23
Ex 9:24
Ex 9:25
Ex 10:7
Ex 10:12 (1)
Ex 10:13 (1)
Ex 10:14 (1)
Ex 10:15
Ex 10:19
Ex 10:21
Ex 10:22
Ex 11:1
Ex 11:3
Ex 11:4
Ex 11:5
Ex 11:6
Ex 11:7
Ex 11:9
(Ex 11:10)
Ex 12:1
Ex 12:12 – 2x
Ex 12:13
Ex 12:17
(Ex 12:23)
Ex 12:27
Ex 12:29
Ex 12:30
(Ex 12:33)
Ex 12:39 – 2x
Ex 12:40
Ex 12:41
Ex 12:42
Ex 12:51
Ex 13:3 (1)
Ex 13:8
Ex 13:9
Ex 13:14 (1)
Ex 13:15
Ex 13:16
Ex 13:17
Ex 13:18
Ex 14:5
Ex 14:7
Ex 14:8

Ex 14:11 – 2x
Ex 14:12
Ex 16:1
Ex 16:3
Ex 16:6
Ex 16:32
Ex 17:3
Ex 18:1
Ex 19:1
Ex 19:4
Ex 20:2
Ex 22:20
Ex 23:9
Ex 23:15
Ex 29:46
Ex 32:1
Ex 32:4
Ex 32:7
Ex 32:8
Ex 32:11
Ex 32:23
Ex 33:1
Ex 34:18
Lev 11:45
Lev 18:3
Lev 19:34
Lev 19:36
Lev 22:33
Lev 23:43
Lev 25:38
Lev 25:42
Lev 25:55
Lev 26:13
Lev 26:45
Num 1:1
Num 3:13
Num 8:17
Num 9:1
Num 11:5
Num 11:18
Num 11:20
Num 13:22
Num 14:2
Num 14:3
Num 14:4
Num 14:19
Num 14:22
Num 15:41

(Num 16:13)
Num 20:5
Num 20:15 (1)
Num 20:16
Num 21:5
Num 22:5
Num 22:11
Num 23:22
Num 24:8
Num 26:4
Num 26:59
Num 32:11
Num 33:1
Num 33:38
Num 34:5
Deut 1:27
Deut 1:30
Deut 4:20
Deut 4:34
Deut 4:37
Deut 4:45
Deut 4:46
Deut 5:6 (1)
Deut 5:15
Deut 6:12 (1)
Deut 6:21 – 2x
Deut 6:22
Deut 7:8 (1)
Deut 7:15
Deut 7:18
Deut 8:14 (1)
Deut 9:7
Deut 9:12
Deut 9:26
Deut 10:19
Deut 10:22
Deut 11:3 – 2x, (1)
Deut 11:10
Deut 13:5 (1)
Deut 13:10 (1)
Deut 15:15
Deut 16:1
Deut 16:3 – 2x
Deut 16:6
Deut 16:12
Deut 17:16
Deut 20:1
Deut 23:4

Isa 30:3

(Isa 30:6)

Isa 30:7

Isa 31:1

Isa 36:6 – 2x

Isa 36:9

Isa 43:3

Isa 45:14

(Isa 51:9) (2)

Isa 52:4

Jer 2:6

Jer 2:18

Jer 2:36

Jer 7:22

Jer 7:25

Jer 9:26

Jer 11:4

Jer 11:7

Jer 16:14

Jer 23:7

Jer 24:8

Jer 25:19

Jer 26:21

Jer 26:22

Jer 26:23

Jer 31:32

Jer 32:20

Jer 32:21

Jer 34:13

Jer 37:5

Jer 37:7

Jer 41:17

Jer 42:14

Jer 42:15

Jer 42:16

Jer 42:17

Jer 42:18

Jer 42:19

(Jer 42:22)

Jer 43:2

Jer 43:7

Jer 43:11

Jer 43:12 – 2x

Jer 43:13 – 2x

Jer 44:1 – 2x

Jer 44:8

Jer 44:12 – 2x

Jer 44:13

Jer 44:14

Jer 44:15

Jer 44:24

Jer 44:26 – 2x

Jer 44:27

Jer 44:28 – 2x

Jer 44:30

Jer 46:2 – 2x

Jer 46:8 (3)

Jer 46:11

Jer 46:13

Jer 46:14

Jer 46:17

Jer 46:19

Jer 46:20

Jer 46:22

Jer 46:24

Jer 46:25

Lam 5:6

Ezek 17:15

Ezek 19:4

Ezek 20:5

Ezek 20:6

Ezek 20:7

Ezek 20:8 – 2x

Ezek 20:9

Ezek 20:10

Ezek 20:36

Ezek 23:3 (1)

Ezek 23:8

Ezek 23:19

Ezek 23:21

Ezek 23:27 – 2x

Ezek 27:7

Ezek 29:2 – 2x

Ezek 29:3

Ezek 29:6

Ezek 29:9

Ezek 29:10

Ezek 29:12

Ezek 29:14 (1)

Ezek 29:16

Ezek 29:19 (1)

Ezek 29:20

Ezek 30:4 – 2x

Ezek 30:5

Ezek 30:6

Ezek 30:8

Ezek 30:9

Ezek 30:10

Ezek 30:11 (2)

(Ezek 30:12) (2)

Ezek 30:13 (1)

Ezek 30:14

Ezek 30:15

Ezek 30:16

Ezek 30:18

Ezek 30:19

Ezek 30:21

Ezek 30:22

Ezek 30:25

Ezek 31:2

Ezek 32:2

(Ezek 32:8)

Ezek 32:12

Ezek 32:15 (2)

Ezek 32:16

Ezek 32:18

Ezek 32:21

Dan 9:15

Dan 11:8

Dan 11:42

Dan 11:43

Hos 2:15

Hos 7:11

Hos 7:16

Hos 8:13

Hos 9:3

Hos 9:6

Hos 11:1

Hos 11:5

Hos 11:11

Hos 12:1

Hos 12:9

Hos 12:13

Hos 13:4

Joel 3:19

Amos 2:10

Amos 3:1

Amos 3:9

Amos 4:10

Amos 8:8

Amos 9:5

Amos 9:7

Micah 6:4 (1)

Micah 7:12 – 2x

Micah 7:15

Nahum 3:9

Hag 2:5

Zech 10:10

Zech 10:11
Zech 14:19
Matt 2:13
Matt 2:14
Matt 2:15
Matt 2:19
Acts 2:10
Acts 7:9
Acts 7:10 – 2x
Acts 7:11
Acts 7:12
Acts 7:15
Acts 7:17
Acts 7:18
Acts 7:34 – 2x
Acts 7:36 – 2x
Acts 7:39
Acts 7:40
Acts 13:17 (1)
Heb 3:16
Heb 8:9
Heb 11:22
Heb 11:26
Heb 11:27
Jude 5
Rev 11:8

Elim

(5 ref. in 4 verses)
Ex 15:27
Ex 16:1 – 2x
Num 33:9
Num 33:10

Etham/campsite and desert

(5 ref. in 4 verses)
Ex 13:20
Num 33:6
Num 33:7
Num 33:8 – 2x
Ethiopia (see Cush)

Goshen

(15 ref. in 11 verses: 12
direct ref. and 3 indirect ref.)
Gen 45:10
Gen 46:28 – 2x
Gen 46:29
Gen 46:34
Gen 47:1

Gen 47:4
Gen 47:6 (1)
Gen 47:27 (1)
Gen 50:8
Ex 8:18 (1)
Ex 9:26

Hanes

(1 ref. in 1 verse)
Isa 30:4

Haradah

(2 ref. in 2 verses)
Num 33:24
Num 33:25

Hashmonah

(2 ref. in 2 verses)
Num 33:29
Num 33:30

Hazeroth

(4 ref. in 4 verses)
Num 11:35
Num 12:16
Num 33:17
Num 33:18

**Heliopolis/On/Beth-
Shemesh**

(6 ref. in 6 verses: 4 direct
ref. and 2 indirect ref.)
Gen 41:45
Gen 41:50
Gen 46:20
(Isa 19:18)
(Jer 43:13)
Ezek 30:17

Horeb (see Sinai – Mount)

Hor Haggidgad/Gudgodah

(3 ref. in 3 verses)
Num 33:32
Num 33:33
Deut 10:7

Jotbathah

(3 ref. in 3 verses)
Num 33:33
Num 33:34
Deut 10:7

Kehelathah

(2 ref. in 2 verses)
Num 33:22
Num 33:23

Kibroth Hattaavah

(5 ref. in 5 verses)
Num 11:34
Num 11:35
Num 33:16
Num 33:17
Deut 9:22

Libnah

(2 ref. in 2 verses)
Num 33:20
Num 33:21

Libya/Put/Pul/Somalia/Cub

(10 ref. in 7 verses)
Isa 66:19
Jer 46:9
Ezek 27:10
Ezek 30:5 – 3x
Ezek 38:5
Nahum 3:9 – 2x
Acts 2:10

Makheloth

(2 ref. in 2 verses)
Num 33:25
Num 33:26

Marah

(5 ref. in 3 verses: 4 direct
ref. and 1 indirect ref.)
Ex 15:23 – 2x, (1)
Num 33:8
Num 33:9

Massah/Meribah

(11 ref. in 8 verses: 10 direct
ref. and 1 indirect ref.)
Ex 17:7 – 2x
Deut 6:16
Deut 9:22
Deut 33:8 – 2x
Ps 81:7
Ps 95:8 – 2x
Ps 106:32
(Ps 114:8)

Memphis/Noph/Moph

(8 ref. in 8 verses)
Isa 19:13
Jer 2:16
Jer 44:1
Jer 46:14
Jer 46:19
Ezek 30:13
Ezek 30:16
Hos 9:6

Migdol

(6 ref. in 6 verses)
Ex 14:2
Num 33:7
Jer 44:1
Jer 46:14
Ezek 29:10
Ezek 30:6

Mithcah

(2 ref. in 2 verses)
Num 33:28
Num 33:29

Moseroth/Moserah

(3 ref. in 3 verses)
Num 33:30
Num 33:31
Deut 10:6

Nile/the river

(58 ref. in 47 verses: 32 direct ref. and 26 indirect ref.)[1]
(Gen 15:18)
Gen 41:1
(Gen 41:2)
Gen 41:3
Gen 41:17
(Gen 41:18)
Ex 1:22
Ex 2:3
Ex 2:5 (1)
Ex 4:9 (1)
Ex 7:15
Ex 7:17
Ex 7:18 (1)

(Ex 7:19)
Ex 7:20
Ex 7:21 (1)
Ex 7:24 (1)
Ex 7:25
Ex 8:3
(Ex 8:5)
(Ex 8:6)
Ex 8:9
Ex 8:11
Ex 17:5
(Isa 7:18)
(Isa 18:1)
(Isa 18:2)
(Isa 18:7)
(Isa 19:5)
(Isa 19:6)
Isa 19:7 – 2x, (1)
Isa 19:8
Isa 23:3
Isa 23:10
Jer 46:7
Jer 46:8
Ezek 29:3
Ezek 29:9 (1)
(Ezek 29:10)
Ezek 30:12
(Ezek 32:2)
(Ezek 32:13)
(Ezek 32:14)
Amos 8:8 (1)
Amos 9:5 (1)
Nahum 3:8 (1)
Zech 10:11

No (see Thebes)

On (see Heliopolis)

Paran (Desert)

(9 ref. in 8 verses: 7 direct ref. and 2 indirect ref.)
(Gen 21:20)
Gen 21:21
Num 10:12
(Num 10:31)
Num 12:16

Num 13:3
Num 13:26
1 Kings 11:18 – 2x

Paran (Mount)

(2 ref. in 2 verses)
Deut 33:2
Hab 3:3

Pathros (= Upper Egypt)

(7 ref. in 5 verses: 5 direct ref. and 2 indirect ref.)
Isa 11:11
Jer 44:1
Jer 44:15
Ezek 29:14 (2)
Ezek 30:14

Pelusium

(2 ref. in 2 verses)
Ezek 30:15
Ezek 30:16

Pi-beseth (see Bubastis)

Pi Hahiroth

(4 ref. in 4 verses)
Ex 14:2
Ex 14:9
Num 33:7
Num 33:8

Pithom

(1 ref. in 1 verse)
Ex 1:11

Put/Pul/Libya/Somalia/Cub

(10 ref. in 7 verses)
Isa 66:19
Jer 46:9
Ezek 27:10
Ezek 30:5 – 3x
Ezek 38:5
Nahum 3:9 – 2x
Acts 2:10

Rameses (= Zoan/Tanis?)

(5 ref. in 5 verses)
Gen 47:11
Ex 1:11

---

1   In Hebrew, the proper name "Nile" does not exist. It is always "the river" that is used. Here, a direct reference refers to a verse where the NIV has used the name "Nile." For the other verses, the phrase "the river" is counted as an indirect reference to the Nile.

Num 9:1
Num 9:5
Num 10:12
Num 26:64
Num 33:15
Num 33:16
(Acts 7:30)

Sinai (Mount) = Horeb (Mount)

(98 ref. in 82 verses: 43 direct ref. and 55 indirect ref.)
Ex 3:1
(Ex 3:12)
(Ex 4:27)
Ex 16:1
Ex 17:6
(Ex 18:5)
(Ex 19:2)
(Ex 19:3)
Ex 19:11
(Ex 19.12) (3)
(Ex 19.13)
(Ex 19.14)
(Ex 19.16)
(Ex 19.17)
Ex 19:18 (3)
Ex 19:20 (1)
Ex 19:23 (2)
(Ex 20:18)
(Ex 24.4)
(Ex 24.12)
(Ex 24.13)
(Ex 24.15) (2)
Ex 24:16 (1)
(Ex 24:17)
(Ex 24:18) (2)
(Ex 25.40)
(Ex 26.30)
(Ex 27.8)
Ex 31:18
(Ex 32:1)
(Ex 32.15)
(Ex 32.19)
Ex 33:6
Ex 34:2 (1)
(Ex 34:3) (2)
Ex 34:4
Ex 34:29

Ex 34:32
Lev 7:38
Lev 25:1
Lev 26:46
Lev 27:34
Num 3:1
(Num 10:33)
Num 28:6
Deut 1:2
Deut 1:6 (1)
Deut 1:19
Deut 4:10
(Deut 4:11) (2)
Deut 4:15
Deut 5:2
(Deut 5.4)
(Deut 5.5)
(Deut 5.22)
(Deut 5.23)
Deut 9:8
(Deut 9:9) (2)
(Deut 9:10)
(Deut 9:15)
(Deut 9.21)
(Deut 10.1)
(Deut 10.3)
(Deut 10.4)
(Deut 10.5)
(Deut 10.10)
Deut 18:16
Deut 29 :1
Deut 33:2
Judg 5:5
1 Kings 8:9
1 Kings 19:8
2 Chr 5:10
Neh 9:13
Ps 68:8
Ps 68:17
Ps 106:19
Mal 4:4
Acts 7:30
Acts 7:38
Gal 4:24
Gal 4:25

Succoth
(4 ref. in 4 verses)
Ex 12:37

Ex 13:20
Num 33:5
Num 33:6

Syene (see Aswan)

Taberah
(2 ref. in 2 verses)
Num 11:3
Deut 9:22

Tahath
(2 ref. in 2 verses)
Num 33:26
Num 33:27

Tahpanhes
(8 ref. in 7 verses: 7 direct ref. and 1 indirect ref.)
Jer 2:16
Jer 43:7
Jer 43:8
Jer 43:9
Jer 44:1
Jer 46:14
Ezek 30:18 (1)

Terah
(2 ref. in 2 verses)
Num 33:27
Num 33:28

Thebes
(5 ref. in 5 verses)
Jer 46:25
Ezek 30:14
Ezek 30:15
Ezek 30:16
Nahum 3:8

Upper Egypt (see "Pathros")

Zoan/Tanis (= Rameses?)
(7 ref. in 7 verses)
Num 13:22
Ps 78:12
Ps 78:43
Isa 19:11
Isa 19:13
Isa 30:4
Ezek 30:14

APPENDIX 4

BIBLE REFERENCES TO PEOPLE AND PLACES OF IMPROBABLE OR DISPUTED AFRICAN ORIGIN

The following are people or places that certain scholars – especially Afrocentric theologians – consider to be African, but that other scholars question. Their inclusion in this list does not necessarily mean that I do not consider them as African, but rather that many others do not.

People of uncertain African origin

Cush, a Benjaminite
Psalm 7 (title)
Cushan-Rishathaim
Judges 3:8, 10
Lucius of Cyrene
Acts 13:1
Romans 16:21?
Nimrod
Genesis 10:8
1 Chronicles 1:10
Micah 5:6
Puah
Exodus 1:15-21
Queen of Sheba
1 Kings 10:1-13
2 Chronicles 9:1-12

Sheba/Sabeans
Job 1:15; 6:19
Psalm 72:10,15
Isaiah 60:6
Jeremiah 6:20
Ezekiel 27:22, 23; 38:13
Joel 3:8
Shiphrah
Exodus 1:15-21
Shulammite woman
Song of Songs 1:5, 6
Simon of Cyrene
Matthew 27:32
Mark 15:21
Luke 23:26
Zipporah
Exodus 2:21
Exodus 4:24-26

Places of uncertain African origin

Cush ("Ethiopia"?)
Genesis 2:13
Cushan
Habakkuk 3:7

APPENDIX 5

PROPER NAMES OF AFRICAN PEOPLE AND PLACES IN THE BIBLE

There are several ways to spell proper names and place names in English, depending on the Bible translation one uses. The King James Bible uses a different spelling at times from the New International Version, or the New English Bible from Today's English Version. In this book I have chosen to use the orthography found in the NIV because that seems to be the English Bible the most commonly used in Africa. The table below gives the orthography of all four of the above-named versions of the Bible in English. If only one spelling is listed all four versions use the same spelling.

New International Version (NIV)	King James Version (KJV)	New English Bible (NEB)	Today's English Version (TEV)
Abronah	Ebronah	Ebronah	Abronah
Alexandria			
Alush			
Anamites	Anamim	Anamites	people of Anam
Apollos			
Asenath			
Aswan	Syene	Syene	Aswan
Baal Zephon	Baal-Zephon	Baal-Zephon	Baal Zephon
Bene Jaakan	Bene-jaakan	Bene-jaakan	Bene Jaakan
Bithiah			
Bubastis	Pi-beseth	Pi-beseth	Bubastis
Candace	Candace	the Kandake (Queen)	the queen (of Ethiopia)
Captain of the guard			
Casluhites	Casluhim	Casluhites	people of Casluh
Chief baker (of the king of Egypt)			

NIV	KJV	NEB	TEV
Chief cupbearer (of the king of Egypt)	Chief butler (of the king of Egypt)	Chief butler (of the king of Egypt)	Wine steward (of the king of Egypt)
Cub/Libya	Chub	Libyans	Kub
Cush	Ethiopia	Cush/Nubia/Ethiopia	Sudan/Cush
Cushi			
Cushite, the	Cushi	Cushite, the	Sudanese slave
Cushites	Ethiopians	Cushites	Sudanese
Cyrene			
Dophkah			
Ebed-Melech	Ebed-melech	Ebed-melech	Ebedmelech
Egypt			
Elim			
Etham			
Ethiopian(s)	Ethiopian(s)	Nubian/Ethiopian	Ethiopian
Ethiopian eunuch			
Goshen			
Hagar			
Hanes			
Haradah			
Hashmonah			
Hazeroth			
Heliopolis/temple of the sun	Aven/Beth-shemesh	On/Beth-shemesh	Heliopolis
Hophra	Pharaoh-hophra	Hophra	Hophra
Horeb			
Hor-Haggidgad	Hor-hagidgad	Hor-hagidgad	Hor Haggidgad
Jarha			
Jotbathah			
Kehelathah			
Kibroth Hattaavah	Kibroth-hattaavah	Kibroth-hattaavah	Kibroth Hattaavah
Lehabites	Lehabim	Lehabites	people of Lehab
Libnah			
Libya			
Libyans	Lubim	Libyans	Libyans
Libyans	Pul	Put	Libyans
Ludites	Ludim	Lydians	people of Lydia
Makheloth			
Marah			

NIV	KJV	NEB	TEV
Massah/Meribah	Massah/Meribah	Massah/Meribah	Massa/Meriba
Memphis	Noph/Memphis	Noph/Memphis	Memphis
Migdol			
Mithcah	Mithcah	Mithcah	Mithkah
Mizraim	Mizraim	Mizraim	Egypt
Moseroth			
Naphtuhites	Naphtuhim	Naphtuhites	people of Naphtuh
Neco	Necho	Necho	Neco
Nile	the river	Nile	Nile/the river
Nubians	Ethiopians	Cushites	Sudan
On	On	On/Beth-shemesh	Heliopolis
Paran			
Pathros	Pathros	Pathros	Pathros/southern Egypt
Pathrusites	Pathrusim	Pathrusites	people of Pathrus
Pelusium	Sin	Sin	Pelusium
Phinehas			
Pi Hahiroth			
Pithom			
Potiphar			
Potiphera	Poti-pherah	Potiphera	Potiphéra
Prison warden	Keeper of the prison	Governor (of the Round Tower)	Jailer
Puah			
Put	Put/Phut	Put	Libya
Putiel			
Rameses	Rameses/Raamses	Rameses	Rameses
Red Sea	Red Sea	Red Sea	Red Sea/Gulf of Suez
Rephidim			
Rimmon-Perez	Rimmon-parez	Rimmon-parez	Rimmon Perez
Rissah			
Rithmah			
Seba			
Shepher	Shapher	Shapher	Shepher
Shihor	Sihor	Shihor	Nile
Shiphrah			
Shishak			
Shur			

NIV	KJV	NEB	TEV
Simeon called Niger	Simeon called Niger	Simeon called Niger	Simeon (called the Black)
Sin			
Sinai			
So			
Succoth	Succoth	Succoth	Sukkoth
Sukkites	Sukkiim	Sukkites	Sukkites
Taberah			
Tahath			
Tahpanhes	Tahpanhes/ Tehaphnehes	Tahpanhes	Tahpanhes
Tahpenes, Queen			
Terah	Tarah	Tarah	Terah
Thebes	No	No	No
Tirhakah			
Zerah			
Zoan			

SELECTED BIBLIOGRAPHY

ATLASES

Baines, John and Jaromír Málek. *Atlas of Ancient Egypt*. New York: Facts on File, Inc., 1980.

Barraclough, Geoffrey, gen. ed. *The Times Atlas of World History*. Maplewood, NJ: Hammond, 1979.

Dowley, Tim. *L'Atlas de l'étudiant de la Bible*. Marne-la-Vallée (France): Farel, 1989.

BIBLES

Alliance Biblique Universelle. *La Bible, Ancien et Nouveau Testament (traduite de l'Hebreu et du grec en français courant)*. Pierrefitte: Alliance Biblique Universelle, 1989.

_____. *La Sainte Bible, nouvelle version Segond révisée*. Paris: Alliance Biblique Universelle, 1993.

_____. Éditions du Cerf. *Traduction Œcuménique de la Bible*. Paris: Société Biblique Française/Éditions du Cerf, 1975.

Barker, Kenneth, gen. ed. *The NIV Study Bible, 10th Anniversary Edition*. Grand Rapids, MI: Zondervan, 1995.

Éditions Excelsis. *La Bible d'étude Semeur 2000*. Edited by Alfred Kuen et al. Charols, France: Éditions Excelsis, 2005.

Felder, Cain Hope, gen. ed. *The Original African Heritage Study Bible*. Iowa Falls, IA: World Bible Publishers, 1998.

Green, Jay, Sr. *Pocket Interlinear New Testament*. Grand Rapids, MI: Baker, 1983.

Harrison, Sean, gen. ed. *NLT Illustrated Study Bible*. Carol Stream, IL: Tyndale House Publishers, 2015. See also Tyndale House Publishers.

Kuen, Alfred. *Parole Vivante*. Braine-l'Alleud, Belgium: Éditeurs de Littérature Biblique, 1976.

Kuen, Alfred et al. *Bible d'étude Semeur 2000*. Charols, France: Excelsis, 2005.

MacArthur, John. *La Sainte Bible avec commentaires de John MacArthur (Nouvelle édition de Genève 1979).* Geneva: Société Biblique de Genève, 2006.

Monks of Maredsous. *La Sainte Bible, version établie par les moines de Maredsous.* Brepols (Belgium): Usines Brepols, 1969.

Société Biblique Française. *La Bible: Ancien Testament et Nouveau Testament: Parole de Vie.* Villiers-le-Bel, France: Société Biblique Française, 2000.

Thompson, Frank Charles. *La Bible Thompson avec chaîne de références.* Miami: Editions Vida, 1990.

Tyndale House Publishers. *NLT Illustrated Study Bible.* Carol Stream, IL: Tyndale House Publishers, 2015.

BOOKS SPECIALIZING IN AFRICA

Adamo, David Tuesday. *Africa and Africans in the New Testament.* Lanham, MD: University Press of America, 2006.

_____. *Africa and the Africans in the Old Testament.* Eugene, OR: Wipf and Stock Publishers, 1998.

_____. *The Place of Africa and Africans in the Old Testament and its Environment.* Ann Arbor, MI: University Microfilms International, 1986.

Adeyemo, Tokunboh. *Is Africa Cursed?* Nairobi: CLMC, 1997.

Bailey, Randall C. "Beyond Identification: The Use of Africans in Old Testament Poetry and Narratives." In *Stony the Road We Trod: African-American Biblical Interpretation,* edited by Cain Hope Felder, 165-184. Minneapolis, MN: Fortress Press, 1991.

Baur, Père John. *2000 ans de christianisme en Afrique, Histoire de l'Église africaine.* Translated by Yves Morel s. j. Abidjan: INADES, 1999.

Bediako, Kwame. *Christianity in Africa: The Renewal of a Non-Western Religion.* Edinburgh: Edinburgh University Press, 1995.

Bullard, Reuben G. "The Berbers of the Maghreb and Ancient Carthage." In *Africa and Africans in Antiquity,* edited by Edwin Yamauchi, 180-209. East Lansing, MI: Michigan State University Press, 2001.

Copher, Charles B. "The Black Presence in the Old Testament." In *Stony the Road We Trod: African-American Biblical Interpretation,* edited by Cain Hope Felder, 143-164. Minneapolis, MN: Fortress Press, 1991.

Cornevin, Robert. *Histoire des Peuples de l'Afrique Noire.* Paris: Berger-Levrault, 1963.

Coulbeaux, Révérend Père Jean-Baptiste. *Histoire politique et religieuse de l'Abyssinie, depuis les temps les plus reculés jusqu'à l'avènement de Ménélick II.* Vol. I. Paris: Geuthner, 1929.

Diop, Cheikh Anta. *Antériorité des civilisations nègres: Mythe ou vérité historique?* Paris: Présence Africaine/édition Club Africain de Livre, 1972.

_____. *L'Unité culturelle de l'Afrique Noire.* Paris: Présence Africaine, 1959.

_____. *Nations nègres et culture.* Paris: Présence Africaine, 1954.

Dunston, Alfred G. *The Black Man in the Old Testament and its World*. Philadelphia, PA: Dorrance and Company, 1974.

Felder, Cain Hope. "Race, Racism and the Biblical Narratives." In *Stony the Road We Trod: African-American Biblical Interpretation*, edited by Cain Hope Felder, 121-142. Minneapolis, MN: Fortress Press, 1991.

McCray, Rev. Walter Arthur. *The Black Presence in the Bible*. Chicago: Black Light Fellowship, 1990.

Oden, Thomas C. *How Africa Shaped the Christian Mind: Rediscovering the African Seedbed of Western Christianity*. Downers Grove, IL: InterVarsity Press, 2007.

Russmann, Edna. "Egypt and the Kushites: Dynasty XXV." In *Africa and Africans in Antiquity*, edited by Edwin Yamauchi, 113-132. East Lansing, MI: MSU Press, 2001.

Sanneh, Lamin. *Whose Religion Is Christianity? The Gospel Beyond the West*. Grand Rapids, MI: William B. Eerdmans Publishing Company, 2003.

Schaaf, Ype. *L'histoire et le rôle de la Bible in Afrique*. Dokkum (Netherlands): Éditions des Groupes Missionnaires, 2000.

Shaw, Mark. *The Kingdom of God in Africa: A Short History of African Christianity*. Grand Rapids, MI: Baker Books, 1996.

Yamauchi, Edwin. *Africa and the Bible*. Grand Rapids, MI: Baker Academic, 2004.

_____. Introduction to *Africa and Africans in Antiquity*, 1-14. Edited by Edwin Yamauchi. East Lansing, MI: MSU Press, 2001.

COMMENTARIES, DICTIONARIES, ENCYCLOPEDIAS

Achtemeier, Paul J., gen. ed. *HarperCollins Bible Dictionary*. San Francisco: HarperSanFrancisco, 1996.

Alexander, Pat, David Alexander et al. *La Bible Déchiffrée*. Valence (France): Éditions LLB, 1983.

Barclay, William. *The Gospel of Mark*. Philadelphia, PA: Westminster Press, 1954.

Brown, Colin, gen. ed. *The New International Dictionary of New Testament Theology*. 4 vols. Grand Rapids, MI: Zondervan, 1986.

Bunson, Margaret. *The Encyclopedia of Ancient Egypt*. New York, NY: Facts on File, Inc., 1991.

Douglas, J. D., gen. ed. *New Bible Dictionary*. Grand Rapids, MI: Eerdmans, 1962.

Douglas, J. D. and Merrill C. Tenney, eds. *The New International Dictionary of the Bible, Pictorial edition*. Grand Rapids, MI: Zondervan, 1987.

Easton, Matthew G. *Baker's Illustrated Bible Dictionary*. Grand Rapids, MI: Baker Book House, 1978.

Éditions Émmaüs. *Nouveau commentaire biblique*. Saint-Légier (Switzerland): Éditions Emmaüs, 1978.

_____. *Nouveau commentaire biblique.* Saint-Légier (Switzerland): Éditions Emmaüs, 1961.

Hackett, H. B., ed. *Smith's Bible Dictionary.* New York: Hurd and Houghton, 1875.

Harris, R. Laird, Gleason Archer and Bruce Waltke. *Theological Wordbook of the Old Testament.* 2 vols. Chicago, IL: Moody Press, 1981.

Hendriksen, William. *The Gospel of Matthew.* Grand Rapids, MI: Baker, 1973.

LaSor, William, David Hubbard and Frederic Bush. *Old Testament Survey.* Grand Rapids, MI: Eerdmans, 1982.

Ligue pour la Lecture de la Bible, rédaction. *Dictionnaire biblique pour tous.* Valence (France): Éditions LLB, 1994.

Pache, René, gen. ed. *Nouveau dictionnaire biblique révisé.* Saint-Légier (Switzerland): Éditions Emmaüs, 1992.

Posener, Georges, Serge Sauneron and Jean Yoyotte. *Dictionnaire de la civilisation égyptienne.* Paris: Fernand Hazan, 1959.

Savage, Gil, Producer. *Compton's Interactive Encyclopedia.* 3rd ed. Carlsbad, CA: Compton's NewMedia, Inc., 1994.

Smith, Jerome, ed. *The New Treasury of Scripture Knowledge.* Nashville: Thomas Nelson Publishers, 1992.

Stedman, Ray. *Introduction aux livres de la Bible.* Marne-la-Vallée (France): Farel, 2000.

Strong, James. *Enhanced Strong's Lexicon* in the Logos Library System. Oak Harbor, WA: Logos Research Systems, 1995.

VanGemeren, Willem, gen. ed. *New International Dictionary of Old Testament Theology and Exegesis.* 5 vols. Grand Rapids, MI: Zondervan, 1997.

Vine, W. E. *An Expository Dictionary of New Testament Words.* Old Tappan, NJ: Fleming H. Revell, 1940.

Walvoord, John F. and Roy B. Zuck, eds. *Bible Knowledge Commentary.* Colorado Springs, CO: Victor Books/Scripture Press, 1985.

Wood, D. R. W., Revision editor (Third edition). *New Bible Dictionary, Third edition.* Downers Grove, IL: IVP Academic, 1996.

Yamauchi, Edwin. "Shishak." In *The New International Dictionary of Biblical Archaeology*, edited by E. M. Blaiklock and R. K. Harrison. Grand Rapids, MI: Zondervan, 1983.

Youngblood, Ronald, gen. ed. *Nelson's New Illustrated Bible Dictionary.* Nashville, TN: Thomas Nelson, 1995.

GENERAL TITLES

Boorstin, Daniel J. *The Discoverers.* New York: Random House, 1983.

Bright, John. *A History of Israel.* Philadelphia, PA: Westminster Press, 1976.

Felder, Cain Hope. *Troubling Biblical Waters.* Maryknoll, NY: Orbis Books, 1989.

Freeman, James. *The New Manners and Customs of the Bible* (electronic edition). Gainesville, FL: Bridge-Logos Publishers, 1998.

Hays, J. Daniel. *From Every People and Nation: A Biblical Theology of Race*. Downers Grove, IL: Inter Varsity Press, 2003.

Shelley, Bruce. *Church History in Plain Language*. Dallas, TX: Word Publishing, 1982.

Smith, David W. *Seeking a City with Foundations*. Nottingham (UK): Inter-Varsity Press, 2011.

Stott, John. *The Spirit, the Church and the World: The Message of Acts*. Downers Grove, IL: Inter-Varsity Press, 1990.

Unger, Dominic J. *Saint Irenaeus of Lyons: Against the Heresies*. New York/Mahwah, NJ: Newman Press, 2012.

Walls, Andrew. *The Cross-Cultural Process in Christian History*. Maryknoll, NY: Orbis Books, 2002.

PERIODICALS

Bennett, Robert A. Jr. "Africa and the Biblical Period." *Harvard Theological Review* 64 (1971): 483-500.

Draper, Robert. "Black Pharaohs." *National Geographic*, vol. 213, number 2 (February 2008): 34-59.

Hays, J. Daniel. "Black Soldiers in the Ancient Near East." *Bible Review* 14 (August 1998): 28-33 and 50-51.

_____. "Moses: The Private Man behind the Public Leader." *Bible Review* 16 (August 2000): 17-26 and 60-63.

_____. "The Cushites: A Black Nation in Ancient History." *Bibliotheca Sacra* 153, number 611 (July-September 1996): 270-280.

_____. "The Cushites: A Black Nation in the Bible." *Bibliotheca Sacra* 153, number 612 (October-December 1996): 396-409.

Leclant, Jean. "Un tableau du Proche-Orient à la fin du XVIIIe siècle." *Bulletin de la Faculté des Lettres de Strasbourg*, number 5 (1961): 252.

Tiénou, Tite. "The state of the gospel in Africa." *Evangelical Missions Quarterly* 37, number 2 (April 2001): 154-162.

Walls, Andrew. "Africa in Christian History." *Journal of African Christian Thought*, vol. 1, number 1 (June 1998): 1-4.

Yamauchi, Edwin. "Afrocentric Biblical Interpretation." *Journal of the Evangelical Theological Society* 39, number 3 (1996): 397-409.

Satisfying Africa's Thirst For God's Word.

Oasis International

is a ministry devoted to fostering a robust and sustainable pan-African publishing industry.

Engaging
Africa's most influential, most relevant, and best communicators for the sake of the Gospel.

Contextualising
content that meets the specific needs of Africa, has the power to transform individuals and societies, and gives the church in Africa a global voice.

Cultivating
local and global partnerships in order to publish and distribute high-quality books and Bibles.

Visit **oasisint.net** to learn more about the resources available from Oasis International or to support its mission.

OASIS INTERNATIONAL LIMITED
Satisfying Africa's Thirst for God's Word